About This

John Pounds is a local hero in Portsmouth, and for a time in the 19th Century his name became genuinely internationally famous. His life, working as a selfless teacher, feeder and clother of the poorest children from some of the most wretched streets of his home town, became a symbol of what Victorian society needed to do to deal with the heart-breaking living conditions of the children of the poor.

Though he had no notion of "founding a school", his example inspired others to teach tens of thousands of children in Ragged Schools throughout Britain.

Countless column-inches were devoted to him in the newspapers of the day, using his name and his life to spread the word of free education for the poor, though none of those commentators ever saw him, let alone met him or spoke to him.

The Reverend Henry Hawkes, of the Unitarian Church, Portsmouth, did. This book is the only account of the character and life of John Pounds that is written by someone who spoke with him on a daily basis.

For those wanting to know the story of John Pounds, what sort of a man he was and how he affected lives not only in Portsmouth by teaching the poor for free, but throughout Britain, this book provides unique source material.

The book also gives a glimpse of the squalor and depravity in the alleys and courts behind the neat facades of the houses along High Street, Portsmouth, and reveals just why John Pounds' work was so important for so many, changing their lives through education, and offering them hope, and a livelihood away from crime.

Portsmouth-themed books from Life Is Amazing

Fiction
The Three Belles Star in "We'll Meet Again"
(by Matt Wingett)
Turn The Tides Gently (ebook)
(by Matt Wingett)
The Song of Miss Tolstoy (ebook)
(by Matt Wingett)
Portsmouth Fairy Tales for Grown-Ups
(edited by Tessa Ditner)
By Celia's Arbour
(by Walter Besant and James Rice)

Non-Fiction
Ten Years In A Portsmouth Slum
(by Robert Dolling, edited by Matt Wingett)
The History of Portsmouth
(by Lake Allen, edited by Matt Wingett)
Recollections of John Pounds
(by Henry Hawkes, edited by Matt Wingett)

Recollections of John Pounds

Portrait of John Pounds,
by Henry Sheaf

RECOLLECTIONS OF JOHN POUNDS

with additional contemporary newspaper extracts

by

HENRY HAWKES, B.A, F.L.S.

Preface by
Erica Davies

Edited by Matt Wingett

Life Is Amazing

A Life Is Amazing Paperback

Recollections of John Pounds,
with additional contemporary newspaper reports

First published 2016 by Life Is Amazing
ISBN: 9780957241398
First Edition

Contents

Preface

by Erica Davies

(Director, Ragged School Museum)

Wealth at death, none.

So ends the entry for John Pounds in the Oxford Dictionary of National Biography. Yet, if Pounds was materially poor when he died, he was rich in the esteem of his fellow citizens who flocked to his funeral in 1839. Nearly two centuries later there is still no consensus on who did open the first ragged school and who coined the term, but there is no doubt that John Pounds' extraordinary dedication to educating destitute children made a deep impression on his contemporaries and successors.

In April 1844, just five years after Pounds's death, four men met in London, all involved in providing free education to "the forlorn and neglected children of the great metropolis." They decided to create the Ragged School Union and they invited Lord Ashley (later 7th Earl of Shaftesbury) to become the president. Their aim was to campaign together on the common interests of ragged schools, and to act as an inspiration and support to anyone who wanted to set one up. One of the key issues for the Union was that the schools should be free and available to the very poorest in society

The need was great because despite its global empire, industrial might and great wealth, nineteenth-century Britain was shamefully tardy in providing even an elementary education for its burgeoning population of children. Public and grammar schools had become the prerogative of the prosperous, and the provision of charity, church and voluntary schools was patchy especially in the inner cities. Anthony Hill, ironmaster at the Plymouth works in Merthyr Tydfil, stated in 1842 "I think the government might wisely leave education alone for a time", even though he founded a school and provided a scholarship.

The role of the ragged school movement in the struggle for free universal education is less well-known than it deserves, largely because of the great diversity of the schools and of their founders. We can only estimate how many ever existed; their informal structure means that records have disappeared for so many of them. Their history is pieced together from tantalising fragments: Charles Dickens' 1846 account of a visit to the Field Lane Ragged School; evocative photographs of the pupils of the Stockport Ragged School from the 1860s; passing references in letters; attendance registers surviving in municipal archives.

We are fortunate that the attendance registers of Dr Barnardo's Copperfield Road Free School (now the Ragged School Museum) survive from 1880 until 1908, when it was the penultimate ragged school to close in London. The entries are a glimpse into a life where income was precarious and chronic illness a looming threat. Families living on the breadline with several children could not afford the school fees for board or church schools which could be as much as three pence per child per week. A significant proportion of the children are described as "fatherless", a stark indication of the struggles their mother faced to provide for her family. One boy's experience indicates the degree to which poverty created a barrier to education: William was 'Sent home from St Luke's for ragged clothes'.

The redoubtable Barnardo was firmly committed to ragged schools from his arrival in London in 1866, opening his own establishment two years later. In Night and Day, the journal he published for his supporters, Barnardo draws a vivid picture of life at his school and it becomes apparent that it functioned as much as a centre of social welfare as for learning. Clothing and shoes were appealed for and distributed. Funds were sought to provide breakfast and at least one good hot meal a week in a bitter winter in 1879, "The meal consists of Irish stew, a good nutritious soup... with a plentiful supply of vegetables". Jamie Oliver would surely approve! Barnardo pricks the conscience of his readers describing how many of the children will have come to school with "nothing but a dry crust for their breakfast," and in a statement which still has resonance today says, "What a cruel mockery it seemed to attempt to instruct half-famished children such as these!". The benefits, physical and spiritual, of excursions to the fresh, clean air of the countryside was an important feature of philanthropy in Victorian cities. In 1881 Barnardo set out, with 2,500 pupils of the Copperfield Road Sunday school, for the fields of Essex. The vast party returned at 7pm to a firework display. The health and safety assessment for such a trip in 2016 would be mind-boggling!

Among the early pioneers of ragged schooling, Thomas Guthrie of Edinburgh wrote widely and insistently about the need for free schools. In his pamphlet, *A Plea for Ragged Schools* of 1847, he argued that education was the key to alleviating poverty and driving down crime. He expressed one of the keys to the success of ragged schools in attracting the children of destitute parents. "Punishments are rare. We work by love and kindness". Guthrie freely acknowledged the inspiration of John Pounds in his own commitment to ragged schooling. The life and dedication of John Pounds is justly celebrated in this anniversary year. The incapacity caused by his accident he turned to the benefit of vulnerable and disadvantaged children. Poor himself, he was resourceful and resilient in providing pastoral care and education for his charges. He lit a flame of compassion which shines still, wherever in the world the struggle for free universal education is not yet over.

Erica Davies
Ragged School Museum
46 - 50 Copperfield Road
LONDON
E3 4RR

www.raggedschoolmuseum.org.uk

Introduction

(by Matt Wingett)

Who was John Pounds?

As Erica Davies writes in the preface, information about the early figures of the Ragged Schools movement is scarce.

Because of his lowly status, no mention is made of the cobbler from Portsmouth in any newspaper before his death in 1839. There is, however, a newspaper entry in the *Salisbury and Winchester Journal* for Monday 10th January 1831, mentioning another man of the same name, which puts into context the importance of John Pounds of Portsmouth's work. It reads, among a long list of similar court sentences:

"Charles Bowley and John Pounds were convicted of robberies. - Judgement of death recorded."

Whether these two unfortunates were illiterate is not known – but by giving his "little vagabonds" an education, Portsmouth's John Pounds may well have diverted some of his pupils from a life of crime – and, possibly, death on the gallows.

During the time that he was teaching in the first half of the 19th century, cities and towns across Britain were burgeoning under the influence of the Industrial Revolution. It was a profound change that led to the breakdown of traditional social controls and to the creation of a massive underclass of children with which society was ill-equipped to deal. Portsmouth had its own problems that exemplified much that was wrong with the country.

Thanks to the Napoleonic Wars, massive investment flooded into the town in the first two decades of the century. The navy in Portsmouth, always huge, was supplemented by a greatly expanded army presence. With thousands of young, single men seeking entertainment, no surprise that drinking dens and brothels abounded. The by-products of such industry – children – were often turned out on to the streets while their mothers worked from cramped, fetid rooms.

Punishments in the Borough for feral children were harsh. As late as the 1840s, children received several weeks' hard labour and a whipping for loitering in the streets. Similarly harsh sentences were meted out for flying a kite or playing marbles at the wrong time or place. An apprentice might receive several months' hard labour for persistent tardiness at work, and two Portsmouth boys were even whipped and imprisoned for fourteen days for playing hopscotch. Child vagrants were punished with hard labour, although imprisonment at least meant a meal was supplied. It seemed that society was organised to label the poorest and most vulnerable as criminals - and deal with them brutally.

In a very real sense, a God-fearing, moral upbringing in the late 18th and early 19th century could be a matter of life or death. John Pounds himself commented proudly that none of his pupils had ever been hanged, though he admitted some had been deported. For the uneducated child, life could mean a disempowered existence, devoid of the basic tools society required for a person to get on, unable to understand the social code or how to apply one's energies within the law. Over the years, it is estimated that John Pounds furnished five hundred of the poorest children of Portsmouth the guidance that few others offered.

Thus we see the importance of John Pounds' work, and understand some of how his name acquired such fame after his death.

Though John Pounds' life is told throughout this book, a brief summary is worth giving here. Born in Portsmouth in 1766, his father was a dockyard sawyer. Pounds himself received scant education and began work in the dockyard at 12. When he was 15, an industrial injury led to him being crippled for life. He learned the trade of shoemaking and set himself up in work as a cobbler in St Mary's Street, Portsmouth.

After he adopted his nephew in the early part of the 19th century, he began to teach him and his neighbour's children to read. Word soon spread, and he was asked by other neighbours to do the same for theirs. Pounds wouldn't take money for his efforts, and indeed, decided he wouldn't accept children whose parents could afford to pay. Thus he taught the poorest children reading, maths, cookery, clothes-mending, shoemaking and other life skills. In doing so, he freed them from a life of helpless poverty. He went on posthumously to become a symbol and inspiration for The Ragged Schools Movement and was a genuinely famous figure throughout the Victorian era.

During his life, however, John Pounds' reputation did not spread far beyond the environs of Portsmouth, although his biographer, Henry Hawkes, does write of visitors to Portsmouth occasionally visiting him, such as a kindly middle-class lady who sent him books, or ex-pupils, sailors and soldiers, returning from far-flung parts to offer him their thanks for educating them.

In Portsmouth, though, he was well known. According to Hawkes, news of his death spread quickly throughout the town; hundreds attended his funeral and a committee was set up to mark his memory. His death was announced in *The Hampshire Chronicle*, and the Portsmouth publisher, Charpentier, produced an engraving, based on his portrait by fellow Portsmouth cobbler and painter, Henry Sheaf (see frontispiece). That the publisher should consider the engraving commercially viable shows Pounds' renown in the town. The unintended consequences of that engraving were that his fame would also spread further afield, as we shall see, later.

Within a few weeks of Pounds' death, the story of a philanthropic, impoverished cobbler teaching reading and mathematics to children of his own class and lower had been retold in numerous newspapers across Britain. Within a few years, he became a point of focus for the growing consciousness that something had to be done about the children of the poor. His blend of selflessness, alongside his humble beginnings, his disability and his manual trade lent themselves easily to a Christian narrative that resonated with reform-minded newspaper editors across the country. In a few years, Pounds' humble life brought him to national note, transfiguring him into a kind of non-denominational patron saint of education for impoverished children.

It is not true to say there were no other schools educating the poor at the same time. In Portsea, less then a mile from where Pounds worked, the Beneficial Society had been schooling charity children from 1755, and during John Pounds' life the Society built a school and meeting house on Old Rope Walk (now named Kent Street), where it still stands, currently used as a community theatre.

In London, between 1798 and his death in 1838, Thomas Cranfield established 19 free schools in the city's most impoverished areas. From 1835, the London City Mission began teaching the poor at several sites. Indeed, in 1840 the Mission first used the term "ragged" in its Annual Report, describing its schools that had been "formed exclusively for children raggedly clothed"- and so a name was created for the Ragged Schools Movement.

What John Pounds did in Portsmouth was not in itself unique, but there was something special in the degree with which he dedicated his life to others with no thought for his own financial or material needs. That story struck a chord with the public. His unique, almost archetypal Christian selflessness provided the growing reformist consciousness with what might be called in modern terms, its *poster boy*. The term is perhaps more accurate than might first be thought. When the Reverend Thomas Guthrie happened upon a Charpentier engraving during a pilgrimage to Anstruther, he became fascinated by his story. Thanks to him, John Pounds' renown was guaranteed.

Guthrie wrote a series of pamphlets arguing for the education of the poor, all citing John Pounds as an inspiration. He argued that Pounds' work could be a solution to the real social problems caused by the growth of cities. He connected Pounds with the newly-born Ragged Schools, describing him as the "Founder of the Ragged Schools Movement". It was good rhetoric, but inaccurate shorthand.

Nevertheless, under Guthrie's activism, Pounds became one of the early inspirations for individuals seeking to set up their own Ragged Schools. Pounds' extraordinarily selfless life was referred to by reformers again and again.

Over the years, Pounds' image became transformed by those telling his story to further their cause. Early engravings based on Henry Sheaf's painting of Pounds teaching in his workshop show a rough and ungainly man with a large head in a cramped room surrounded by boys and girls. A later, more romanticised image appears on the cover of this book. Taken from a Victorian magic lantern slide, it shows a handsome-faced craftsman with lustrous locks and firm jaw teaching boys from complete books. Hawkes, by contrast, tells us Pounds often used scraps of paper and single pages while teaching both sexes.

An engraving in *The Illustrated London News* of 1857 (see page 205) shows Pounds transformed further. Taken from a watercolour by E H Wehnert, "A New Pupil For John Pounds" features a spacious emporium adorned with birdcages, with Pounds surrounded by well-fed, well-clothed children mainly at their leisure, some lying on the floor looking lazily at a book, another pair of boys discussing a model yacht, others standing around with a country squire's air of easy authority, while Pounds, his face a mask of noble piety, assesses a new pupil dressed in rags. This has very little to do with the earnest attention Hawkes says his pupils paid to their teacher, nor the hard work he encouraged in them, or the toys he made for them, such as an "old guy carved out of a carrot".

Such images may partially come from the difficulty artists of higher classes had in comprehending the genuine poverty in which Pounds lived. It is a sobering reminder, when you stand outside the reconstruction of his shop at the John Pounds Unitarian Church in Portsmouth (the original, destroyed in World War II is pictured on page 23), of how cramped it was, with as many as 40 children crammed into its close, dark walls.

So, after his death, the name of John Pounds came to stand for something more than John Pounds himself. It stood for a movement. Over the years, writers compared his work with that of William Wilberforce the great anti-slaver; John Howard, the prison reformer; or, later, Florence Nightingale, the pioneering nurse. The difference is that those other individuals knew they wanted to change society. Pounds did not. Pounds lived within the close walls of Portsmouth, modestly and unambitiously plying his trade. He did what he did out of instinct and out of pleasure in acting selflessly. That in many ways, is a great achievement of its own.

In this book, Hawkes attempts to rein back some of the more extreme interpretations others put on his life. He questions the title given him by Guthrie as "The Founder of Ragged Schools" and attempts a polite "warts and all" portrait of the man, describing him as dirty and – quite authentically – capturing his local Portsmouth voice. That Hawkes also seeks to turn him into a local saint is equally apparent – nevertheless, the Pounds story is told in good faith and with good heart by a writer who clearly genuinely admired him, and, most importantly, actually knew and regularly spoke with this extraordinary son of Portsmouth.

Matt Wingett, Southsea, 2016

NOTE:

At the back of this book, I offer a brief timeline of some events in the Ragged Schools Movement, and how they connect to Pounds.

I have also included extracts from contemporary newspapers and books to show a little of how the crippled philanthropist of Portsmouth inspired others after his death.

About Henry Hawkes

Henry Hawkes, Unitarian Minister, was born in Dukinfield, Cheshire in 1805, into a family of Unitarians. He attended Glasgow University where he obtained a Bachelor of Arts degree and in 1833 was appointed minister of the Unitarian Chapel on Portsmouth High Street.

Inspired by John Pounds, in 1835, Hawkes founded a Sunday School for the children of the poor.

Over time, Hawkes became a strong advocate of Pounds' teaching methods, which emphasised kindness and persuasion rather than compulsion, and asserted mutual respect between teacher and pupils as the most effective means of inspiring children to learn.

Intimately acquainted with Pounds and his neighbours, Hawkes's descriptions of the lives of the poor in Portsmouth, and his detailed accounts of the dark alleys where the poor lived desperate lives give a powerful evocation of the period.

Hawkes was also central to Pounds' funeral arrangements and raised donations for the modest memorial stone which still exists in the churchyard today.

Recollections of John Pounds was published 45 years after the death of Pounds, after the profound influence of his life on educators had been played out. At times florid and deeply sentimental, at others perhaps overly pious for modern tastes, it nevertheless gives a strong impression of the town at the time, and of the character of John Pounds and the works he did. For that, successive generations are grateful.

The initials and the spaces in place of proper names imply real persons and places.

H. H.

Recollections of John Pounds

I.

A few days after I came to reside at Portsmouth, in the spring of 1833, a lady said to me laughingly, "Have you been introduced to the old cobbler yet?" Seeing that I was at a loss to know whom she referred to; "O you must go and see the old cobbler;" she said in a somewhat more serious tone; but mingled with pleasantry. "He's a remarkable man; quite a character! and does a great deal of good, in his own quiet, humble way. Besides, he is to be one of your new Flock; and a very constant one:—in an evening; but he is never there in the morning. They say he stays at home in the morning to cook his Nephew his dinner. He has adopted his Nephew; and the young man lives with him. But he is always there in an evening; nobody ever knew him absent,—or late. He's always one of the first. The early comers are sure to see John Pounds in his place. He sits in the left gallery going in, at the farther end, near the pulpit; and has commonly a cluster of little children about him. For he has taken a fancy to keeping a school:—if—school—we may call it!—such a crowd of children, all huddled together, in his very little shop; and he teaches them while he goes on with his cobbling! Many of the poorest of them he partly feeds and clothes. His shop is full of them. Oh, such a little bit of a shop! One wonders how he gets them all in. And yet in that poor little place he has commonly thirty or forty children at once; sometimes more; all happy about him. On a fine day you may see a row of them sitting outside in the street, on a little form, just under his little tumble-down window."

"What are his terms?"

"Terms!"—and she laughed heartily. "He has no terms! He won't receive any thing for it. He gets about him the poorest and most destitute; he seeks out those that can't pay. Friends would gladly give him something occasionally in the way of remuneration; but he always refuses it. No one has ever been able to induce him to accept any thing for it."

"What has he to live upon?"

"We don't know. But he can't have much, if any thing, besides what he earns by his cobbling; and he can't earn much by that; for his work, though they say it is strong and serviceable, is but of arough sort. Every thing about him, and his manner of living, seems very bare and scanty; and would look wretched, but for his own happy contented spirit, and his host of happy little faces. And he has his shop crowded with bird-cages, and baskets for his cat and kittens, and young birds, and other animals;—any thing he can help to make happy! The place is full of life and cheerfulness. But you must go and see him; and he will tell you all about it himself; for he dearly loves to talk about all his doings, to any one that will listen. He has a very independent spirit, and a most benevolent heart; indefatigable in doing good; but all in the humblest way; most unpretending, and obscure. Mrs. E—, of A—, calls him a philanthropist! She says, he's an honour to mankind!"—with a smile. "We took her to see him once, in the midst of his busy little school; cobbling, and teaching his scholars! And she was highly delighted. She calls him—a public benefactor!—She has repeatedly sent a bundle of their children's cast-off clothes for his poorest scholars; which he has always received very gratefully, and made the best use of for them. He will accept any thing for the poor children; but nothing for himself."

"Has he kept this school long?"

"Yes, many years. But you must not expect to find it much like a school. It is more of a gathering together as many children as his shop will hold; with nothing like system or classification. His crowd of little boys and girls cluster about him like a swarm of bees!—and with very much of the same sort of constant hum and buzz!—all at their ease! It is quite a pleasant sight to see them; they all look so happy together. And yet he has some of the roughest of the rough. But he has a way of attaching them to him; so that he can keep them all in good order:—if we may call such a formless sort of doings—order!"—with a good-natured laugh. "They always treat him with the greatest respect. They all love him; and would do any thing to please him."

"How old is he?"

"We think, between sixty and seventy. But he looks older; he is so spare and gaunt; so meagre-looking; and his features are deeply furrowed."

"Is he much helped?"

"We think not. Very few seem to take much notice of him. A few friends occasionally give him some books, and slates, and other things useful in teaching. But he goes on in his own quiet, unpretending way of doing good; happy and unobtrusive; apparently without a thought, or a wish, beyond his own immediate usefulness;—and that—is never-ceasing!—But you must go and see him, and judge for yourself. Mr.— will have pleasure in taking you."

Mr.— happened to come in just then; and kindly offered to take me the next morning; to which I gladly agreed.

II.

The next morning, about ten o'clock, we were on our way to the old cobbler's. It was a beautiful morning in May; the sun was shining bright, and the air was refreshing. Going out of High Street by Golden Lion Lane, we entered St. Thomas's Street, and turned to our right. "As you are new to Portsmouth," Mr.— said, "it may perhaps be interesting to you if I point out some of the characteristics of this garrison town." "I shall feel much obliged to you," I said, "for all such information." "Those fine large elm-trees, crossing the end of the street, and overtopping the houses with their fresh green leafiness, grow on the walls. The walls are constructed partly of stone, but chiefly of earth, and large timber trees grow upon them in many places. You may see part of the wall below, and the parapet rising as high as the lower branches. That is the extent of Portsmouth within the walls in that direction; the north-east. Portsmouth has its own walls and fortifications; and Portsea has its own walls and fortifications. We are now in about the centre of Portsmouth within the walls." "It seems a short distance," I said, "for twice that length to be the average diameter of the town." "Portsmouth within the walls is not a large town; but outside, the building is extensive, and is fast spreading; chiefly in the Landport and Southsea directions.

"This street turning out of St. Thomas's Street at a right angle to our left is St. Mary's Street; the street in which the old cobbler lives."

"I should not have expected to find him living in so good a street."

"You'll see it different soon."

When we had gone a short distance down St. Mary's Street, I was struck with the appearance of an apparently new building, with four handsome columns in front, and asked Mr.—what it was. "The Philosophical Society," he said, "built it a few years ago for their meetings. It contains a good lecture-room, a laboratory, an excellent museum, and a valuable, though not numerous, library of reference.

The library is open daily as a reading-room for the members. A mass of rubbishy old houses stood at that corner; which was cleared away to make room for the present building.

"From this point, you see how completely the character and appearance of the street alter. All before us is now a scene bespeaking profligacy and its attendant vices and wretchedness.

"All looks deplorable."

"At the farther end of the street you see the walls again, crossing it. The trees rising above the houses, grow upon the wall; a continuation of the line of elms you saw crossing the end of St. Thomas's Street. The door-way under them is a sally-port, leading through the walls to Portsea."

"What is this large brick building, bordering the narrow street between it and the Philosophical Society's building; apparently bordering the street all its length?"

"It does border the street all its length. It was used in the war-time as a Government stores, in connexion with the victualling department for the navy. It is now used as a bonding store. The street is called King Street; a short street, leading to Quay Gate; which you would see just beyond, but for that corner of the bonding store. Quay Gate leads through the walls to the Town Quay."

"King street seems a dull dismal street. I see nobody in it, but those dirty children, loitering about in rags, as if uncared for." "The neighbourhood we are now going into swarms with such poor neglected little things.

"The bonding store borders another short narrow street on the other side, called Crown Street; also going down to Quay Gate. Crown Street is much more frequented, but of a low disreputable sort.

"Now turn to this other side of St. Mary's Street. This broader street opening out of it on our right is Warblington Street. There is the wall again crossing it at the end, with the continuation of the same line of elms growing upon it, overshading the tops of the houses. Warblington Street runs nearly parallel with St. Thomas's Street and High Street. It is another wretched street of the same disreputable sort; abounding in profligacy and loathsomeness. You see those poor, miserable, abandoned creatures; with no self-respect:—all this densely-populated neighbourhood harbours crowds of such utterly wretched inhabitants. Dirty children straggling about everywhere, as if nobody cared for them. That is the sort the old cobbler looks up. The more forlorn and cast away, ragged, starving; the more he seems bent on winning them

John Pounds' house, St Mary's Street, Portsmouth, late 19th Century

into his little shop; and he has a way of doing it that never seems to fail. And when he once gets them into his shop, he makes them comfortable and happy. Some poor dirty things are in rags and tatters, almost naked, when he brings them in; and he clothes them, with cast-off things that friends give him for the purpose; and he keeps them in readiness. In the cold weather he keeps up a blazing fire. And we never hear him complaining, that his scholars play truant, or are unwilling to come to school!

"Look at that miserable soldier; lounging about, as if with no object. He has probably broken leave, and been out all night; and will soon be picked up, and taken off to the guardhouse. But come, we'll move forward."

As we went along St. Mary's Street, it was thronged with revolting sights of intemperance and bloated degradation:—women of the grossest appearance, sitting on door-steps, or lounging about, lazy and gossiping; their voices and language—heart-rending to hear; and their loud laugh of utter self-abandonment:—men—haggard, dark-looking, wretched; smoking—as if from desperation:—children scattered all about, in dirt and rags; some—playing; but their very sports implying the saddest neglect and degradation.

"What a sad wretched scene we are in!"

"Yes; and you don't see the worst of it. St. Mary's Street, Crown Street, Warblington Street,—all this crowded neighbourhood,—abound with dark alleys—leading into back courts, filled with dissolute, abandoned occupants.—And these back courts and dark alleys are the feeders for the old man's school."

"I have been surprised to see so many well-dressed, respectable people, ladies and gentlemen, passing along this street, in both directions."

"St. Mary's Street," Mr.— said, "notwithstanding its loathsomeness and degradation, is one of the principal thoroughfares between Portsmouth and Portsea, for persons on foot.

"Just glance into this bit of narrow paved road on our right, so crowded on both sides with small houses. This is Armoury Lane; an inlet into the Colewort Barracks. The barracks are behind this mass of poor houses; with a burial ground intervening. They are occupied by Royal Artillery. And a few doors further on—you will come to the old cobbler's shop."

"On which side of the street is it?"

"On this."

"Let us cross over to the other side; for I wish to have a good look at him, and his house, and his doings, before he knows we are coming."

We crossed over. "There it is;" Mr.— said; pointing to a little weather-boarded thing, standing separate by itself, between higher houses. "And there's the old man, sitting at his little open window, mending an old shoe; and his little shop full of scholars about him. You hear the cheerful buzz of their voices. Quite at their ease, you see. Look at those little things, lolling over the half-door, with their heads and arms leaning out for a little fresh air. And there's a row sitting outside in the street, just under the old man's open window. And look at his bird-cages hung up outside,—How merrily the birds are singing! as if they would out-vie one another."

"The house," I said, "does not look much more than two yards wide." "And the height up to the eaves," Mr. M— added, "is little more than twice the breadth. The shop is not quite five yards from front to back; and is only about two yards high from floor to ceiling.

"And in that little place the good old man gathers about him his thirty and forty children at a time; and makes them happy, and keeps them busy at their lessons!"

"The house has only two rooms; the shop and a chamber over it. You might see the opening of the little twist of a stair-case leading up to it in that corner opposite the door, but for those children sitting on the steps."

"I see their heads rising one above another."

"They have little else to sit on; only two or three old boxes, and a little form or two. Most, you see, are standing; some leaning against the wall, others crowded close together. No chairs to sit on;—no room for such luxuries here!"—Mr.— said, with a good-natured laugh. "Don't laugh so loud; he'll hear us."

"The upper half-door is almost always open all day long, whatever the weather. On this side of the house you may see the wall is of brick; but only as high as the chamber floor; so on the other side. All the rest is of wood; front, back, and sides, mere weather-boarding. One wonders how it can have stood so long; forty or fifty years, or more; we don't know how long."

"The shop looks very dark and dirty. And what a poor little window that is the old man is working at! with its little diamond panes, so thickly covered over with dust:—at this end, so sunk down out of the level;—the frame and leadings look very weather-worn and crazy. The whole house seems covered thick with dust; and of long standing."

"Probably never disturbed," Mr.— said, "since the house was built." "So weather-worn, there is no telling what colour it was when first painted; black, or blue, or what."

"You observe the house stands separate from the higher houses on both sides; except the low bit of wall on each side connecting them; each wall with a door in it. Those doors lead into an open court at the back of the old man's house, common to the neighbours."

As I stood looking at the old man, through his little open window, at his work, cobbling; it was with very mingled feelings. A tallish boy was standing beside him reading; while the old man went on mending his old shoe. He looked rough and self-neglected. He had no hat or coat on. His shirt, very dingy, was open at the collar and chest; the sleeves were rolled back above the elbows. His face, neck, chest, arms, and hands; all were dark, as if seldom washed. There was a repulsive coarseness about his features. His voice was harsh and loud, as he spoke to the children. What he said, and his manner of saying it;—all would have given me the impression of coarse vulgarity; if I had not heard so much good of him.

But there was something about him, which, the more I looked at him, and observed his manner of doing things, impressed me—with something superior, through all. His head was large and manly. His features were strongly marked; and, with his deeply furrowed countenance, bespoke deep thought and feeling. A large pair of spectacles rested on his broad open forehead. His long arms, though somewhat spare, were muscular and sinewy; implying great strength. His hands were large, and full of vigour.

"What's y'at, ye rascal there in the corner? I'se pay int' ye, if you's not mind, you wagabond!" The old man suddenly said this in a loud harsh voice, turning sharp round, with an eye full of fire; and he seized a stick, and shook it fiercely at the boy.

Mr.— smiled; and said, "Come, we'll go over, and I'll introduce you to him."

III.

"Well, Mr. Pounds, here you are." "Yes, here I bes." "Busy, as usual." " Yes, I'se always something to do." "I've brought our new Minister to see you." The old man deliberately raised his head from his work, and said, "Yer sarvant, Sir:"—and fixed his large eye full upon mine, with a penetration, that at once I felt,—There's strength of character there.

"I'm glad to be introduced to you, Mr. Pounds;" I replied.

"I'se have a good friend," he said, "in Dr. Scott, I has. And so's many another. Once when I wants some Bibles and Testaments for my poor little things to read out of; thinks I, I'se go to Mr.—; he's a clergyman; he's give me some Bibles and Testaments for 'em. So I goes to Mr.—; and I asks him if he's give me some Bibles and Testaments for my poor little things to read out of. But he says to me; 'I'se tell you what it is, my man; I'se no Bibles and Testaments to give away; but let your scholars bring their halfpennies and pennies to me; and when they's brought enough halfpennies and pennies, I'se let 'em have a Bible or a Testament.' Poor things! And where's they to get their halfpennies and pennies to take to him? They's no halfpennies and pennies. No.—And so I says to myself; I'se go to Dr. Scott; he's a good man; he's give me some Bibles and Testaments for 'em. So I goes to Dr. Scott. And they asks me in; all so kind! And he says; 'Yes, Mr. Pounds, I'se give you some Bibles and Testaments for your scholars.' And he goes upstairs, and he brings me down his arm-full o' Bibles and Testaments. 'And here's some other little books,' he says, 'for your scholars to read out of, and larn their verses from. And when they's worn out, come again, Mr. Pounds; and I'se give you some more.'God bless him! We's all miss him very much. You's like to hear 'em read a bit." "If you please."

"Here, you rascal wi' the curly wig! come and show the gentleman what you's a-doing." And a fine intelligent little boy brought a bit of broken slate, with a long-division sum on it. The slate was clean, and the figures were well formed, and the sum, as far as he had gone in it, was correct. "Here's a sum that there rascal in the corner's ben an' done;" handing his slate to me. "The wagabond! he can do 'em when he likes." It was a double rule of three sum; done correctly; the figures, neat and clear.

"Here, Lizzy, come and read for the gentleman." And a nice little girl, with clean bright face, and neatly dressed, evidently well taken care of at home, came and climbed up the old man's knee, and put her little white arm round his dark rough neck, and he gave her a kiss, and she looked very happy. A cat came with her, brushing against his leathern apron, as if pleased with all that was going on. "Now, Lizzy, here's the sixth chapter of the Gospel according to Matthew; it's what our Saviour's saying to the multitude, as he sits on the mountain side." And she read the chapter through with a clear pleasant voice, and with scarcely any hesitations, and as if she felt it. All the other children were still, and listening, as if they were interested in what she was reading. "That 'ill do, Lizzy" And he gave her another kiss. "Now go to puss and the young birds in the corner." And she jumped off his knee merrily; and puss went with her to the basket and the young birds in the farther corner.

"That's my cat, Sir. There's ne'er another cat in all the neighbourhood round can come up to my cat. She's a-nestling my young birds for me. She takes to 'em and brings 'em up as if they's her own kittens. And she's not let any other cat or dog come near 'em. One day a butcher's lad comes by, and sees my cat driving a big dog away from the door. 'You's a fine cat there, Master,' he says. 'Yes,' I says; 'she brings up my young birds for me; and she's not let ne'er another cat or dog come near 'em. I'se a big bull-dog at home,' he says; 'she's make nothing of him.' 'You's best not try,' I says. 'But I will though,' he says. And he's a-going off to fetch his big bull-dog. I says to him; 'You's not a-going to do that 'ere?' 'But I bes though,' he says. 'You's best not,' I says; 'I'se not be answerable for the consequences.' But he goes off, and brings his big bull-dog. Just before he gets to my door, he spirts it up-like, all keen and eager. And just as he comes to my open door;—'There 'tis!'—he says;—'In with y'!'—An just as his big bull-dog's a plunging in all among my poor little things—they's all so frightened, —poor things!—my cat springs on dog's back, and begins a-clawing back of his head. Dog turns up his mouth to bite at her. My cat strikes her claw into his eye. Dog ducks down his head, an turns up t'other side to bite at her. My cat strikes her claw into that eye. Dog bobs down his head again. An so they goes on; till dog bolts down street, with my cat on his back. Poor thing! By the time they gets to the sally-port;—if he isn't blind o' both eyes. But it's all the lad's fault. He didn't ought to do it. He's not do it again in a hurry.

"What's that you's got in your hand, Polly?" And a very little girl on the floor beside Lizzy and puss said, "A buttercup, Mr. Pounds." "Buttercup? Bring it to me, Polly, and let's look at it." And the little girl brought it to him, and he lifted her up on his knee, and gave her a kiss. "Spell butter, Polly." And the child spelt butter. "What colour's butter, Polly?" "Yellow, Mr. Pounds." "Spell yellow." And the child, with a little help from the master, spelt yellow. "And this flower's yellow, like butter. Now spell cup." "Kup." " No, Polly;—Cup. They doesn't know, Sir, how C spells like K. Now mind that, Polly; c—u—p, cup. And now look down into the flower; it looks like a cup; doesn't it, Polly?" "Yes, Mr. Pounds." "And so they calls it a butter-cup. Where's you get it, Polly?" "On the walls. And there's daisies too." "Buttercups and daisies! Who makes the buttercups and daisies, Polly?" "God; Mr. Pounds." "And God takes care of 'em in the dark night, and when the storm blows hard. And when the storm's over and gone, and the sun shines out bright again, there's the pretty buttercups and daisies again, all so bright and pleasant for us to look upon. Isn't it very kind of God, to make so many nice things for us?" "Yes, Mr. Pounds." "Red roses, and white roses, that grows in the hedges, and smells so sweet; and cowslips and primroses; and the pretty birds, singing all day long so merrily, to make us glad. There's no end to all the good things that God's always doing for us. And we's love him, Polly." "Yes; mother says so." "And we's try and do what 'ill please him, Polly." And the old man gave her a kiss. "There, go to Lizzy and puss and the little birds in the basket." And he lifted her lovingly off his knee; and the little thing went happily to Lizzy and puss and the young birds in the basket.

All the other children had been listening, very still, to what Mr. Pounds was saying to Polly. As soon as it was over, there was a sudden buzz of many voices:—"I'se go and get him some buttercups at twelve!"—"And I'se get him some daisies; there's lots on the common!"—"I knows a bank where some woilots grows. I'se go and get him some o' they; I'se soon be back again; it's only three miles off."

"What's y' all a-talking about so busy?" "Flowers, Mr. Pounds!"—a lively little voice said, full of confidence and fun. "Flowers;—spell flowers." And the boy spelt flowers. "Well, there's a time for flowers, and a time for work;" the old man said cheerfully. "Now to work again." And they all settled down to their lessons again, well pleased and happy.

"Billy, come and say your pretty verses:—How doth the little busy bee." And a rosy-cheeked little boy, not more than three or four years old, came eagerly pushing head foremost through the crowd, and took his stand beside the old man;—scarcely higher than his knee;—and looked up at him with a loving smile; and repeated without any hesitation, and as if he felt and liked them, those favourite verses of Dr. Watts's, beginning,

How doth the little busy bee
    Improve each shining hour,
And gathers honey all the day
    From every opening flower!

All the children seemed fond of them, and listened with bright countenances, as if they could never hear them too often. "You's be a busy bee, Billy!" "Yes, Mr. Pounds." "Not a lazy chap; good for nothing." And the old man took the child fondly up in his arms, and kissed him. "There, Billy; that 'ill do till next time." And the little fellow was soon out of sight among the crowd of taller boys.

"Can't ye be quiet there, you wagabonds on the stairs? I'se be at ye, if you's not mind;"—turning with a sharp look at two biggish lads, full of their fun. The lads were still in a moment; not as if unwillingly; but looking at their old master with love and reverence; and their slyly looking at one another, with a good-natured smile; as if they felt the rebuke was just, and kindly meant. "They's no evil intent in 'em, Sir; they rascals; but I'se forced to keep 'em under a bit sometimes. They knows it's all for their good.

"Dick Saunders;" and one of the taller boys came and stood beside him. "Harry Jenner;" and another came; apparently about the same age. "Tom Richmond;" and a little fellow came, and stood with them; younger, and much shorter than the others; but full of life and intelligence. "Thinks I, one day, Sir, a long time agone, they lads as I'se a-larning 'em their sums, they's not always have their slates with 'em ready like—when they goes into business; so, thinks I, I'se put their slates in their heads for 'em;"—with a comical smile and tone; and the boys smiled, as if they understood his meaning, and appreciated it: —"and then they's always have 'em with 'em ready!—Now, lads!" And they were all attention. "Answer first as can; and him as blunders, t'others set him right. Quick, lads!" He then began to ask them questions in arithmetic: first, in addition; beginning with easy questions; which made the boys smile as they answered, as if it was play-work. But he soon went up to larger and larger amounts; which all three answered instantly, and correctly; till he came to numbers so large, and somewhat complicated, that I was astonished that in every instance one or other answered every question right; and very rarely was any one of them at all at a loss. "Now, for substraction." And he began as before, with rather simple questions; which the lads seemed to think too easy. But he gradually went on to more difficult; and almost all of them they all three answered readily. "And now, Sir," he said, turning to me, "you's please an ask 'em any questions you likes out o' the multiplication table." "With pleasure, Mr. Pounds." And I began, as he had begun, with rather easy questions; and the lads smiled as they answered. But I gradually went on to higher numbers;

and finding that they all three answered every question quickly and correctly, I tried them with what seemed to me the most difficult questions in the table; but they answered them all instantly, and without a blunder. "Now we's have some division sums; long and short divisions, mixed like."

"Thank you, Mr. Pounds," Mr.— said; "I think we must be going now." And I very cordially thanked him; and said: "I have been very much interested, Mr. Pounds; and I hope to have the pleasure of seeing you again soon."

"Yes, I'se be at Church o' Sunday. I'se always there of an evening. Ye sees, Sir, my Neffy's a journeyman shoemaker. And a good, steady, industrious lad he is; though I says it. And there's only one day in a week that he's have a comfortable dinner like; and that's o' Sunday. So I stops at home o' Sunday mornings to cook my Neffy his dinner; poor lad! But I'se always go to Church o' Sunday evening; and some o' my little wagabonds wi' me;—them as likes. No; I never forces 'em to go to Church. No; I says to 'em o' Saturday; Now, all you as likes to go wi' me to Church to-morrow, I'se give 'em a half-holiday o' Monday. So there's always some as likes to go wi' me to Church o' Sunday. Poor things! there's some on 'em's no clothes fit to go in. So I keeps some bettermost sort o' clothes here in my shop for 'em; fit to be seen in o' Sundays. And they comes here, and puts 'em on in my shop; and goes wi' me to Church; and looks like other folks; respectable like. And then, after Church, they comes back wi' me, and takes 'em off again in my shop; and I takes care of 'em again, ready for 'em next Sunday." "Thank you, Mr. Pounds! Good morning." "Here, you rascal on the steps there! come and spell a bit for the gentleman before he goes. And a rough-looking chubby lad, with a broad laughing face, and a plentiful head of hair, came to him. "What's this?" the old man said, grasping a hand-full of the lad's hair. "My wig!"—with a touch of fun, and wincing. "My wig?—ye rascal!—Spell wig." The boy seemed at a loss, and stood silent. "That W, Sir, 's a hard word to larn 'em to spell with. They's a long time coming to it. W—i—g, lad." And the lad spelt wig; with a roguish look. "What's I give you then?" the old man said, as roguishly; giving the lad a smart blow on the shoulder; and all the school laughed out heartily. "You gives me a blow, Mr. Pounds." "Spell blow." And the boy spelt blow. "Where's I give it you?" "O' my shoulder." "Spell shoulder." The lad tried, and blundered. "Try again, lad." And he tried again, and blundered again; and so, several times. At last he succeeded, with some help from the master. "There! go along with y';" giving him a good-natured push. "And mind, lad; you's always lay a good shoulder to the wheel;—all your life, lad."

IV.

It was no easy thing to get away from the good old cobbler. For though we had repeatedly bid him Good Morning, he had always something else to tell us, or show us; his heart was so thoroughly in all he was doing. At last—we were determined! But as we went away from his door, I could not help feeling sorry for him; he seemed so desiring to tell us something else about his doings.

"We won't go back the same way that we came," Mr— said; "we'll move onward; and you shall see a little more of the old man's district, as we may fairly call the little compact sphere of his never-tiring usefulness.

"This sally-port leads through the walls to Portsea. But before we enter it, look into these narrow openings to the right and left, between the walls and the houses. These narrow lines of road are called lanes. They lead to other sad disreputable haunts of vice and infamy. This lane on our right passes by the ends of Warblington Street, St. Thomas's Street, and High Street. This to our left, leads to a place called Prospect Row; notoriously bad; one of the most wretched and abandoned of all the disreputable places in this densely crowded neighbourhood. And from these vile sinks of wretchedness the good old cobbler seeks up his poor little lost ones, 'that nobody cares for;' as he so touchingly expresses it. You would observe when he was at his shop, that some of his scholars he had from more respectable homes; but he diligently seeks up the most neglected and forlorn.

"We'll now go through the sally-port. Have you been this way before?" "No; and I am very desirous to know all you can tell me about the neighbourhood, for the old man's sake. What a good kind creature he is!—notwithstanding all his roughness. But I wish he were cleaner." "We all wish that. But it has always been so with him. But on Sundays you'll see it different. Then, every thing is clean and proper about him; both as to his person and dress."

Passing through the sally-port, we came out upon the moat; which we crossed over by a footbridge. "Those are the Portsea walls before us, with those fine timber trees growing upon them. This broad sheet of water spreading immediately to our right, is the mill-dam; fed by the tide. It works the garrison mill; that brick building bordering it on our left. The gate just beyond the mill is called Mill Gate. It opens through the walls into Portsea. Our purpose does not require us to go into Portsea. We will take the opposite direction, and turn round this corner of the Portsmouth moat, and go along the straight carriage road, bordered by the moat on our left, and this high brick wall on our right.

"That dirty, ruinous row of upper windows just within the Portsmouth walls is Prospect Row; the wretchedly degraded place I mentioned to you at the sally-port. It extends, parallel to the wall, and almost close up to it, to the lower end of Crown Street, and nearly to Quay Gate."

"What is this high brick wall close to us on our right?" "The boundary of the Gun Wharf. These are artillery barracks, inclosed within the same line of wall. And this building next to the barracks is the Custom House.

"Here the Portsmouth moat terminates, in this direction. Its waters pass through that iron grating into the Camber; as that bason just beyond it, so crowded with trading vessels, is called. That is part of the Town Quay, close beside the Camber, bordering it on the left; and there is Quay Gate, opening out upon it through the Portsmouth walls. Just within Quay Gate,—Prospect Row, Crown Street, and King Street, meet us at a centre. All this neighbourhood is continually frequented by the good old cobbler, in his searching rounds of benevolence.

"We will not go into Portsmouth through Quay Gate; I wish to take you over this swing-bridge, crossing the mouth of the Camber, into that little ill-looking street just beyond.

"But stop for a moment. As we stand here on the centre of this bridge, with the Camber on the one side of it, so full of trading vessels, and this narrow approach to it on the other, also crowded with trading vessels; you see the whole extent of accommodation provided at Portsmouth, with its fine Harbour, for any thing like merchant shipping. Government have always set themselves against encouraging merchant shipping at Portsmouth. They have always seemed desirous to preserve our port altogether, or as exclusively as possible, for the Royal Navy. The Harbour, one of the finest in the world, opens just beyond this narrow entrance. But you will have a better view of the Harbour from another point.

"We will now go along East Street. You see, it is crowded with poor small houses on both sides;—poor dirty children scattered about everywhere. Observe these narrow alleys on our right, as we pass along. They lead through this dense mass of houses to another part of the Town Quay. This also is part of the good old cobbler's district; into which he comes untiringly, to pick up scholars.

"East Street, you see, is but a short one. This larger street, crossing the end of it at right angles, into which we now enter, is Broad street; commonly called 'Broad Street, Point;' Point being the general name for all the part we are now on; jutting into the Harbour. During the war-time, Point was constantly thronged with sailors and persons connected with the shipping. It is still the principal part of Portsmouth for sailors and watermen.

"We will turn to the right. A few steps, you see, and we are at the end of the street. And there—the Harbour opens full before you; with the ships."

"A fine view indeed!—It seems to go up as far as that range of hill."

"The Port does;—about four miles. It is only this lower part of the Port, where the ships are, that is properly called the Harbour. That line of hill is Portsdown; a long chalk range. This is the Gun Wharf, bordering the Harbour immediately on our right; the ground so dark covered over with guns spread out upon it. Those heaps are stacks of shot. Next to the Gun Wharf beyond, bordering the Harbour, is the Dockyard. On this opposite side is, first, the town of Gosport; coming down to the water's edge. And that extensive mass of brick-building next beyond Gosport, also close to the Harbour, is the Royal Clarence Yard; the new offices for victualling the navy."

"What is the breadth of the Port?"

"Just beyond that further corner of the Dockyard, the Port suddenly widens to great extent, east and west; but very irregularly; several miles across in some parts, at high water. The mouth of the Harbour, as you have no doubt observed, is comparatively narrow." "Yes." "A great advantage for our ships; for so vast a body of water flowing out with every tide is continually ploughing so narrow a channel deep.

"That ship near the Dockyard is the Victory. She was Lord Nelson's flag-ship at the battle of Trafalgar; on board of which he was shot, and died. She is now used as the flag-ship for the Port Admiral."

Just then, the flag-ship began firing a salute. Mr.—, inquiring what it was for, was told, it was in reply to a foreign ship, just come up to Spithead.

"Come," he said, "we will now return." Leaving the Harbour, and going along Broad Street in the opposite direction:—"That gate at the end of the street," he said, "is King James's Gate. It opens through the walls into High Street; and you will find you have come round to the point from which we started. And I shall have shown you pretty nearly the whole circuit within which the poor old cobbler has lived all his life; or thereabouts; seldom going beyond, but for an occasional ramble into the fields, or over the Hill."

V.

When we had passed through King James's gate, and were in High street, I warmly thanked Mr.— for all his kindness! and bid him Good Morning; for I wished to be alone; and think of all I had seen and heard of this good old man. I crossed the Grand Parade. The General was there, with his staff, trooping guard. The band was playing "Rule, Britannia!" There was a gay crowd of lookers-on; interspersed with ill-looking idlers, lurking about; both men and women; and children playing everywhere. I hastened through Spur ravelin, and went out upon Southsea Common. "Oh! blessed fresh air!"—I seemed to say to myself, as I came out on the open glacis. How different from those noisome haunts of infamy and wretchedness, in the midst of which that good old man has chosen to live!

What is it—that gathers all those children about him so lovingly? He can do what he pleases with them. His word is law. And they do it,—whatever he says,—with delight; and love him for it. His personal appearance is altogether against him; so dark, and coarse, and not clean; altogether self-neglected. And that loud harsh voice was at times shocking; revolting. Still, there was something about him, that, with all his coarseness of look, and harshness of voice, and abruptness, and rough usage, bespoke a loving heart, and kind cherishing spirit, that was very endearing. How happy that little girl seemed, sitting on his knee reading!

But what a poor bit of a place for a school!—And so many crowded into it!—scarcely room for them to turn about:—the roof, so low; the walls, so dark and dirty; and crowded with bird-cages, and other things; his little shelves, heaped with old boots and shoes, cups and saucers and mugs, tattered books and broken slates; all meagre and poverty-stricken. Still, there was an air of happiness and comfort in all that busy group. The old man was happy at his work, cobbling, in the midst of his loving family! For they all seemed like an happy family! So loving, and peaceful, and united! And he rules—the Master-spirit—among them! But he rules—a Father—among them, all love; and loved by them all!

As I was thus walking thoughtfully over the common toward the Fire-barn, the twelve o'clock gun fired from the King's bastion; and soon after, some children came running out from Spur ravelin, spreading joyously over the common, stooping down here and there, as if to pick up flowers. Some came running eagerly toward the furze bushes beside the Fire-barn; where I was now standing; enjoying the fine open view over Spit-head; with ships lying at anchor, and yachts sailing about; and the Isle of Wight beyond, giving the effect of lake scenery.

The first boy that came running up rushed headlong in among the furze bushes, and was instantly out of sight. Others came running close after him:—"We's get him such a lot o' flowers for this a'ternoon!"

Then came running a little girl, all life and activity, with a ringing voice, calling out merrily, "I'se got him some o' they pretty little flowers—that looks like a little bird flying away!" "Pink, and blue, and white!" exclaimed another. "And here's one," said the first boy, coming out from among the furze bushes, "pinky white. Isn't it a little beauty?"—showing it to them with delight. "They calls this—blush colour."

"Here's some woilots;" said another. "Yes, but they's not sweet woilots. They's only dog woilots. Bob's run out to Copnor, to get him some real sweet woilots." "I knows 'em;" exclaimed another: "they grows on a green bank there." "Yes, under a hedge;" said another: "I'se seen 'em." "So's I!" said a very little voice, in a tone of delight and triumph:—"Father carries me on his back to see 'em." "Yes, but Bob's not find 'em a-blowing now;" said the first boy: "it's too late for 'em."

"I'se get him some o' these yellow furze blossom;" said another. "Mind you's not prick your fingers;" said another, laughing. "I'se not care for that. I'se get him some. They's very pretty. And they smells sweet; like honey."

These, I thought, are some of the happy children we saw with the good old cobbler this morning.

"Oh, look here!" exclaimed a little girl, just come up, panting for breath; "isn't this a pretty daisy?—pink all round the edges!—Oh, you little darling!—White and pink !—I'se take it home, and give it Mr. Pounds!"

"I'se get him some groundsel for his birds!" said an eager lad, grasping a hand-full. "And I'se take him some chickweed; they's very fond of it;" said a little voice beside him. "I often gets him chickweed for his birds;" said a stout lad; "and so does brother Jack, and cousin Jenny." "And they long spikes!" exclaimed another; "they calls 'em canary seed." "I knows 'em;" said the first boy; "with broad leaves like. Mr. Pounds calls 'em plantain." "How the birds likes 'em!" said a lively little fellow, looking up, with bright face; "I likes to stand and watch 'em peck at 'em; they likes 'em so!" "I'se have a bird o' my own soon;" said another; "and I'se get him plenty o' they plantain spikes; and plenty o' groundsel too, and chickweed."

"Hark,—that lark!"—exclaimed the first boy; looking up, and standing erect and firm; listening intently. "How clear he sings! And so far off!"

"I'se not see it;" said a little boy; turning up his face, and putting both hands before his eyes, to screen them from the sun.

"But y 'ears it, lad!"

"But its so high up in the sky."

"That's it's natur, lad. It's a sky lark. Mr. Pounds says, there's ground larks too. And sky larks, that flies so high, builds their nestes down on the ground. They sky larks' nestes ben very hard to find; they's done down so nice and close like; all down in the grass. You's tread on 'em, if you's not mind. The old birds covers 'em over so, to keep 'em safe and warm."

"Oh, yes!" exclaimed the merry little girl with the ringing voice, full of life and enthusiasm; "don't you remember Mr. Pounds showing us that lark's nest in that field over the Hill?" "Yes!"—several voices at once; "with two young ons in it." "And how careful he covers it up again;" said the first boy, very seriously. "And when we offers to take they young birds home for him; and Dick says, 'Ye knows, Mr. Pounds, your cat's 'ill bring 'em up for you;' Mr. Pounds says, 'No; it's cruel to put a sky lark in a cage.' A sky lark's natur is to fly up high in the sky. It darts up on strong wing. And when you puts it in a cage, it darts up, and hits against the top o' the cage; and comes knocking down again.—Poor thing!"

"Poor thing!"—tenderly sighed several voices.

I turned homeward—with a heart full of gratefulness and admiration, at this new proof of the excellent influence the old cobbler was so happily cherishing. Blessed old man!—Who shall tell the extent of the good thou art doing?—So humble—and unpretending. But thou shalt be blest. For they cannot recompense thee.

VI.

Passing the next day, at noon; all was still in the little shop; except the birds singing. No little crowd of scholars; his little tumble-down window was open, and the upper-half of the street door was open; but his bench was vacant. The old man was asleep in his old arm-chair; his cat sitting on his knee, comfortably tucked up, seemingly asleep too. Two very little children were amusing themselves on the floor; very quietly, as if careful not to make any noise to wake him. They had probably shared his dinner with him. The bit of fire was out; as if it had done its work till tea-time. Near the grate were some potatoe-peelings, and a sauce-pan.

Passing again on my return, just after two o'clock, all was changed. No stillness now! The little shop was full to overflowing of children; some with slates, or bits of slates; some with books; some with only a single leaf out of some old worn-out book, learning their lessons; some with flowers; some amusing themselves with playthings. And the old cobbler was sitting on his bench at work, at the open window, mending a boot; all life and authority! the growing spirit of that busy, happy group! loving, and loved! His cat was sitting on his shoulder, looking about, interested in every thing. The birds were singing loud, enjoying the lively scene.

"Johnny, when's you bring me you's boot to mend, with the big hole in it?" "Any when, Mr. Pounds," "Any when? Now, ye rascal! Off with you!" And the little fellow ran out, laughing and full of glee; and was soon back with his old boot; and gave it to the kind old man, with love and respect. The old man took it from the child with a tender seriousness; and turned it about and about, and looked at it with such searching care;—all the children were hushed to stillness, and loving respect. He had probably done the like for some of them. "I'se make a good job of it for you, Johnny." "Thank you, Mr. Pounds."

"Dick, here's a sum for you;" handing a slate to one of the bigger boys. He was one of the three I had questioned in the multiplication-table the day before. "What rule's it in?" "Rule of three, Mr. Pounds." "Right. What sort?" "Double rule of three." "Right again. Now, quick, lad. But, mind, no blunders. Slow, and sure. But, quickest best; so long as there's no blundering." At once the boy was leaning with his back against the wall, intent on doing his sum.

"Sandy, come here, lad." And a quiet-looking little boy, with chubby cheeks, came to him. "What's this, Sandy?" touching the boy's nose with his finger. "My nose, Mr. Pounds." "Spell nose, Sandy." And the boy spelt nose. "What's this?" laying his broad hand on the child's head. "My head, Mr. Pounds." "What's it good for?" "Doesn't know, Mr. Pounds." "No nor nobody else. Fill it full o' larning, Sandy! Then it's be good for something. Here, go and larn this." And he gave him a torn leaf with some verses on. "I knows you like 'em; they's very pretty verses; 'Birds in their little nests agree.' And you's all agree, and be good friends together, like the little birds in they's nestes." "Yes, Mr. Pounds;" several little voices; "we's all be good friends together." "That's it, lads."

"What's that you's a-doing, Joe?" "Nothing, Mr. Pounds." "Then keep your nothing to yorself; and don't molest your neighbur."

"Here, Georgy, here's some verses for you." And a beautiful little girl, with open blooming countenance, came and received from him another leaf, out of an old worn-out book. I knows you's like these pretty verses, Georgy:

'Hop about, pretty sparrow, and pick up the hay,
'And the twigs, and the lamb's-wool, and moss;
'Indeed I won't hurt you, my dear little Dick!'

"You's not hurt a poor little Dick, Georgy?" "No, Mr. Pounds." And all the others seemed to say so too, by their looks. "No; let 'em all live and be merry!" "Yes, Mr. Pounds!"—a crowd of little voices, very emphatic. "There, Georgy; go an' larn yur verses; and as soon's yur know the first verse, come an say it." And she went out and sat down on the little bench in the street, just under his open window, and began reading the verses aloud to herself; another little girl close beside her looking over too; and another, on the other side, leaning against her shoulder, enjoying hearing her read.

A drunken man was passing. "Look at that drunken fellow;" the old man said very solemnly; and all were fixed upon him; eyes and ears. "What a beast he makes of himself! Nay, worse than a beast. Beastes never get drunk. Never get drunk as long as ye live." "No, Mr. Pounds;" several of the older boys, very seriously. "That's the abuse of God's good gifts; and they's be punished for it. Never get drunk. Look, he can't stand straight. He's a-trying to stop, and he can't; he's all in a totter. He's despised by every body that sees him. And he's no comfort in himself. He despises himself. And it's all for drink. Never get drunk, as long as ye live." "No, Mr. Pounds."

"Tom, my lad, come and read the first chapter of Genesis; how God created the heavens and earth, and all things therein! Here's a Bible for you." And a stout intelligent boy, of rather superior expression of countenance, received the Bible with reverence; and read the chapter, with a clear voice and pleasant expressiveness; all the rest listening, very still, and full of interest. When he had finished, the old man said with grave tenderness; "Who created this world, Tom, you lives in, and made it so good for us, and filled it with so many beautiful and pleasant things; all to make us happy?" "God, Mr. Pounds." "And you's love God, Tom; and try and do all as you can to serve him, and please him?" "I'se try, Mr. Pounds," "That's it, lad. Try, and do your best; and God 'ill bless you. Here, take the Bible with you, Tom; and read on for yourself. And make it yur Friend all yur life. It 'ill fit you to go to heaven, and be happy for ever." The lad took the Bible gratefully, and went and sat down on the stairs, and bent over it, with self-devoting earnestness. And a pleasing seriousness dwelt over all.

"Doesn't that linnet sing sweet, Lizzy?" the old man said in a gentle voice to the little girl who read to us the day before, and who was now leaning against his knee, listening to it. "Yes, Mr. Pounds. I do so like to hear it." "So does I, Lizzy. Who made it, Lizzy?" "God, Mr. Pounds." "Yes. The great and good God, who created the heavens and the earth, made that little linnet, to sing so sweet and happy."

VII.

The following Sunday evening, I saw John Pounds turning round the corner of White Horse Street into High Street; with a group of his scholars about him. It gave me a view of the old man's deformity to an extent I had no idea of before; though several friends had spoken to me strongly of it. He would have been a tall man, six feet high, or more, if he could have stood erect; but, as he walked, his body, from the hips to the shoulders, leaned so much forward, that his long back was nearly parallel with the ground. One hip bulged largely out.

But his neck and head turned up with lively vigour; full of self-respect and manly assurance; and showed a countenance all life and animation. His eye was keen, and very observant; but apparently only for things near to him; he seemed not to take any notice of any thing at a distance. He strode along with determined alacrity. In his right hand he grasped a strong straight stick; which, stretching out his long arm in a line with his prostrate back, he struck down perpendicularly, with a force that made the flags ring. His legs were long, rather spare, but well formed, and very energetic. His feet were large, and full of active strength. His strides were long and rapid.

Friend after friend greeted him kindly, as he strode along; some seemed desirous to stop him, and have a chat. He returned their greetings with marked respect and kindliness, but did not stop to speak with any. He was going to the House of God! And it seemed as if nothing could induce him to linger on the way.

It was very impressive to look at him now, and compare his appearance with what we had seen him a few days before, at work in his shop, in the midst of his crowd of scholars. As Mr.— told me it would be on Sunday, all now was very different. Every thing about him was clean and becoming, and bespoke a careful regard to person and dress. Hands and face were well washed. His gray hair, bristling plentifully from under his large broad-brimmed hat, had evidently been combed and brushed. His shirt collar was white. A black stock was neatly fitted just under it. His waistcoat was buttoned up to the top button. His large dark-brown frock coat, which flapped widely about him, was well brushed. His tight snuff-coloured knee-breeches were buckled neat and close, just under the knee; his bluish-white stockings were very clean. His large strong shoes were very black and bright.

A tallish youth, of staid demeanour, was walking near him; probably one of his former scholars some years before, and now gratefully attached to him from maturing respect and affection. A little girl fondly held him by his left hand, trotting happily beside him. His other scholars all looked peaceful and happy; with no strict restraint, but moving along with a cheerful propriety. The consciousness of the Lord's day, and that they were going to the House of God, seemed to imbue them all with a feeling of reverence, and serious pleasantness.

The time for the service to commence was a quarter to seven o'clock. About a quarter of an hour before that time John Pounds peacefully entered the House of God, and was quietly followed by his scholars.

VIII.

Some weeks after, going to Chapel one Sunday morning, I saw some one standing talking with the Secretary of the Congregation that I had not seen before. He was standing with his back to me; a square-shouldered man, about medium height, well-proportioned, strong-looking, erect and firm on his feet, with a prepossessing ease. As I came up to them, the Secretary said, "Let me introduce you to Mr. Lemmon; many years a Member of the Congregation;" and explained, that he was master of a trading vessel, and was consequently very much away from Portsmouth. "Yes," Mr. Lemmon said, in a pleasant manly voice, "that is the reason I have not been able to speak to you before. I only returned from Jersey last night." Conversing with them a few minutes, my approaching duties required me to bid them Good Morning. But I said to Mr. Lemmon; "If you will favour me with your address, I shall be happy to call on you." He said, he lived in the lower part of St. Mary's Street; the third house from the sally-port, on the right hand side of the street going towards the walls. As I left them, saying, I hoped soon to see him again, he gave me a smile, that assured me of an excellent spirit.

There was something in Mr. Lemmon's appearance and manner that pleased me at once, and left a very pleasing impression to dwell upon. Though there was evidently not much culture, and his living in the lower part of St. Mary's Street implied that he was in but a lowly condition of life; there was a native dignity about him; a manly openness of countenance and expression, intelligent, and expressive of good feeling, an ingenuous self-possession, that made it a delight to converse with him. His eye was bright, observant, and penetrating. His dark ruddy complexion, sunburnt and weather-beaten, seemed to tell of years of faithful endurance in his sea-faring life. His manner was respectful, and with a manly self-respect, somewhat elevated; but nothing assuming; no undue self-assertion. His conversation was ready and flowing, well expressed, with a clear utterance. A pleasant propriety pervaded all he did and said; imbued with a gentle urbanity.

I was so much interested in him, that the next morning I called on the Secretary, desiring to know more about him. He told me, that Mr. Lemmon had been for some years a widower; that he had now living with him, in his small house, several grown-up daughters, and some little grandchildren; and though they had only one room, and that a small one, for their sitting-room, in which they chiefly lived; there was always an appearance of comfort and propriety; go in when you might. His means must be small, for such a family; but all showed good management. The grown-up daughters were industrious, in a humble way; and there was a prevailing good spirit in every thing about them.

"Has he always led this sea-faring life?" "No. When a youth, he was employed in the Arsenal at Woolwich; in the foundry department. There he continued for some years; faithful to all his duties; respected and trusted by those under whom he served. From Woolwich he was honourably transferred to the Gun Wharf at Portsmouth. Here he gained the like esteem and confidence by his constant good conduct; and continued in this employ till near the end of the war; when he entered the merchant service; and worked his way on, till he became master of a small trading vessel; the Elisabeth. He has now pursued this sea-faring life nearly twenty years; and is still in full vigour of life. He has been master of several trading vessels, one after another; respected and trusted by all who have had any dealings with him. Going from port to port, he has seen a good deal of various society, in a small way; and has gained considerable knowledge by it, and practical experience."

That afternoon, I went to call upon Mr. Lemmon. It was between three and four o'clock. I readily found his house; the third door from the sally-port. The street door opened directly into their sitting-room; with three steps down from the level of the street to the floor. Mr. Lemmon was at home; and his three grown up daughters were with him in the room, and several of his little grandchildren. The room was indeed a small one, and seemed to serve as kitchen as well as sitting-room. But there was an air of comfort and cheerfulness about it. Though there were so many persons in it, there was no appearance of crowding or inconvenience. The daughters were quietly at work, and the children were amusing themselves quite at their ease. Mr. Lemmon placed me in what I felt sure was his own armchair, in a quiet corner beside the fire; just opposite the window; which was a large one in proportion to the room. It was very clean and bright. All the furniture was bright and well dusted; every thing in the room looked clean, and well arranged. I was glad to see along the window-sill a row of flower-pots, with healthy plants; geraniums, a fuchsia, a rose-tree, and some mignionette; all showing good management.

"I think I see a little friend there I've seen before."

"Our Lizzy! Yes, she told us you had been to see the school."

"And I had the pleasure of hearing her read."

Just then the street-door burst forcibly open, and in came John Pounds, holding a large tea-kettle in his out-stretched hand;—no hat or coat on, his shirt sleeves rolled back above the elbows, neck and chest bare. "I'se come to borrow your fire to boil my kettle:"—and he strode across the floor, and put it on the fire,—all in a moment. All smiled.

"Yer sarvant, Sir. I'se not know you's here."

"How do you do, Mr. Pounds?" "I'se very well, thank God! I'se come, ye sees, Sir, to boil my kettle. My fire's gone out; and I always knows I'se a fire here to boil my kettle."

. "Yes, Johnny; and in any house you like to go into, all the neighbourhood round;" Mr. Lemmon said, with a warm heart. "They're all glad to see him come in, Sir, and to do any thing for him they can; to show their love and gratefulness for all the kind things he's always doing for them."

"No more o' that, Lemmon. It's for us all to live neighbourly-like, and help one another all us can. Ye sees, Sir, Lemmon an me's known one another before. We's ben boys together."

"Aye, Johnny, almost babes together. For when I was a babe in arms, you were not a very big boy;"—with a smile of pleasantry. "No; about six or seven, I s'pose." "That's it, Johnny; only six years difference between us."

"Yes, Sir; we's ben play-fellows together; Lemmon an me. An when I'se brought home on a stretcher out o' the Dockyard,—a heap o' broken bones, an out o' joint; Lemmon's soon wi' me then; little lad as he was then. Only eight or nine, Lemmon?" "That's all." "And he stays wi' me, night an day; and does for me like a nurse, he does."

"Ah, Johnny, that was a bad job for you; that fall into the dry dock."

"I'se not know that, Lemmon. I'se a lively young chap then; full o' fun; up to every dodge. And who's know, but I'se ben like many another young chap,—gay an thoughtless,—wi' their larkings an their foolery? But they broken bones quiets me a bit. An I'se rubbed on very well, I has; thank the Lord!"

"Mr. Pounds, I'm admiring the size of your tea-kettle! It covers the fire, and partly the hobs on both sides! And it seems to be quite full; judging from the bubbling about the lid!"

"Why, ye sees, Sir, it isn't all for me, like. Many's the poor little thing's belly's empty when they comes to me;—poor things!—an they's have no tea at all, if I'se not give 'em some o' mine. An I likes 'em to have plenty. Yer sarvant, Sir." And he whisked the kettle off the fire, and strode to the door. "Are you going, Mr. Pounds?" "Kettle boils." And the old man was instantly gone; pulling the door to after him with lively energy.

"How full of life and vigour he is!"

"Yes!" said his friend. "Old age does not do much to lessen his activity; nor his lameness and great deformity;—poor, dear Johnny!"

And the friend's face coloured; and a tear started to his manly eye; and he hung down his head, for a few moments. Resuming with a tremulous voice:—"He's as active in his usefulness as ever."

"How old is he?"

"Nearer seventy than sixty. It is written in their old Family Bible, that he was born in the year 1766; the 17th June;—this very month!"

"You said, Mr. Lemmon, you were only six years younger. You bear your age well."

"I have very much to be thankful for;—bless the Lord!—I've never abused a good constitution. I've enjoyed life; but I never gave in to those mad pranks that make a wreck of life;—a misery, and a disgrace.

"It was in this house, Sir, that Johnny was born. His father was living here then. He was a carpenter in the Dockyard. After that, they removed to another house, nearly opposite; where they lived many years. That house was afterwards pulled down to make way for the building of a larger one; that which you see there, on the other side of the street. It was then that Johnny went and took that poor little weather-boarded thing a few doors farther up the street; and there he has lived ever since."

"What schooling had he?"

"Not much of that. He was apprenticed to the Dockyard at twelve years of age; and after that he had no more schooling. And what he had before was very little; and that little, but of a very humble sort. For his father had but small means for a growing family. And schools for children of small means were not so good then, as they are now. No Lancasterian schools then; no National schools. Oh, the blessings provided for children now!

"When poor Johnny began to get better from his fall into the dry dock, and could work a little, they put him apprentice to a shoe-maker; for it was clear he was too much crippled ever to go back to the Dockyard; and by that he has maintained himself."

"How long has he been in that house he now lives in?"

"It was in 1803 that he first went into it; the year of the threatened invasion!"

"Has he kept his school there all that time?"

"No; the latter sixteen or seventeen years. We can't say just how long. There was no exact time when we could say it began. It came on very gently and easily at first.

"Lar, Sir ! there's no telling the good our dear old friend has always been doing in that little shop of his;—poor little bit of a thing as it is.

You'd be astonished;—the hundreds of poor children he has taught there; and many he has clothed and fed. And they all love him; and would do any thing for him. He's the friend of all the neighbourhood round. None of the neighbours, but respect John Pounds; and wish him well. But he never seems to think of this. He only thinks how he can do them good. And he's been like a doctor among them! If any's sick; he goes and sees all about it, and learns what they want, that would do them good; and he goes home and makes basons of gruel, and takes it to them; and nice hot broth; or cooks them a good beaf-steak,—at his own little fire; or a mutton-chop;—and takes it to them hot!—and all so kindly!—to look at him;—great, coarse, ugly fellow,—as a stranger might think him;—striding along, with his long legs;—half doubled down, from his accident;—no coat on,—no hat on;—his hair all rough and bristling out;—as you saw it just now!—And so dark and dingy too. More so than need be; and we've often told him so; and said, we wished he'd use more soap and water. But it's all to no purpose. It's his way; and it won't alter now.

"But to see him going with his nice things,—so quick and lively, striding along!—hot, and well cooked, and all by his own hands!—Night or day, it makes no difference to Johnny! Hot weather or cold, wet or dry; all the same to him; if any poor sufferer wants his aid. And he'll sit by them, and talk with them, and comfort them!—Yes, like a loving Pastor, he will! And he makes it all so plain, and simple, and pleasant; and it's all so full of heart! They can all understand it, and feel it comforting to them! And he'll do for them any kind thing,—like a nurse;—so thoughtfully, and tenderly!—rough as he looks. Nothing comes amiss to Johnny; if he can but do any poor creature good by it. Nothing's too good, or too nice, for him to go and buy for them, as far as his poor earnings will let him;—if it's the thing his poor sufferer needs. And if it wants special care in the cooking and preparing; he'll do it all himself; and all with the nicest care. And then he'll take it to them;—all so kind and pleasant;—it's a blessing to see him come in!

"But,—for himself,—he's all as sparing. He never indulges himself in any of these nice things.

His way of living is the plainest and simplest possible. No one ever hears of John Pounds cooking a dainty dinner for himself. Except at Christmas!—On Christmas day, he always likes to have his roast-beef and plum-pudding!—and plenty of it!—But all the neighbourhood are welcome to come and share it with him!—But all the rest of the year,—all is hard with Johnny. No indulging himself in the way of eating and drinking:—that he may have the more of his little means,—to bless others with!—He often makes me think of our Divine Master:—'who went about doing good!'"

"And, no doubt,—he has often felt that blessedness, spoken of by our Saviour:—'It is more blessed to give, than to receive.'"

"Ah, yes!—dear Johnny!" Mr. Lemmon said, with full heart.

IX.

On my way back to my lodgings in High Street, I had to pass the old cobbler's shop. As I drew near, I heard many children's voices, chattering and laughing all together. The upper half of the door was open, as usual; and his little tumbledown window was open too. Looking in:—there was the good old man in his glory!—in the midst of a host of little girls and boys, crowding about him, with merry laughing looks and voices! His birds seemed to enjoy the life and noise, and were singing loud. His cat was all alive, purring, and rubbing against the children. The old man, like a Father Bountiful among them, was sitting in his old arm-chair, with a large loaf grasped in one hand, cutting thick slices of bread, with quick alacrity, and spreading them plentifully over with butter; and then cutting them into halves, and giving the half-slices into the eager hands outstretched for them. He had no table; there was no room for a table. But on a shelf, close beside him, I saw a great tea-pot, and some mugs and cups, and a great sugar-basin heaped with sugar, and a great lump of butter beside it; and near them, there were two more large loaves in readiness, and another great lump of butter, and plenty more sugar.

"Has y' all got some bread-an-butter now?" "Yes, Mr. Pounds!" many voices at once. "No, Mr. Pounds, I'se not." "And I'se not, Mr. Pounds." "Two's not. I'se cut ye some, lads." And he cut another good thick slice, and buttered it plentifully, and cut it in halves, and gave it to them.

"And now you's have some tea." And he began to fill cups and mugs very fast. "An y' all likes plenty o' sugar!" "Yes, Mr. Pounds!" a crowd of voices. And the good old man laughed merrily; "I knows that!" And he quickly put a good large spoon-full of sugar into every cup and mug; while the children looked on with longing eyes; and the old man,—happy in making them happy!—instantly gave a cup or a mug full to every out-stretched hand.

"An now you's all some tea too." "Yes, Mr. Pounds!" Then he gently raised his hand, and all the children were hushed in silence; and he said with loving gratefulness and tender solemnity: "Bless the Lord for all his goodness!"

After a short pause, the old man said with a joyful voice, "Now we's have a good tea !" And the children set to heartily. And he took the remainder of a loaf, and cut a piece of bread for himself; the same thickness he had cut for them; they saw no difference; but he was more sparing in buttering it. And then he filled a mug of tea for himself; just like their's; no difference; except that he did not indulge himself so bountifully with the sugar.

"I see now, Mr. Pounds, why you wanted your tea-kettle so large!"

"Yes,—the little wagabonds!—I likes 'em to have enough. And I'se another kettle a-boilon next door. Run, Jem, an' see how it's a-getten on. An' tell 'em, we's want it soon. Nay, stop, Jem, an' bring it. Save 'em the trouble; kind craturs as they bes!" And a brisk lad brushed sharply past me, coming out full of mirth. "But some on 'em's very hungry though;"—giving another thick half-slice to a poor famished-looking lad, looking up imploringly beside him; who had devouringly eaten the first half-slice;—and another half-slice to another voracious lad, pushing his way through the crowd to him. "An thirsty too; isn't ye, Kitty?" "Yes, Mr. Pounds; very! My mug's empty again. Please fill it; quite full, Mr. Pounds!" And the old man filled it quite full;—with a comical smile. "Here, Kitty;" giving it to her very carefully. "Mind you's not spill it." "No, Mr. Pounds." Her eager grasp soon spilt some. "There, Kitty, you's ben an spilt some." "It's so full, Mr. Pounds." "Well, Kitty, you says, please fill it, quite full; but I knows you's a-going to spill some." The old man spoke gently and kindly, with a pleasant smile; but very impressively. "You's not say, quite full, next time, Kitty!" "No, Mr. Pounds." This was said in a thoughtful tone; her cheek colouring.

"Here comes Jem with the kettle!" And the lad came toiling in, with a look of triumph!—the big kettle swinging backwards and forwards down low between his spreading legs; his back and shoulders leaning forward; but looking merry, with his shining cheeks! "Thank y', Jem." "You's welcome, Mr. Pounds." "Now you's all have enough! Here's some bread-an-butter for y', Jem; an there's a mug o' tea cooling for y', when ye wants it." "Thank y', Mr. Pounds." "Mr. Pounds, here's little Rory's none." Ha, Rory, lad, I'se not see you." The poor little sickly child, deadly pale, and emaciated,—stood motionless near the good old man; and seemed to have no heart to speak, or stir. "Rory, you's no bread-an-butter." "No:"—in a faint voice. "An no tea." "No." The old man gently drew the poor child to him; and, putting his arm lovingly round it, said; "You's not at school the morning, Rory:"—tenderly and kindly. "No." "Why's ye not, Rory?" The child stood silent. "Where's ye be the morning, Rory?" "Nowhere." "Has y' have any dinner, Rory?" "No." "Any breakfast?" "No." "I'se give y' some bread-an-butter, Rory; an if you's a-ben at school the morning, you's have some dinner too." I observed, that he cut the bread for this poor starving child much thinner, than for the hearty ones; and he buttered it carefully, and very nicely. "Here, Rory; here's some bread-an-butter for y'; an I'se give y' some tea too." The poor sickly thing received it languidly. It seemed too faint with starvation to have any heart to begin eating it; I quietly observed it awhile, without its knowing it. To begin with, it had no vigour—to do much in the way of eating. But when it had eaten a little, the good old man, who had been silently watching it, gave it a mug of tea; but first, he quietly poured some cold water into it, to cool it. "Here, Rory, 's some tea for y'." The child gulped it down instantly. "Some more." "Yes, Rory, I'se give y' some more tea." And he kindly took the mug from the child, the moment he offered it. But, I observed, he was rather slow and deliberate about what followed;—still quietly watching the child. When it had eaten a little more of its bread-an-butter;—then the old man poured a little more tea into the mug, and some more cold water to cool it; not more than half a mug-full altogether. "Here, Rory!—here's some more tea for y'!" The child put out its poor little white hand for it eagerly, and drank it off at once. "Some more, please, Mr. Pounds!" "Yes, Rory, I'se give y' some more." This was said in a very kind cherishing tone; and the poor child seemed to feel it revivingly. But the old man was still quietly watching it; and gave it time to eat more of its solid food; which it now seemed to begin to relish; and then he gave it another half mug-full; which it drank more leisurely; and seemed to enjoy it. And the old man gave it a loving kiss. "Mind, you comes to school tomorrow, Rory." "Yes, Mr. Pounds!"

"An now, has y' all have a good tea?" "Yes, Mr. Pounds!—an thank y'!"—a host of happy voices. "Who gives us such a nice tea?" "God! Mr. Pounds:"—many voices:—in a subdued,—beautifully solemn and tender tone. "Yes, darlings!—God gives us all these good things. An we's bless God for 'em all; an try an do all us can to please him." "Yes, Mr. Pounds!

X.

Stopping one morning at the old cobbler's open half-door, to have a chat with him, and look on the busy scene of life and improvement and happiness so full of vigour about him, I observed some books beside his left elbow very much worn, and coming to pieces; and I said, "I think, Mr. Pounds, you want some new books." "Why so?" he said. "Because those just under that birdcage seem to be coming to pieces." "So much the better." "How can that be, Mr, Pounds." "Why, ye sees, Sir, when a book's new like, an all tight together, it sarves for only one at a time; but when it comes to pieces, every leaf sarves for one. Besides, I doesn't always larn 'em out o' books. Here, you curly dog! Joe, lad, when's ye coming? Stir yourself, lad; quick, lad!" And a fine strong boy, with curly head, about twelve years old, came to him, colouring, as if he thought he had not lost much time in coming; but there was a loving smile of respect too, more prevailing in his countenance. "What's slops, Joe?" "What father wears." "Spell slops, Joe." And the boy spelt slops. "Any other sort o' slops, Joe?" "Yes, Mr. Pounds; what's in that bucket." "Right, lad. Spell bucket." After a blunder, the boy succeeded in spelling bucket. "Now spell pump, Joe." And the lad smiled; for he saw what was coming; and he spelt pump. "Now, Joe, take bucket to th' pump an empty slops out, an bring it back full of fresh water. Dick." "Yes, Mr. Pounds." " You go too, an help Joe." And the lads ran off with the bucket; glad to be set free, and get into the open air; and frisked about, full of redundant life.

"Tom Tit. They calls him Tom Tit, Sir, 'cause he's such a plump little round fellow! But he's sharp enough, the little rascal." And a very little boy came to his knee, with bright face, and sparkling black eyes, and a quick smile, that looked ready for any fun. "Willy Dale." And a meek boy came and stood beside him, about the head and shoulders taller than the plump little fellow; slender and delicate, but full of gentle life and fine perception. He had a fair complexion, blue eyes, beautiful features, and flaxen hair, that flowed gracefully down to his shoulders; his clothes fitted him neatly, and had evidently been made for him, with a simple air of refined taste; but their colours were faded, and their textures seemed thin and slight. Every thing about him seemed to imply tender care, but extreme poverty. "Ye likes a bit o' fun, Tom, doesn't y'?" turning with a waggish smile and tone to the plump little fellow. "Yes, Mr. Pounds; so does you!" "Yes, lad, I does! I likes a bit o' fun as well as any on ye; an y' all knows that!" "Yes, Mr. Pounds!"—

many joyous voices. "I likes fun, an I likes work. A bit o' fun makes work go light an easy. But fun, an no work, brings a man to grief in the end. Now, which o' you two spells fun first?" Tom Tit spelt it instantly; while Willy Dale seemed scarcely to have had time to think about it, in his gentle way. "Now, Tom, spell run!" And he spelt it like lightning. "Off with y'! run to th' pump, an help 'em bring back bucket." And off he sprung; and a good-natured laugh followed him as he ran out, overflowing with fun.

The meek little boy seemed depressed, that he was not allowed to go too; and stood sad and silent. "Willy, dear," the old man said tenderly,—with gentle hand patting his fair cheek; "what's sunshine?" "When the sun shines, Mr. Pounds." "Spell sunshine, Willy." And the tender child spelt sunshine with simple sweet voice, that flowed like music. "Does y' like sunshine, Willy?" "Yes, Mr. Pounds. Don't you?" "Yes, Willy. God gives us sunshine to cheer us an make us happy; an it's for us to enjoy it thankfully; an bless him for his kindness. Now, Willy, off with y'! Run to 'em at th' pump; an get a breath o' sunshine!" It was beautiful to observe, how still and pleasant all the school were, while this little conversation was going on with the tender child. Every syllable of his sweet silvery voice and artless utterance was heard clear and impressive; listened to with delight by them all. And when the old man said to him—"Off with y'!"—in his merry way, his light step bounded off with a native grace,—that even the rough old cobbler followed him with charmed eye, till he was out of sight! And then he said, as if recollecting himself; "I sends 'em out a bit, now an then, ye sees, Sir, for a little fresh air, an to stretch their limbs like; for we's rather thick on the ground here. An then they comes in again bright an fresh, an ready for work again."

"Here they comes with the bucket!" exclaimed a loud voice at the door, in a tone of admiration. And the boys came up to the door with it, full of glee. There was no little stir to make way for its coming in; for the crowd of children were packed close up to the door. "Here's a bustle you's a-maken!" said the old man merrily. "Spell bustle—who can." Several tried; but blundered. Only one spelt it right. "Jem's right. Spell it again for 'em, Jem, lad." And the boy spelt it again, with a clear voice, and deliberately, while they all listened. "Now, you's all remember, spell bustle like Jem. Put th' bucket down, lads; an thank y'." "You's welcome, Mr. Pounds:"—with frank heartiness. "Mind my cat, in her basket." "Yes, Mr. Pounds; we's not hurt pussy; will us, pussy?" "Now, all to work, again." And all were soon still, and happily at their lessons again;—save one. "You rascal there, what's you a-doing?" "Nothing, Mr. Pounds." "Nothing? Then come here, an I'se give y' something to be doing. I'se not like idlers. How far's ye know in this?" giving him a multiplication-table. "To five-times, Mr. Pounds." "Larn six-times. Quick, lad! An as soon's ye knows it, come an say it. Look sharp." "Yes, Mr. Pounds." And the boy went, and, standing straight up in the thick of the crowd, set earnestly to work learning it; and soon came with bright look, and said it without a blunder. "Good lad! Now larn seven-times.

"What month's this?"—to all the school.

"September."—"October."

"October's right. Last week's September; now's October come in. Now autumn's come. Spring for flowers; an autumn for fruits. All at once now. Answer first as can. What fruits' ripe now?"

"Crabs, Mr. Pounds."—"Ah, Jem, lad, you's ben at the crab-trees." "Yes, Mr. Pounds; that crab-tree you showed us over the Hill; so full of blossom; pink, an white, an crimson, all mixed together; oh, so beautiful!" "Full o' blossom; an now they's full o' fruit; an fruit's ripe. How long ago's that when they's in blossom?" "About five months, Mr. Pounds." "Right, Jem:—in the merry month o' May!—when the flowers comes out so gay! an the birds—they's all a-singin!" And the old man looked round on all the children, joyous and thankful, as if he would inspire them with the same thankfulness and joy at the remembrance!

"Any more sorts o' fruit ripe now?" "Yes, Mr. Pounds;—blackberries."—"Hips an haws, Mr. Pounds."—"Nuts."—"Sloes and bullaces."—"Horse-chestnuts."—"Acorns."—"Beech-nuts."—"That 'ill do lads; there's lots more.

"I s'pose you sometimes pricks your fingers when you's a-gettin blackberries." "Yes, Mr. Pounds!"—several voices, with a wincing laugh. "What's blackberries fruit of?" "Brambles." "Where's you mostly find brambles a-growing?" "Along hedge-rows and among wild bushes." "Does mother make pies an puddings o' blackberries?" "Yes! they's so good! An we goes an gets baskets full, an sells 'em." "That's right, lads. Arn an honest penny, when's y' can; an help father and mother keep y'." "Yes, Mr. Pounds!"—many voices, heartily.

"What trees bears acorns?" "Oak trees, Mr. Pounds." "The oak of old England! Our ships ben built of oak. An our brave sailors likes to sing 'Hearts of oak!' What's they mean, Jem, when they says—'Hearts of oak?'" "Strong for duty." "Right lad. They calls our ships the wooden walls of old England. What's they mean by that, Jem?" "'Cause they keeps us safe from our enemies outside." "Right, lad; with our brave sailors a-board. But if all's be good friends, an neighbourly like; that's be best for all. All's be safe then, an good friends, an no fighting. But they's a long time coming to this.

"What sort of a tree does horse-chestnuts grow on?" "A great broad tree, that grows high, with long spreading branches, an large handsome leaves, an beautiful white flowers, that stands straight up, in long bunches." "Well done, Jem!" the old man exclaimed with joy, as if proud of his scholar. "But you says, the flowers ben white." "Yes, Mr. Pounds." "So they looks, when ye sees 'em far up the tree. But take a horse-chestnut flower into your hand, an look at it close; an you's find, the white's beautifully spotted wi' red and yellow, inside. Does any on ye like to eat horse-chestnuts?" "No, Mr. Pounds; they's not good to eat." "What's they good for then?" "Nothing, Mr. Pounds, but to play with. We plays marbles with 'em; an throws 'em at one another; all in fun, ye knows." "But that's not all they's good for. When God Almighty makes horse-chestnuts, he means 'em for good. Horses feeds on 'em, an they likes 'em; an so does sheep; an stags an deer in the Forest.

"Hips an haws, you says. What's hips the fruit of?" "Rose-trees along the hedges." "What's haws the fruit of?" "Hawthorn bushes, that grows along the hedges too." "Right, Dick. The hawthorn bears haws, an it has thorns; an so they calls it hawthorn. Does y' care to eat hips and haws much?" "No, Mr. Pounds; not much. Hips ben nice-tasted, but they's little hairs in 'em, that tickles our throats; an haws ben nearly all stone." "No, they's not much good for man to eat; but birds likes both hips an haws, and they feeds on 'em all the winter through. An we's praise God for his goodness in providing food for the birds." "Yes, Mr. Pounds;"—several voices, with simple, touching solemnity.

"Does they call the hawthorn blossom by any other name?" "Yes, Mr. Pounds; they calls it May." "Right Flemming. Why's they call it May?" "'Cause it flowers in May." "Right again, lad. There's another bush common along the hedge-rows, that bears white flowers. The flowers comes out three or four weeks before the May. What's they call that?" "Blackthorn, Mr. Pounds." "Right, Jenks; the blackthorn. It's branches ben very dark-looking, an it has sharp thorns; an so they calls it blackthorn. It's white flowers comes out before the leaves. Does the May flowers come out before the leaves?" "No, Mr. Pounds. The branches ben covered with young leaves, bright an green, before we finds any flowers come out." "Right, Jem. Any other difference atween the blackthorn flowers an the May flowers?"—A long silence. Not one answered. "Why, lads, next April,—if it please God to let you live so long,—be on the look-out along the hedge-rows; an you's see plenty o' blackthorn in flower. Take hold of a branch, an you's find the flowers scattered like, all over it; only one or two together; not many flowers close together in a bunch. An so's they scattered all over the bush. Then next month, May, look out for the hawthorn, when it comes into blossom; an you's find the flowers o' the hawthorn not scattered all over the bush, like the blackthorn, but a bunch here, and a bunch there, a good many flowers together in a bunch." "Yes, Mr. Pounds;"— a sweet little voice, full of life;—"an sometimes the white May flowers has some pink in 'em;—oh, so pretty!" "Right, Polly. That's another difference atween 'em; for the white flowers o' the blackthorn never has any pink in 'em. That is, I means,"—the old man said cautiously; —"I'se never see a blackthorn flower have any pink in it. I always finds 'em all white.

"What's they call the fruit o' the blackthorn?" "Sloes." "Right, Jem. What colour's ben sloes?" "Black; when you rubs off the whitesh mealy dust that covers 'em." "Right again, Jem. What ben sloes like?" "They's like little plums." "So they bes, lad. Any other wild fruit that you finds like sloes; only bigger?" "Yes, Mr. Pounds; bullaces." "Right. Sloes grows on bushes; does bullaces grow on bushes?" "No, Mr. Pounds; I has to climb up a tree to get bullaces." "What colour's a bullace?" "Mostly black, like sloes; but sometimes, Mr. Pounds, I'se find bullaces yellowish green, with some red in it, when they's quite ripe." "They calls that a variety, Jem, when they's not black; 'cause black bullaces ben commonest. Jem, lad, which does you like best to eat; bullaces, or sloes?" "Bullaces. I'se not eat more than one sloe at a time; or two, at most; 'cause they's so sour like, an bitter. But fine ripe bullaces ben almost as good as plums." "But birds like sloes;" the old man said. "An God makes 'em all good for something. An we's bless God for his goodness. We sees his goodness everywhere, wherever we goes. An we's be very thankful." All were very still, as their dear old master said this. All seemed to feel it reverently, and gratefully.

After a pause for a few moments; which I felt to be sacredly impressive:—"What's nuts grow on?" the old man said,with fresh liveliness. "Hazels!" exclaimed many lively voices. "You's stick's a hazel, Mr. Pounds!" "Yes, lad, it is. An a good friend its a-ben to me, many a year. It's ben wi' me many a mile;—that good hazel stick o' mine. I goes into Havant Thicket, an I cuts it for myself. I looks about for a good straight stick, an a good strong on. An I cuts it with a hook at one end; to pull down branches with, when they's too high to reach without it." "Yes, Mr. Pounds, you pulls 'em down for us; an we gets flowers an acorns from 'em, whiles you holds 'em down for us;" several lively little voices. "Yes, dears. An I puts a thick piece of iron on t'other end, wedge-like." "Yes, Mr. Pounds, you digs roots up for us with it." "Oh, I'se such a nice daisy-root at home.—You digs it up for me in Tipner Lane. I waters it 'most every morning. Oh, such pretty flowers! White, an pink all round the edges!" "Bes it in flower now, Polly?" "No, Mr. Pounds; but you says, its flowers 'ill come out again next year." "Yes, Polly dear!—if it pleases God to let you live till next spring, you's most likely see its pretty flowers again; pink an white." "Yes, Mr. Pounds." And the child looked thoughtful and happy.

"Well now, nuts ben ripe, an blackberries ben ripe, an bullaces, an acorns, an horse-chestnuts, an lots more o' nice things; an I means to go a bit of a walk to the Hill next week; an all you as likes to go wi' me, I means you to go too; an we's have a good day of it." "What day, Mr. Pounds?" "Saturday, in next week; if it's a fine day. What day's this?" "Monday." "Well now, all you as means to go wi' me to the Hill on Saturday in next week;—mind now, you's come to school meanwhiles, every day, both morning an a'ternoon; or else you's not a-going wi' me to the Hill next week." "On Saturday-a'ternoon, Mr. Pounds?" "No Jenks, I'se wrong there; Saturday-a'ternoon's a holiday; you's not come then." "Sunday too, Mr. Pounds." "Right again, lad, I'se wrong there too. I'se ought to say; every day, morning an a'ternoon, save Saturday-a'ternoon and Sunday." "I'se come!"—and "I'se come!" and "I'se come!"—in rapid succession.

"An you's see the beautiful trees in all their autumn glory! Ash-trees an lime-trees turns bright yellow in autumn; horse-chestnut-trees turns rich orange, an yellow, an reddish brown; beech-trees turns deep red brown; oaks turns deep red brown, an bright yellow, an other beautiful colours, all mixed together. An all the trees together, spread out far an wide over the country, makes it look very rich an beautiful, in this glorious month of October!

"Now, these ben the glorious things you's a-going to see wi' me next week, if you's be good, an comes to school meanwhiles." "I'se try an be good;"—"An so's I;"—several subdued voices;—as if not quite confident; —but desiring.

"Mick Robins." "Please, Mr. Pounds, he's not here." "Not here? How's that?" "He's ill, Mr. Pounds." "Ill? What's matter with him?" "He's got the fever, Mr. Pounds." "Fever? Run, Lizzy, and ask his mother all about it; an tell her I'se come at twelve." And off she ran, without waiting to get her bonnet. "Georgy, peel taties; an you's have a taty when they's boiled. Bessy, make some nice gruel; an I'se take it to little Mick at twelve; an I'se tell him, Bessy sends this to thee, Mick!" And the child set about it with a blooming smile.

"Mr. Pounds, if there's any thing we can help you with for your invalid"—

"Bless y', Sir, if I'se not forget you's here. But poor little Mick! I'se thinking of him. We all loves him; an we's all very sorry for him."

"If there's any thing you want for him, that we can get; please let us know."

"I will, Sir; an thank y'."

"Good morning, Mr. Pounds."

"Yer sarvant, Sir."

XI.

On the Tuesday morning after the Saturday that John Pounds had arranged to take his scholars a ramble to Portsdown, I wished to speak to him, and went to his shop; but to my surprise I found the door shut. The little tumble-down window was open, and his cat was sitting at it, keeping watch. But there was no sound of children's voices, and the old man was not there. A woman, with a child in one arm, and leading another by the hand, came over from the other side of the street, and said respectfully; "Mr. Pounds, Sir, is gone over the Hill with his scholars for the day, and won't be back till evening; if I can take any message for him—"

I thanked her, but said I need not trouble her; and went on to Mr. Lemmon's, to know more about it.

As I began my inquiry,—"Oh yes!" exclaimed one of the little grand-children, running to me;—"such a lot of 'em! And we went to see 'em off! Didn't we, Lizzy?All so merry!" Lizzy smiled, but did not speak. She looked sad. "I thought Saturday was the day for the excursion." "So it was;" Mr. Lemmon said; "but the day looked dull, and likely for rain; so Johnny put it off. Last night he said to a neighbour, that we should have a fine day today, and he meant to go to the Hill, and take his little vagabonds with him; as he expressed it;" and Mr. Lemmon smiled.

"And it is a fine day!" "Yes;" Mr. Lemmon said; "Johnny seems to be weather-wise. He often tells us what sort of weather we are going to have; and I never knew him wrong. So last night before he went to bed, he packed up provisions sufficient for them all to have plenty during the day's ramble. The very little ones could not go; for he often takes them sixteen or eighteen miles, or more, before they get back. It's about six miles to the top of the Hill; and that makes it twelve—back again; and they go a good deal farther, rambling about, just where their fancy leads them. Sometimes he takes them into Havant Thicket; sometimes, as far as Nelson's monument, over against Wickham.

"This morning, Johnny was up and stirring by five o'clock; getting a good breakfast ready for the children. And he went to two of his strongest and most active lads, and told them he meant to go to the Hill today; and bid them run and tell the rest; and say, that all who wished to go with him, might come to his shop as soon as they liked; and breakfast would be ready for them all at six; and he meant to start at seven. They soon came running in; and before the time breakfast was ready, all were there that meant to go. And some of the very little ones, too young to go, came to see them off! The breakfast which he had prepared for them was a good substantial one; that they might start in good condition for the day's ramble. At six, he began helping them all bountifully. 'Now, are ye all served?' he said, looking round upon them. 'Yes, Mr. Pounds!' they all replied. The old man gently raised his hand:—and all were still. And he said, solemnly: 'Bless the Lord for his goodness!' After a little pause;—they began; and all were at work in right good earnest.

"The provisions which they were to take with them for the day, he had packed up in several bags. These bags, when first he began these excursions for the children, had a long string fastened to them; so that the boys might sling them over their shoulders, and have their hands and arms at liberty. But he soon improved upon this; and instead of a string, he fitted a leather strap to each bag, with a buckle at one end, and long enough for the boys to adapt it comfortably to their own height; and the flat strap was pleasanter to their shoulders. One bag is always much the largest. This he carries himself. And very often, in such rambles, when any of the younger ones begin to get tired, and can't well keep up with the rest, he takes them up on his back, first one, and then another, and carries them miles together. One wonders how he can do it; so lame as he is, and so deformed. But the heart's the thing! And as they go rambling about, quite at their ease, he's on the look-out in all directions, and shows them all sorts of things; any thing that he thinks will interest them; and stops and explains things in his pleasant way, at any moment, whenever any one comes running to him, with any thing to show him, or ask him any questions; or he turns aside with them, whenever they want him to go and look at any thing they can't bring to him. Whatever interests them, interests him; and they can't help seeing that he is interested in it, and that he takes pleasure in telling them all about it. And this keeps up their life and spirits. His kindness and patience among those poor children seem inexhaustible. Nothing seems to weary him, while he is doing all he can for them. And his strong hazel stick has a hook at the end; and with this he pulls down branches of trees, and shows them any thing upon them; flowers, or fruits, oak-apples, or caterpillars; and sometimes, other plants growing upon them. And when they come to water; as a running stream, or a pond, or a watery ditch; and there are water-lilies, or other plants growing,—floating on the surface, or growing deep down in the water;—he draws them to him with his hooked stick, and shows them to the children. The other end of his stick has a lump of iron fixed to it, narrowed like a wedge. With this he digs up roots for them; and they bring them home; and he gives them flower-pots, or makes them wooden boxes, to grow them in. Any thing that will please them, and do them good. Nothing's a trouble to him, that will give them pleasure, and help to store their hearts and minds with happy thoughts, and good feelings.

"And in the midst of all these kindnesses to others, dear old Johnny has his own deep, sacred delights. October is a favourite month with Johnny. He likes to go over the Hill in October, to enjoy the rich autumnal tints in the trees. You may perhaps know, that from the top of the Hill, looking inland, there is a good deal of beautiful woodland scenery?"

"Yes; I have repeatedly walked there to enjoy the fine views we have, in all directions, from the top of Portsdown; and from the first I have been delighted with that view you speak of, looking northward."

"Johnny always delights in woodland scenery. He rejoices in the bright fresh growing colours of spring; but the solemn richness of autumn seems peculiarly to impress him:—deeply;—delightfully. And he delights to take the children with him, and let them feel the same pure, elevating joy."

"They'll see the autumnal scenery in its glory—this brilliant day!"

"They will. When his crowd of happy scholars had done their breakfast, and were chattering and laughing all together; Johnny takes out his watch, and sees that it is nearly seven; the time he told them he meant to start. Johnny's very exact; when he says a thing, he means it.

When he told them seven—to start, they knew he meant to start at seven. 'Now, have you all had enough?' he said. 'Yes, Mr. Pounds! and thank you!' they all answered. 'Then get ready to start; it's nearly seven.' And he gave a bag each to several of the stronger boys, to carry; and while they were joyfully slinging them over their shoulders, and buckling them to their right length; he adjusted the largest bag to his own back; and put his large broad-brimmed hat on, and got his strong hazel stick:—'And now, are ye all ready?' he said, looking round on them all with loving eye. 'Yes, Mr. Pounds!' all exclaimed with glee. 'Then, we'll start.' He kissed the little ones that could not go with them; and promised to bring them home some nice flowers and nuts, and some acorns, with their pretty cups, and horse-chestnuts, to play at marbles with. Lizzy looked up, and smiled; but still looked sorrowful, that she could not go with them.

"Oh, to see the neighbours round, as they started! All along St. Mary's Street, as they went, and at the ends of Crown Street and Warblington Street, young and old came clustering out to greet them! —Mothers, with their babes in their arms; fathers, and grown-up brothers and sisters, came from their work to see them off; all with kind words, and looking so glad and happy! Johnny seemed to stride along in triumph, as he went along with his merry host about him, and turned into Warblington Street, and was soon out of sight at the other end of the street.

"Warblington Street, you may perhaps know, is the direct road out of St. Mary's Street to Landport Gate?" "Yes." "If indeed, any road," Mr. Lemmon added, with a significant smile, "can properly be called direct, from any street to any principal outlet, in this fortified place; where all the skill seems to be to prevent the enemy having any direct way in.

"Passing through Landport Gate, and crossing the moat, and going through the ravelin, they were out on the London Road.

"My daughter here had told him not to trouble himself about the breakfast leavings:—(there's no waste with Johnny;)—for that she would come and clear them away after they were gone. So there was nothing of that sort to delay them.

"In the evening, as they return from these long rambles, they come loaded with flowers and ferns, and other interesting things that they have gathered, according to the time of year. And then, when they get back, they're ready for something! And Johnny brings them all with him into his little shop; where there's a good substantial tea ready for them!—plenty of good thick bread-and-butter,—all ready cut:—for them to begin at once;—for they're ravenously hungry!—And the tea's ready made, and only wants pouring out; and kettle's boiling, ready to go on making more. That's one of his kettles there; that big one beside the fire; which he brought to us, to have it boiling by the time they come back; and another he's taken to another neighbour's; and it's sure to be boiling in right time. And my daughter here will go and have every thing nice and ready for them. And we're as happy at home—helping to have every thing nice and pleasant for them when they return, as they are to come and enjoy it! And dear old Johnny's the happiest amongst them!—No signs of weariness with him; till they're all well fed and refreshed; and gone to their homes. And then, he sits down in his armchair, and goes to sleep!"

XII.

"Mr. Lemmon, did you ever go with them on any of these pleasant rambles?"

"Once; seven or eight years ago; I can't say exactly what year. It was in the spring of the year; in the merry month of May! as Johnny likes to call it. And a very pleasant day's ramble it was. I remember it all as clear as if it was yesterday. And many's the time I've thought of it with pleasure since."

"I should like to hear all about it, if it would not be troubling you too much."

"Oh, no trouble, Sir. My time's my own; for I happen to have nothing to do this morning. And I shall like to live it over again!"

"Yes; one of the great,—the invaluable blessings of happy memories!"—I said. "And in this manner, our good old friend may now be giving some of those children, going with him this fine autumnal day, the same kind of happiness, for them to live over and over again, at happy intervals, through life!—some of them, perhaps, to brighten their old age, and delight others with."

"Yes," he said, in a deep earnest tone of feeling:—"so he has been doing for hundreds!—Dear old Johnny!—Sailors, out at sea; soldiers, in barracks, and in hospitals; think of John Pounds; and bless him!"

Lizzy brought a little stool, and placed it beside her grandfather's knee, and sat down, to hear all about the day's ramble.

"The evening before his intended ramble with his scholars," Mr. Lemmon said, " Johnny called upon me, and said, 'Lemmon, we're going to have a bit of a walk over the Hill tomorrow,—my little vagabonds and me;'—(he always talks of them so; but its all in kindness;)—'will you go with us?' I said, Yes, I thought I should like it; if it was a fine day. 'No fear of that,' he said; 'we shall have a fine day tomorrow; you'll see.' And it was a fine day! one of the most beautiful days, in that bright, rejoicing month of May!"—It was delightful to see Mr. Lemmon warm up so glowingly to the happy remembrance! All was living to him afresh!

"We were to start at seven o'clock. Johnny was up at five; getting things ready. For all those of his scholars that were going, might come and have breakfast with him, at six o'clock. And a good large party he had for breakfast. And the breakfast he got ready for them was a substantial one; and plenty of it. For Johnny had always the notion, that to enjoy a long day's ramble, they should have a good breakfast to start upon. By seven o'clock, all were ready and in high spirits for starting. He had the night before packed up abundance of solid provisions in several bags, to serve for all of us all day. As for anything to drink; he took nothing for that. He trusted to our coming to some fresh water, when we wanted to drink. And he knew all the country round so well, from his own frequent rambles, that he could easily manage that we should be near enough some good fresh water, whenever it was time for us to stop, and have a good solid meal. The largest bag he retained, for himself to carry; and distributed the other bags among the strongest boys; who slung them over their shoulders exultingly; and soon had the straps buckled, each to his own liking. Now, you big lads, he said, take it turn about, carrying the bags, and relieve one another. And now it's seven o'clock. Let's start, lads!

"We did not go out by Warblington Street and Landport Gate that time; but turned down St. Mary's Street, and came past this house, where we are now sitting, and went through the sally-port close by, and through Mill Gate, into Portsea; and along St. George's Square, and crossed Queen Street near Lion Gate, and went out by Unicorn Gate, and so to Stamshaw Lane. Leaving Tipner Lane to our left, we turned into the fields on our right, and the children ran off in all directions, shouting and laughing at the height of their voices.

"While we were within the range of the towns, Johnny did not like them to be boisterous. There was not much restraint in his way of treating them; for he always wished them to have as much freedom as was consistent with good conduct; but there was a feeling with them all, that while they were in the towns, there was to be no noisiness or roughness in their mirth. And I don't recollect, that once during that happy day of free enjoyment, he had to check any one of them. But when they got clear of the towns, all were free to run off where they liked, and do what they liked; so long as they did no mischief.

"The fields between Stamshaw Lane and Port's Bridge were chiefly pasture land; so that the children could run about free, without any fear of doing mischief. And the fresh morning air, the bright sunshine, the birds singing, lambs sporting about, spring-time with its lively green, and flowers everywhere, and the feeling that they were free to enjoy themselves; all filled them with joy and gladness."

"And, no doubt, their knowing their dear kind old master was looking on, pleased to see them happy, added largely to their happiness."

"Ah, yes!" Mr. Lemmon said fervently; "no doubt! no doubt!

"After the first out-burst of their joy, running wild, making as much noise as they could; they, gradually became more quiet in their pleasures. Some rambled about the fields, picking up primroses and daisies; some stood still, listening to the birds singing; some went along the hedges, gathering roses, and honeysuckle, and May, which were plentifully in blossom. Now and then, they seemed to be looking in at a bird's nest. Johnny had no wish to hurry them along. He wished them to have time to look at any thing that caught their interest. They were now in the midst of those delights that he would have them enjoy with all their heart. Still, when there was nothing to cause delay, he kept his way onward toward the Hill. But when any child came to him, he was ready to stop at any moment, and listen to all it had to say; and was all life and interest in whatever interested the children. There were no signs of haste or impatience while any child wanted him to stop and explain any thing. Still, through all, I could perceive, his onward purpose was—to the Hill.

"A little lad came running to us, with something bright and green in his hands. 'Mr. Pounds,' he said, almost out of breath; 'what's this, so bright and green? It grows all along the hedgerow, a long way.' Johnny received it from the boy very respectfully. If it had been the king, he could not have been more respectful, 'They call it Traveller's Joy,' he said. It is not in blossom yet. You found no flowers upon it?' 'No,' said the boy; only leaves.' 'No; it's too early for the flowers. It's a clematis; but they call it Traveller's Joy. Its leaves are so bright and green, spreading plentifully over the hedges, a long way together; and its flowers, when they come out, are a greenish white, and look bright and gay; and when the flowers go to seed, every seed has a longish feathery tail, curling out from one end, almost as white as the flowers; and they glisten in the sunshine: so that they brighten the hedgerows all through spring and summer and autumn;—in spring, with their bright green leaves; in summer, with their white flowers, so plentifully spreading; in autumn, with their white feathery seeds, sparkling in the sunshine; all looking so pleasant and cheerful along the road-sides:—I've often thought,' Johnny said, with a brightening countenance, 'this is why they call it Traveller's Joy; it cheers the traveller on his way.'

"As we were going through a corn-field, Johnny stooped down, and picked up a little scarlet flower, which he told us was the scarlet pimpernel. 'This little flower,' he said, 'they call the Shepherd's Weather-glass; for it opens in fine weather, and closes when rain's coming. Is it closing now?' Many eyes crowded round to look into it. 'No, Mr. Pounds; it's wide open.' 'Yes, it tells us we're not likely to have rain to-day.' And we had no rain, all day. Johnny went on to show us, that that little flower, so bright and scarlet, was beautifully varied inside with a little purple, and a yellow spot in the centre.

"Just then, a boy ran up to him with a scarlet poppy in his hand. Johnny took it with marked interest and pleasure; and, leaning on his stick with one hand, he held out the poppy in the other, for them all to look at it, together with the scarlet pimpernel; and said:—'These two are the only sorts of scarlet flowers that I have ever found growing wild;—the scarlet poppy and the scarlet pimpernel. All of you try and see if you can find any other scarlet flower growing wild. And if you do, show it to me.' 'Yes, Mr. Pounds!' several exclaimed; 'we'll try; and we'll bring it to you.' 'That is, if you find it!' Johnny said, with a smile; that implied, he did not think it very likely.

"When we came to Port's Bridge, it was between nine and ten o'clock, and Johnny said, 'Joe, my lad, bring us your bag; let's see what's in it.' The bag was full of sea biscuit, broken into moderately large pieces. 'Biscuit!' Johnny called out aloud, for them all to hear. 'Now, here's a piece for every one that likes to come for it; and those that don't want any, needn't come.'—A burst of laughter!—and all were directly about him like a swarm of bees. As each received his piece of biscuit, they dispersed, and some jumped up on the walls of the bridge, and sat down upon them, and began eating their biscuit. Others climbed up on the adjoining rails; others lay down on the grass. Johnny and I took a piece, and sat down among the children, to enjoy it; for our several miles' walk and the fresh air had given us a hearty relish for it.

"When Johnny had finished eating his biscuit, he rose, and stood on the bridge, and, resting with both hands on his strong hazel stick, he said;—looking round on all the children, as they were resting themselves:—'What point of the compass do we turn to, when we look down towards Portsmouth?' 'South, Mr. Pounds;' several of the bigger boys answered. 'What's to our north?' 'The Hill.' 'Yes, Portsdown Hill;' Johnny added, by way of explanation. ' What's this piece of water to the east of us?' Only one voice answered; 'Langston Harbour.' 'Right, Jack,' he said with cordial approval. 'And on the other side of Langston Harbour you see Hayling Island, bordering it all down to the sea. What's the piece of water to the west of us?' 'Portsmouth Harbour.' 'Yes;' he said : 'sometimes called the Port of Portsmouth. On the further side of it you may see Portchester Castle; at the water's edge. In the war-time, Portchester Castle was used as a prison; many French prisoners were imprisoned there. It is now only a ruin. Lower down the Port towards Portsmouth, is a long line of ships lying in ordinary.' 'What does that mean, Mr. Pounds?' a sharp little voice asked. 'Ships that are laid by, and not in active service, and not preparing for active service, are said to be laid up in ordinary. This creek,' he said, 'that goes under the bridge, east and west, joins our Port with Langston Harbour, and makes an island of the land south of us. What is this island called?' 'Port sea Island;' only one voice answered. 'Right again, Jack!—Or, the Island of Portsea; it has both names. From this point, we leave the Island of Portsea, and go out on the main land. I should have liked,' he said, 'to have taken you down to the mud below, to show you some interesting plants that grow in it; but you see the creek is fast filling with water.—The tide's coming in, and very strong. We shall have a high tide today; the wind's blowing in with it. Low water would be better for us; for some of the plants are covered by the water, every time the tide comes in; and when the tide goes out, it leaves them open to the fresh air again. Perhaps, another time I may show them to you.' ' Oh, yes, Mr. Pounds! please do!'—many eager voices exclaimed; 'and let it be soon, Mr. Pounds!' The old man smiled; and said, lovingly; 'Well, well; we'll see.'

"As Johnny leaned on his stick, and stood thus talking, he seemed in no haste to move forward. He kept them a long time, listening, delighted, to his interesting and instructive conversation. I thought he seemed to be lengthening it out for the purpose of giving them a good long rest, before they came to the Hill. When he thought they had rested long enough, he suddenly said,'Who can see that lark, singing up in the sky?' Those that were lying down, jumped up to look; and all were intent—looking up, trying to see it. 'There 'tis!' exclaimed one. 'Where?where?' the others eagerly exclaimed, crowding close up to him. 'There,—that little black speck;'—pointing to it. 'It twinkles like;' the boy said;—'You see it,—and you don't see it; and then you see it again;—the sun's so bright.'

"'Now, lads, we'll start again;' Johnny said gaily; and strode away with his accustomed alacrity. And all the children ran off, capering about, full of fun and frolic, making the air ring with their merry voices.

"At Port's Bridge we left the fields, and came out on the London Road. All along that straight level line of road to Cosham, the high thick hedges, with their grassy banks and ditches, were our chief objects for observation and search. I observed, that Johnny, while he walked fast, with his long strides, kept his eye very much on the hedge-banks. At one place, stopping suddenly, he seemed to examine something on the side of the bank, about half way up; and gave a call, that they all understood, and came flocking about him; and he said; 'Look at that little hole in the bank;'—pointing to a fresh-made hole in the earth, about an inch across, or perhaps less. 'Look! Don't you see the earth, like dry dust, moving gently out from inside the hole, and running down the bank outside?' 'Yes, Mr. Pounds;' several of the nearest said, almost in a whisper, with subdued wonder. 'What makes it come out?' 'Wait awhile,' he said, 'and you'll see.' Presently, the body of a large bee began to appear; moving backwards from within the hole, and pushing the finely crumbled earth out before it. 'That big humble-bee's what pushes it out. It's going to make its nest there; and it's first clearing room for it.' When it had pushed it all out, and the opening was clear of it, the bee went back into the hole again, and disappeared. The hole was just large enough for the bee to move along, but seemed not large enough for it to turn round in. Soon, and one of the boys exclaimed; 'Oh, look! the dust's moving out again!' And another little heap of finely crumbled mould came moving forward as before; and as it ran down from the entrance of the hole, the body of the bee began to appear; moving backwards towards the entrance of the hole, and pushing it out before it. And when it had pushed it all out, and the entrance of the hole was clear and open, the bee went into the hole again, and disappeared. And so it went on. We did not see the head of the bee once. Johnny said; 'This sort of bee does not live like bees in a bee-hive, many together; it lives alone; and makes a house for itself. Who teaches it to make that house for itself to live in?' 'God, Mr. Pounds:'—several said; with feeling and reverence. 'Yes;' Johnny said. 'They call it by some fine name;'—(Johnny meant Instinct;)—'but it's God,' he said very decidedly, 'that teaches the bee how to make its house, and have a home ready for its young ones, when they come. Come along; we'll not hurt it.' 'Oh no, Mr. Pounds!' several of the children exclaimed heartily. 'And we'll not hinder it at its work, making its house so cleverly.' He said this with a reverent smile, and a beautiful touch of pleasantry mingling with it. And all the children seemed to feel it with the like reverence and pleasure.

"While we were on the road from Port's Bridge to Cosham, the Rocket Coach passed us on its way to London. Frank Faulkner was driving. And when he saw Johnny, in the midst of his scholars, he took off his hat to him, and gave him a friendly greeting." "Our friend Mr. Faulkner," I said, "has repeatedly spoken to me, and always with high esteem, of the good old cobbler in St. Mary's Street; as he designates him." "Ah, yes!" Mr. Lemmon said, with a good-natured laugh;—"that's what people always call him:—the old cobbler!—Dear old Johnny!

"The little town of Cosham, you probably know, is very near the foot of Portsdown?" "Yes." "Soon after the Rocket had passed us, and began to be seen above the houses, going up the Hill, we entered Cosham; and, without a word or a look from their dear old master, all the children were quiet and orderly, moving forward with cheerfulness, but with no noisy voices. When we had nearly passed through this little town, Johnny rapped at the door of one of the farthest houses, and a motherly-looking woman came and opened it. 'Misses,' Johnny said, 'these lads are very thirsty; will you kindly let 'em drink at your pump?' 'Yes, Mr, Pounds;' she said pleasantly; 'and welcome.' And she went in and brought her arm-full of mugs and cups and basins; and Johnny strode to the pump, and began pumping. All the children drank eagerly, and brightened up refreshed. Johnny drank last. And then he took back the cups and mugs and basins, and thanked the good woman. And we started afresh.

"The children ran direct for the Hill; frantic with joy; and were soon seen spreading up the open down. Johnny and I walked steadily forward, side by side, in friendly conversation; which I enjoyed exceedingly; and have often called to mind since, with fresh pleasure.

"As we were going up the Hill, I asked him to let me carry the bag a while for him; but it was not without difficulty, that I could persuade him to let me help him. When I felt the weight of the bag, I thought;—Dear old Johnny!—how little do they know how thou hast been toiling for them!—And then the pleasant thought occurred;—it won't be so heavy to carry home again!

"He now left the lads entirely to themselves. No restraint now. And they ran about in all directions, scattering far and wide, perfectly free; just as their fancy took them. He knew that when the dinner-call was given, they'd all be sure to be there then!

"'What a good, kind Heavenly Father we have, Lemmon!' he said to me in a fervent voice, of deep devotion and gratefulness;—'to make all these pleasant things for us!—to create all these happy children, to enjoy his goodness!—and make this world of our habitation so pleasant and beautiful for them! It's all for his children's good. Almighty God needs none of it for himself. It's for us—he makes it so good, and so pleasant. How can any of his children—not be grateful, and try to be dutiful,—for so much loving-kindness?'

"As Johnny and I was thus in earnest conversation on all the delights about us; a lad came running up to him with something in his hand; and said eagerly, 'Please, Mr. Pounds, what's this?' Johnny stopped at once; and received it from the boy with care and serious regard; and told him; 'It's what they call a fungus. It belongs to the same family as the mushroom. Don't you like mushrooms?' 'O yes, Mr. Pounds! We go out and pick them up in the fields; and bring them home to mother; and mother roasts them before the fire for us, and we have them for dinner. They're so good!' 'Well, this fungus belongs to the same family as those nice mushrooms, that you eat for dinner. But this is not fit to eat; this would poison you. There are a great many different sorts of fungus; some are good to eat, and some not. So, mind; some would kill you! And he gave it back to him, with such a kind, loving interest!"—And his friend was moved—in telling it.

"The boy went away very thoughtful; and began to show his fungus to others; and seemed to be earnestly telling them about it what Mr. Pounds had just told him.

"Johnny and I started again. And he strode along up hill with his characteristic vigour; and felt, I must exert myself to keep up with him! And so,—to the top of the Hill.

"'Stop, Lemmon!'—he said, as soon as we came to the top of the Hill; —'Let's turn round,—and have a look. Isn't this a glorious scene?'—He spoke with a warmth of enthusiasm—that warmed my heart to hear it. —'What a breadth of water!—right and left!—There's Portsmouth down there, right before us; and the Harbour, with the shipping; and Spithead; and the Isle of Wight. To our left, there's Langston Harbour, all down to the sea; and Hayling Island, and Havant; and so on to Emsworth and Chichester; all well wooded, as far as we can see. And the day's so clear, we can see Chichester spire in the distance. Now turn right:-—and there's our own Port, in its glory!—fast filling with water, spreading for miles, length and breadth, up to the very Hill. No other Port, they say, to beat it, in the world!—And there's Portchester, with its old castle, and their fine old trees; and that woodland scenery beyond, stretching towards Botley and Wickham. Now turn north, and look inland. What a glorious sight!—Hill and dale, beautifully varying one another; so richly wooded, all about; and green fields and hedge-rows opening between; with all the bright fresh colourings of spring-time; full of present delight; and full of promise—for a bountiful summer and autumn; and food and comfort for winter!'

"After a short pause:—quite still, and silent,—as he rested with both hands on his stick,—looking enraptured at the scene:—'Come, Lemmon!'—he said, with a sudden change of tone, and look;—so characteristic of his thoroughly excellent spirit:—for, with all his fun and jocularity,—there was no levity;—nothing at all—savouring of the irreligious.—No,—dear Johnny!—He is a soul—all—truly religious;—happy, self-devoting,—in his all-pervading piety:—An Israelite indeed, in whom there is no guile:—as our Divine Master once said.

"But now, he spoke with a touch of fun:—'Come, Lemmon!' he said; 'let's go to the Running Walks; and see how the little rascals 'ill run down 'em!'—And they did run down them—like mad!—shouting and laughing all the way!—The only wonder seemed to be, that some of them did not break their necks.

"You may perhaps have heard, that the Running Walks, as they are called, go steep down into a beautiful little valley, just over the Hill?"

"I've been over the Hill, and down into that beautiful little valley; and have looked up the Running Walks, so steep, from down below."

"Then you know the fine clump of trees in the valley, not far off, surrounded with nice short grass."

"I've been into that beautiful clump of trees, and enjoyed its embowering shade, with some friends; so peaceful, and secluded; as if shut in among the high massive bushes so abundantly scattered all around."

"It was there that Johnny had fixed upon for our having our dinner."

"I think he could not have chosen better."

"We all thought so.

"He went in under the trees. The birds were singing delightfully; in full voice. I took the great bag of provisions off my shoulder, and gave it to him. And he gave his call for dinner. And the scholars nearest us took it up, and called out to the others, 'Dinner! Dinner!' And others sent it forward; and—'Dinner! Dinner!'—went on sounding farther and farther off; and they were all very quickly with us; and seated themselves round their dear old master; some, on the grass; some, on crags of stone; some, at the roots of trees; all, just as they found most comfortable, or convenient. And some talked with delight of the buttercups and daisies they had seen; 'thousands and thousands! We got our hands full!' they said. Some told of the many sheep feeding all over the down; and lambs playing among them; all so happy! One told, laughingly, of a young foal they saw; 'with such long legs! It made us laugh so, when it tried to run a bit!' Some saw a fox, a long way off. 'It bounded away, so light and swift!' one said, with a look and tone of admiration:—'soon out of sight.' Some saw some rabbits, and some young ones; and they ran after one, and tried to catch it; 'but they were so soon in their holes.'

"Johnny was pleased to listen to his scholars; and went on busily preparing to serve out the feast. When he had spread out on the grass before him what he thought enough of the good things to begin with:—eggs, boiled hard; a great piece of boiled beef, already cut into slices; plenty of bread, and several large pieces of cheese; and potatoes, both boiled and roast:—and all was in readiness:—he raised his hand; and all were still:—and he said with solemn feeling:—'The Lord be praised for his goodness!'—Then,—after a pause,—he said,—with a cheerful, loud voice;—'Now, who shall be helped first?'—'Mr. Lemmon!'—they all shouted out. I confess, it brought a tremour all over me; and I felt a tear or two running down my face. He then helped the others. And all set to in right good earnest.

"When all had eaten to their satisfaction, Johnny said: 'Now, we'll have a good long rest here. Do what you like; set still; lie down; go to sleep; every one, just what you like.' Some sat down on the grass, and began showing one another the flowers and other interesting things they'd picked up. Others lay down, and went to sleep. Some walked leisurely away among the bushes. All pleased themselves. And Johnny began packing up the things, to have them in readiness when the time came to start again. Several of the children came to him, and said: 'Mr.

Pounds, let us help you.' ' Yes, lads,' he said, 'you shall help me. I like a helpful spirit. That's the way to be happy through life; and the way to make others happy too.'

"When the things were all packed up, Johnny said to me: 'I've been thinking, Lemmon, as this is spring-time, and all the hedges and fields and copses are full of life and beauty, we'll not go along the top of the Hill to-day to Nelson's monument, as I take them sometimes, for the fine open scenery; but we'll turn inland, and take them all about the fields and hedge-rows, and into the woods and copses, and along the green lanes; and show them all the interesting things there.' I agreed with him, I thought this would be best. So this was decided. He then sat down on the root of an old elm, that curved up about as high as the seat of his arm-chair at home, and leaned the side of his head and shoulder against the tree, and went to sleep.—Good old Friend of them all! It was very pleasant to look at him—resting himself,—fast asleep; renewing all his energies, to start again with them, refreshed, to be the delight of them all!"

"And what did you do, Mr. Lemmon?" "I went to sleep, too!"—with a laugh. "When Johnny and I woke up refreshed, we saw several of the children fast asleep near us. Johnny whispered to me; 'We'll not wake 'em. Nature's the best judge.' And not till the last sleeper woke up of himself, without being disturbed,—did Johnny allow the shout to go forth—for the fresh start.

"All gathered about him. But before we started, Johnny said to them:—'Now, we're going into fields, and into copses, and along green lanes; and mind, you're none of you to be doing any mischief. You're none of you to be breaking down young plantation trees; you're none of you to be breaking through fences; or you'll be getting yourselves into prison. And we're to have no running over the young corn, and no trampling down the meadow-grass. 'No;' he said:—'We're come out to enjoy ourselves; not to do mischief. We'll have no mischief at all, mind. Or you'll not come over the Hill with me again in a hurry. Mind that.'

"As we were coming out from among the trees where we had been dining, the boy whom he called Jack came to him, and said: 'Mr. Pounds, I've been looking about for a pretty white flower that I once found here, and I can't find any of them. They grew scattered about under the trees, and near them outside.' 'What sort of a flower was it, Jack?' 'A rather large flower, at the top of a very slender stalk; six or eight inches high. And some of the white flowers had some purplish pink outside; very pretty.' 'How many flowers grew on the stalk?' 'Only that one.' 'Were there any leaves on the flower-stalk?' 'Three, close together, a little way down below the flower, with very short stalks. The leaf-stalks were longish, and came up from about the root.' 'How long ago is it since you saw these white flowers?' 'The month before last.' Johnny stepped aside a little way, and stooped down near a tree, and gathered some dark green leaves; and, showing them to the boy, said, 'Was this the sort of leaf?' 'Yes, Mr. Pounds, that's it!' he exclaimed, delighted. 'It's what they call the Wood Anemone, Jack. It's rather late for it now. It blossoms earlier in the spring.' 'But can't I take a root home, Mr. Pounds, and grow it in a flower-pot, for next spring?' 'Yes, lad; I'll dig you a root up. And he began to dig some roots up for him, with his iron-wedged stick. 'Don't you trouble, Mr. Pounds; let me do it;' the lad said; and was going to take the stick out of his hands. But Johnny said: 'No, Jack, my lad; I'd better do it; for the stalks grow deepish down, and are very tender under ground, and easily break; and you would very likely break them; for they don't go straight down to the root, but turn about, here and there.' And as he went on digging, he said, 'Always get at least two roots of a plant, if you can, that you want to take home and grow; lest one should die. Here are three for you, Jack.'

"It was beautiful to see, how gratefully the boy received them; and how pleased Johnny was to give them.

"'Now get a fresh dock-leaf,' he said; 'or some fresh green grass; and wrap the roots up in it; to keep them cool and moist; or else they'd soon die. And every now and then, when we come to some water, dip the roots in, to moisten them afresh.'

"And so he stopped and dug up roots of other plants, for others of the children, who wished to take them home, and grow them. And he never did it as a trouble; but always as a delight; however often they came running to him; well pleased to do it, as pleasing them; and cherishing in those children a beautiful, healthy spirit for life.

"Jack's a man now; in the Civil Service; steady, and respected; and in a fair way for getting on well in life."

"And so," I said, "are many others, I believe, of his former scholars."

"Yes;" Mr. Lemmon replied; "few that have been long with him, but have turned out well; both men and women. There have been some unhappy exceptions; but very few. Drink—was their ruin.

"We now moved forward from the clump of trees where we had our dinner, and Johnny went deliberately to a majestic oak, and stood looking up at the lower branches. The season was a very early one, and that fine old oak was almost in full leaf. After looking up awhile, as if searching for something, he lifted up his hooked stick, and carefully drew down a leafy branch, and broke off a bit with some leaves on it; and gave his well-known call. The children came flocking round him, full of expectation; and he showed them, on one leaf, a light orange-coloured spot, inclining to yellow ochre, like a blister on the leaf; and said;—'A sort of fly did this. It made a little hole in the leaf, and laid an egg in it, and left it. And a little rim rose round the egg, and made a little nest for it. And the rim went on growing higher all round till it covered the egg all over; as you see it now. This little yellow spot is a young oak-apple; and the fly's egg is inside it. The young oak-apple goes on growing, till it is as large as a marble; as you've seen them.' ' Yes! Yes!' several of the boys eagerly exclaimed. ' Well;' Johnny said; 'the egg hatches inside it; and then it's a maggot. And the maggot changes, and changes, till it comes to be a fly. And this fly eats its way through the side of the oak-apple, and comes out, and flies away. Apples,' he said, 'are the fruit of apple-trees; but oak-apples are not the fruit of oak-trees. Acorns are the fruit of oak-trees. The oak-apple is a disease to the oak-tree; caused by that sort of fly that I've just told you of.'

"His scholars listened in silence and wonder; and he left the leafy bit of the branch in the hand of one of them, while the others crowded close up, looking intently at it;—and Johnny moved gently away; leaving them to themselves.

"He had not gone far, before a boy came running to him;—'Oh, look, Mr. Pounds! isn't that tree a beauty?—covered all over so thick with those beautiful blossoms!—pink, and white, and crimson, all together !' 'Yes,' Johnny said, 'it is a beauty. That's a crab-tree.' 'How I wish I could get some of those flowers!' 'Do you?' Johnny said; 'I'll get you some.' And he took out his pocket-knife, and with his hooked stick he pulled down a branch, and cut off a beautiful bit, with plenty of flowers, some fully open, and some only just peeping out of the bud, with some shining green leaves amongst them. How delighted the boy was, as he gave it to him! And Johnny was as much delighted, in seeing his scholars so happy.

"Johnny considers the crab blossom one of the most beautiful of our wild flowers."

"I think so too;" I said.

"'Mr. Pounds!' exclaimed another lad, coming eagerly to him from another direction, almost out of breath:—'Oh, there are such nice white flowers swimming in the water yonder! Come and see!' And he went with him to the water; and was pleased to see some of the children lying all their length on the grass, with their lips down to the water, drinking. Others stooped down to the water, and dipped their hands in; and drank out of the hollow of their hand. He rejoiced to see their bright faces, as they looked refreshed.

"'Look, Mr. Pounds!—there are the pretty white flowers,'—taking hold of his hand, and pulling him to the water. 'They're white buttercups,' he said. 'Shall I get you some?' 'O yes, please, Mr. Pounds!' And he stretched out his hooked stick, with his long arm, and drew some of them near enough for the children to gather them.

"And so we went on; turning in any direction, wherever any thing of interest seemed to invite us. And we were continually finding something new to interest us:—till,—I thought,—I perceived Johnny was quietly working his way homeward. He said nothing about it. He left the children as free as ever, to do whatever they pleased; and he did not take any direct line towards Portsmouth. But I could see, that with all his turnings aside, and his zigzaggings, to please them, he managed to keep the lead steadily homeward.

"After we had left the water some distance, one of the children who had brought the white buttercups with them, came to him with sorrowful face:—'Oh, look, Mr. Pounds;' he said in tone of sad lamentation:—holding the flowers up in his hot hand:—'See how my white buttercups are dying.' 'It's because they're water-buttercups;' he said. 'Water-plants won't look fresh long out of water. But take some home, and let them float in water, and they'll soon brighten up again.' 'Oh, how I should like to take some roots home,' the boy said, 'and grow them in water!' 'Ah' so should I!' another, and another, said; with brightening desire. 'Well, come, lads, I'll go back to the water with you, and get you some roots for you to take home.' All the children, with joyful voices, ran back for the water; and he got them some roots; and showed them how to do them up, so as to keep them cool and moist; and then again set his face homeward. And the children came away delighted; bringing their treasures with them!

"By the time we were nearly at the bottom of the Hill, all were hungry again. And Johnny called for all the bags, and we sat down upon the grass, and he emptied them all out; and gave us another plentiful meal. This was to be the last place where we were to have anything to eat before we got home. And I observed Johnny, in packing up what remained of the provisions, without saying any thing, put it all into his own large bag; and gave back the smaller bags to the boys, every one empty; so that they should each have the pleasure of carrying home their bag, without any weariness from its being at all heavy. Some of them seemed to notice this; for they looked at their dear old master in silence; and, I thought, with a feeling of grateful sorrow, that he was determined to have all the burden to carry himself.

"We were now between four and five miles from Portsmouth; and Johnny let the children enjoy another good long rest, before starting again. After they had done eating, and had been resting awhile, and all seemed very still and quiet; a little boy, lying on the grass, said; 'Mr. Pounds, tell us a nice story.' And without hesitation, Johnny told them a nice story; which entertained them all; and while it amused them, in his simple way of telling it, the spirit of the story was beautiful, and morally elevating.

"Soon after he had finished telling the story, another lad said; 'Mr. Pounds, please, will you sing us a song?' And Johnny laughed, and sang them a song. He's not much at singing. But they were all pleased; and he was pleased in giving them pleasure.

"At this last place, there was no water for us to drink. So Johnny took us down to Cosham, and called at the house where we had stopped to drink at the pump on our way up in the morning. But before he knocked at the door, the door opened; and the same kind motherly-woman came with a smile, and said; 'I saw you coming, Mr. Pounds! and here are some mugs and basins ready for you.' Johnny received them with thanks, and distributed them among his scholars, and went and began pumping. And they all drank joyfully. Johnny drank last; and he drank very heartily, and seemed greatly refreshed. And when he had done, he said, very gratefully, 'Thank God!'

"All started again in fresh spirits. But before long, some of the younger ones began to be very tired; and Johnny took them up, first one, and then another, and carried them on his back; and was seldom without one on his back many minutes together, till he put the last gently down in his own little shop.

"From Cosham, we came back all the way along the London Road; and entered Portsmouth by Landport Gate, and came along Warblington Street, into St. Mary's Street, and so into Johnny's shop.

"At Port's Bridge, we had another good rest. And then we made our last start for home. The elder boys were still lively and active, and roamed about where they liked; but Johnny told them on the way, to come into his shop when they got back, and there would be something for them to eat. And a good hearty tea was ready to welcome them, as they came in; with plenty of thick bread-and-butter!—Just as he has provided for their return this evening;—when they will come home with their autumn gatherings; and ravenously hungry!"

I looked involuntarily at the big kettle beside the fire; and thought of the other big kettle at the other neighbour's.

"I've not told you," Mr. Lemmon said, "any thing like all we did and enjoyed that happy day. These are a few samples, to show you the kind of rambles Johnny takes his scholars."

"Thank you, Mr. Lemmon! I feel very much obliged to you. No wonder his scholars are so attached to him. Would that many more who have the care of children—had his spirit!'

"I wish so too;" Mr. Lemmon said, very feelingly.

"I dare say," he said to his little grand-daughter, who had been sitting at his knee, listening to the day's ramble, "you'll go, Lizzy, and meet them when they come back, and see if Mr. Pounds has remembered to bring you the acorns he promised, with their pretty cups."

"If, grandfather? He's sure to. He said he would."

The grandfather smiled; well pleased at her vindication of her dear old master. "I'm sure he will, Lizzy, if he can. Our dear old friend always means what he says. And he faithfully fulfils every promise, if it is possible."

XIII.

Winter set in early; the cold was intense; but it seemed to make little difference to John Pounds. He was seen striding along the street, early and late, without hat or coat on, his neck and chest bare, his shirt-sleeves rolled up above the elbows; carrying his good nourishing things, that he had been preparing, to comfort his poor suffering neighbours.

One keen frosty morning, after a severely cold night, as a beautiful little boy came running jumping in, with shining rosy cheeks;—"How's Polly Wilkins, Jemmy?"—the old man said. "She's dead, Mr. Pounds." "Dead?—Polly—dead?"

Yes, Mr. Pounds; she died last night." "Poor little Polly!—The Lord bless her;—and take her to himself!—She's be happy—there. We's all to go, Jemmy. Some goes first; some follows after. But—we's all to go,—

when our time comes. The Lord grant us—be ready,—when he calls us. Dear little Polly! We's not see her here any more. But we hopes, we's all meet in heaven. The will of the Lord be done!" The old man said this —with simple, deep feeling:—and all were still. All felt it.

"Here, Carry!—run and take these to poor little Willy;"—and he handed to her a warm plate of roasted apples; carefully covered over with another warm plate. Both plates looked clean and bright;—all very nice. "And ask mother, Carry, if he's getting better." "Yes, Mr. Pounds!"—with a delighted earnestness. "You's not mind the snow, Carry?" "No, Mr. Pounds!" And off she bounded full of joy. And all the rest looked after her pleased.

XIV.

One evening, some weeks after Christmas, the servant announced, —"Mr. Pounds"—"Ask him up."—As I welcomed him into the room, I was glad to see he had his coat on, and his large broad-brimmed hat in his hand; for this seemed to imply he was come for a lengthened call. Receiving his hat from him, I showed him to an arm-chair beside the fire; and he settled himself down in it comfortably. I offered to take his strong hazel stick; but he retained it; and sat holding it firmly in his right hand, and seemed to feel comfort in leaning upon it. The fire was blazing bright; and the good old man sat looking at it with a smile, as if enjoying the light and the warmth.

He had several times called on me before; but those calls were by day-light; and then he came just as he rose from his bench; with no hat or coat on; his shirt sleeves—not pulled down from above the elbows; his grizzly hair bristling out in all directions; hands, face, chest, all very dingy. Those day-light calls were always very short; and then he would not come in; but stood at the front-door, and I went down to him, to attend to all he wished to say, and have done. But now, in this evening call, he came in full Sunday dress. His waistcoat was buttoned up to the top button; his shirt-collar was fastened neatly under his chin, and looked white; and his black stock was nicely fitted just below it; hands and face were well washed; and his plentiful gray hair had been combed and brushed into moderate order. His snuff-coloured breeches were buckled neatly at the knee; his light-coloured stockings looked very clean; his large shoes were well blacked, and shone in the fire-light. As he entered the room, it was with a pleasant smile of self-complacency, as if he felt he was come for a better sort of call.

It was very pleasant to look at him, as he now sat comfortable in the arm-chair beside the fire. His deformity was scarcely apparent. He seemed—a tall man, sitting at his ease; well proportioned, of manly, energetic frame; full of life and vigour; with a countenance—bespeaking strong mind, and lively benevolence; an eye—full of fire; and with an air of pleasing self-satisfaction.

He had always an object in his calls:—some one of his scholars, that he wished to tell me about; or some poor neighbour, that he wanted something for. It was always some—one—thing. And he went direct to it; stating the good he wanted to do; and the very means, he wanted for doing it. It was always something immediate; something practical; some solid good. It was always something for somebody else; never, any thing for himself.

He now told me at once the purpose for which he was come. And as soon as this was provided for, he went on, with scarcely a moment's interval, to tell me of something else; and went on to other things, with his never-failing readiness and abundance;—telling of his doings with his scholars, and poor neighbours; always something personally about him; all heart and soul in it; as if he could never have told enough about them.

"No! "—he said,—suddenly,—abruptly,—in the midst of our conversation;—and very vehemently:—"I'se have nothing to do with their quarrels. I never meddles wi' none on 'em:—and I never will. I keeps myself to myself; and I leaves them to their own consarns. I'se not meddle wi' their squabbling. They comes to me sometimes, an asks me to settle their disputes; when husband an wife's been a-quarreling like. 'Mr. Pounds,' she says, 'come an speak to my husband. He's been a-beating me; he's not listen to reason.' But I says, 'No. Go home, an settle it between yourselves. I wants to have nothing to do with your disputes. I wants to live peaceable all round.' And I will.

"At the back o' my house, there's a bit of a tenement; a poor little bit of a shed; scarce enough for any body to live in it. There's but a narrow bit of a court between us. Some poor lost things lives there. They's stowed very thick together. I often hears 'em at their nonsense; but I keeps myself to myself; I'se have nothing to do with 'em;—poor lost craters! Their chamber window fronts my chamber window. In hot summer nights I lets my chamber window bide open, to have some fresh air coming in. An they lets there's bide open; an I hears 'em at their laughing an joking;—poor lost things! An they calls out to me. But I says nothing to 'em. Sometimes, on a fine summer's morning, very early, not time to get up yet;—and it's nice an light;—an my birds ben all a-singin:—I likes to lie in bed reading my book. An they sees me lying in bed reading my book; an they laughs at me, an passes their jokes on me. But I takes no notice. I never answers again:—poor lost things!—I goes on reading my book. But any time, if I'se be able to do 'em good;—then I'se always ready an willing. I sometimes takes 'em a bit o' my dinner; an then they's very thankful; an treats me very respectful then. Poor things!—they's often have no dinner at all, if I'se not take 'em some o' mine.

"No, Sir!—When I first goes to that house o' mine;—that's thirty years agone;—an more:—thinks I,—I'se now be settling down where I'se have plenty o' squabbling, if I chooses to meddle with it. But, no; I'se not pester myself wi' their broils an their quarrellings. I'se let 'em go on as they likes; I'se not hear it. I'se make better use o' my time. I'se not quarrel wi' none on 'em; and they's not quarrel wi' me. An I'se not an enemy in all the neighbours round. An there's not a crater on 'em all that I owes any ill will to. An they's all ready to do any thing for me. They tries, who does it first. One comes in, an takes my kettle, when my fire's gone out, an boils it on their fire for me! Another's make my Neffy a bit of a pie, or a pudding, or so, for his dinner;—poor lad! Another comes in, an says; 'Mr. Pounds, your place wants doing up a bit.' An so I clears off, an goes a walk along the walls. It's when my little rascals ben all gone, ye knows, Sir. An by the time I comes back,—good crater!—she's done up my place, an put things to rights."

"You remind me, Mr. Pounds, of that afternoon, when I was sitting by Mr. Lemmon's fire-side, chatting with him and his family; and suddenly the street door burst open, and you came in with your kettle; and you went straight to the fire and put it on!—telling them, your fire was gone out. You seemed as if you were at home in their house." "Oh yes!—dear souls!—I'se as much at home with 'em as they's be themselves;—God bless 'em! An I larns their Lizzy." "Yes, I heard her read, when I first came to see you. And I thought she read very nicely, for such a little girl. And it was very pleasant to see her sitting on your knee while she read, and looking so happy!"

"Yes, I'se had many a good chance o' making a good bit by that school o' mine. But I says, 'No:—I'se maintain myself independent by my trade.' An that's all I wants. And I'se not take a penny from any body for larning 'em;—poor little things!—And I never has taken a penny for it:—I'se say that; I will."

"But, Mr. Pounds, if you had accepted pay from those who could afford it, and who would have had pleasure in giving it, you might have done more good with it." "No; less good. They as can pay's not the ones for me. I tells 'em, they's send their children to a pay school. They's not bring 'em to me. I'se not have 'em. Many's the gentle-folks, in good circumstances in life, says to me, when they sees how my little rascals ben a-getting on;—'Mr. Pounds, why's you not take scholars for pay, an have some o' the better-most sort? We's send you our's, if you's let us pay for 'em.' But I says,'No. You as can pay for your children's larning, send 'em to schools meant for 'em. Mine's for a different sort. I wants they as nobody cares for. They's they for me!—poor things!—what's to come on' em, if I'se not take 'em in hand? An if there's some as can pay, an some as can't pay; there's be a jealousy atween 'em. An they as can't pay's fall off. An they's what I wants to have in my school.

"They often hurts my feelings;—very much, they does;—ladies an gentlemen;—what I hears 'em say, as they passes by my shop; an sees it full o' my scholars; all going on so happy together. The Port Admiral goes by my shop one day last week, an some fine ladies with him. And as they's a-passing by, they looks in; and I hears one o' they fine ladies say: 'That old fellow makes something by that school. See how many he has.'—No!"—he said with great vehemence and indignation;—"I'se never made a penny by my school! And I never will!

"But, ye knows, Sir, I'se not refuse to receive what kind friends sometimes gives me for the poor children. No; I says—'Thank y'—' for that; an takes it; an does the best with it I can for 'em. Sometimes, strangers stops at my door, as they's a passing; an looks in, an speaks kindly; and seems pleased; and they gives me,—some, a shilling, it may be; some, sixpence. And I says, 'Thank y';'—for it. But it's all be laid out for the poor children. Never a penny of it goes for myself."

"Do you get much help in that way?" "No; very little. But,—thank the Lord!—I rubs on very well;—I does. Sometimes, when a new regiment comes in; or a ship comes up to Spithead; some fine young fellow comes, an stops at my door, an looks in;—a soldier, or a marine, as may happen; or a sailor;—and has a bit o' talk wi' me. And he turns out to be one o' my old scholars! And they likes to come an see the old place again; and I likes to see them again; an they knows it. An they talks about old times, when they's be with me. An they tells me all about what they's ben a-doing since; knocking up an down, all over the world:—poor lads! T'other day, the Billy-ruffon comes into Harbour, to be paid off; and a fine able-bodied seaman comes—leaning over my door,—and stands—looking in at me. 'Who's you?' I says. 'Don't you know me?' he says. 'No;' I says. 'But,' he says, 'I knows you! Don't you remember Dick Saunders?'

'Yes; but you's not that little Dick Saunders.' 'But I bes though;' he says. 'An you's a fine able-bodied seaman! with they good-conduct stripes on your arm!' 'Yes; but it's all along o' you!'—he says. 'Here;—and God bless you!—here's this for your scholars.' And he gives me five shillings. And I says, 'Thank y', my lad! — and God bless you!' And he turns his face away; and wipes his eyes with his sleeve. And I'se 'most ready to cry too;—as I looks after him.—Bless the lad!"

"Mr. Pounds, how is it, that you get all these poor children about you?"

"Why, ye sees, Sir, I'se tell ye. I wants they as nobody else cares for. They's they for me. An so I goes along Crown Street, and Warblington Street, an down to Town Quay, an East Street, an all about the back courts and alleys; and I keeps my eyes about me;—an when I sees a poor little starved thing, that nobody cares for, poking in the gutter;—That's the one for me!—And I goes gently to it."—And as the old man spoke, his manner, and tone, and look, softened to an endearing tenderness.—"And I says:—'Will y' have a taty?'"—And he bent gently forward in his arm-chair, as if he saw the poor child before him, at the moment.—"And I has a boiled taty ready in my pocket. And I pulls taty part out o' my pocket. An when he sees taty, he says, 'Yes.'"—And the old man smiled.—"And I gives him the taty. And he begins eating it. An whiles he's eating his taty, I moves off. But not so fast, ye knows, Sir, but he can keep up wi' me. But I takes care,—before he's done eating his taty,—I'se be in my shop. An he follows me into my shop for another taty. And as sure as he comes in once, he comes again!"—And the old man looked up, with a bright warmth of love and triumph!

"Poor things!—Many's the one that comes to me leaves home in the morning with a bit o' breakfast;—not enough of it, an wants more:—Some, none at all, till I gives 'em some:—an they doesn't go home till night; they stays wi' me to be out o' the way. An so I gives 'em a bit o' my dinner; or else they's have no dinner at all;—poor things! And when I'se done my dinner, I leaves 'em to themselves; whiles I gets a bit of a sleep in my arm-chair. I always has a bit of a sleep in my arm-chair after dinner. It freshens me up like for 'em, when they comes in the afternoon. Why, Sir, you's scarce credit it. People's no notion how some o' they poor things lives. I'se tell ye. One day, when I'se done my dinner, I leaves the pan on the hob, an the water in it taties been boiled in; an taty peelings on the floor. An there's two poor little things as I'se ben an given a bit o' my dinner to. They's a-playing together on the floor, whiles I gets my sleep in my arm-chair. The warm water I leaves in the pan's to wash things up with, when they's all gone in the afternoon. Well;—when I wakes up;—I looks about;—Where's taty peelings?—thinks I. None there. I looks into the pan;—no water in it. If those poor little things hasn't ben an eaten up all the taty peelings, and drunk up all the water taties ben boiled in! Poor little things! But, ye knows, its something warm; and it all helps to fill their poor little empty bellies!"

"What was it, Mr. Pounds, that first made you think of having a school?"

"I'se not think of it at all. It comes of itself like. My Neffy, ye sees, 's born cripple. Both feet's turned in like, and overlapping one another. That poor cripple, thinks I, 's be but a trouble to 'em at home; an they's plenty more to do for, with their small means; I'se take it off their hands. So I goes, an says to 'em, 'Your little Johnny's be but a trouble to ye; I'se take him off your hands, if ye likes; an bring him up, an do for him; an you's clear of him.' An so they talks a bit together; an then his mother says; ' Yes, John; you's have him; for we knows you's do your duty by him.' 'No fear o' that!'—I says. So I takes the poor little thing in my arms, an brings him home wi' me into my shop. That's when Johnny's about a year old.

"But, thinks I, my little Johnny's wants a playfellow to play with him. So I goes to Lemmon; an I says, 'Lemmon, my little Johnny's want some play-fellows to play with him. Let your little ones come an play with my little Johnny. An they's lose none o' their schooling by it. I'se larn 'em their lessons all the same; an they's lose nothing by coming an playing with my little Johnny.' An Lemmon says; 'Yes, John, they's come; an I'se be pleased they's be with you. I'se satisfied they's lose none o' their larning by coming to play with your little Johnny.' So they lets 'em come; and I larns 'em their reading, an spelling, and their verses. Lemmon's little ones ben older than my little Johnny by several years; an they's a-reading a bit when they first comes. So I gets my little Johnny on; and he soon knows all his letters; an soon begins to read a bit; and they's all soon a-reading nicely together. And they plays with Johnny, and Johnny plays with them; an we's all very happy together. And I larns 'em to spell little easy words; and hears 'em say their pretty verses; and they has their little slates; and I larns 'em to write a bit, and do little sums. An they delights in it. An neighbours passes by, an sees 'em all so pleasant and happy; and they stops, an looks in;—and one says, 'Mr. Pounds, will y' kindly let my little ones come and larn lessons with your little ones?' I says; 'Yes; bring 'em.' And they comes, an plays together; and I larns 'em all alike. And another neighbour stops, an hears 'em read so nicely, an sees 'em so busy with their little slates; and says; 'Mr. Pounds, will y' let my children come an larn with yours?' I says; 'Yes; bring 'em.' An so they goes on coming, till my shop's full;—and more than full."

"Yes, I almost always see a row of them sitting out in the street, whenever I pass."

" No; I'se not find in my heart to say 'No;' whiles there's room to stow another. For, ye knows, Sir, many's o' that sort as comes to me, nobody's know what's come of 'em, if I'se not take 'em in. I'se had some of the roughest;—I has;—the wagabonds! But I will say this:—I'se never had one come to condign punishment!"—in a tone of triumph!—Then,—more subdued; and deeply serious:—"I'se had one,—now an then, ye know,—'s been transported-like.—But," suddenly brightening up again,—"I'se never had one as come to condign punishment!—I will say that for myself!—I will!" "How many have you now, Mr. Pounds?" "Why,—about forty, or so. But—they's rather thickish on the ground. And I keeps my window open all day, an door open;—upper half;—or they's be 'most smothered;—poor things! But they's all very happy together. An they's never loath to come; an they never wants to go;—save at twelve an four;—an then—they runs off like mad!—the little rascals!

"One morning, a poor woman stops at my door, respectable dressed, and decent looking; and she's two nice little children with her,—a boy and a girl; nicely dressed an clean. But they all looks very sad. And she says, with a gentle voice;—timid like,—as if she's afraid to speak :—'Mr. Pounds, what's your charge for letting these two little things come to your school?' So I looks up, and I says:—'Missus!—my charge—is—Nothing!—Let 'em come, an they's be welcome!'—To see her then!—How she brightens up!—She looks so!—An then,—you's a-thought,—she's a-going to cry;—poor thing!—An so I gets up fro' my bench, an I lays down my hammer an lap-stone, and I opens the door;—lower half, ye knows, Sir."—"Yes."—"And I takes 'em gently by the hand,—the pretty little things!—an I brings 'em in. And all t'others ben so glad to see 'em come in!—And she says, 'Thank you, Mr. Pounds!'—And then she says;—an she gives 'em such a loving look!—'Now, you's be good; an mind what Mr. Pounds says.' 'Yes, mother;' they says;—so sweet an clear—An she moves gently off. I thinks she's a-crying. For she takes out a white handkerchief, an puts it up to her eyes.—God bless her!—Poor thing! She's seen trouble:—we's sure o' that.

"This all comes o' that fall o' mine into the dry dock."

"How so, Mr. Pounds?"

"Why, ye sees, Sir, I'se only fifteen years old then. An they discharges me fro' the Yard, as incapable. Then,—how's I to live;—crippled? So they puts me 'prentice to a shoe-maker. I'se ought to have a bit o' pension for that fall o' mine into the dry dock; breaking my bones, an putting 'em out. They's not all right now. It's that as makes me walk so lame. But they's never made that clear out; and I'se never had a sixpence for it. But I'se rubbed along very well without it;—thank the Lord! Ye sees, Sir, there's a great deal o' sitting in my trade. An whiles I'se a-sitting all day long on my bench, working at my trade, I'se be able to tend all they little rascals. I hears 'em read, an say their lessons; and it's no hindrance to my trade. My works a-going on all the same. Sometimes I lays down my tools a bit; and looks over their sums, an their writing, an sets 'em fresh lessons, to be larning; an then I goes on mending my shoe again. If I'se not have that fall into the dry dock, to tie me down to my trade; who's say, what a' become o' me? For I'se a brisk young chap then."

"Whenever I have stopped, Mr. Pounds, to look in at your open door, during school hours, I have always been very much pleased to see the cheerfulness prevailing among you. There was always a prevailing life and pleasantness in your school. The children seemed to be doing their work as a delight; not as a drudgery. It has been delightful to me, to see you all so busy and happy."

"Yes, we's all very happy together;—thank the Lord!"

"I have scarcely ever noticed in any of your scholars any thing like weariness, or want of interest. They all seemed full of life and attention while you were teaching them. They applied themselves with readiness to the lessons you gave them to learn. None seemed to feel it a hardship."

"No; they knows it's all for their good. And I keeps my eyes about me. And if I sees any one getting a bit tired; an drooping like; I takes no notice; but lets him go on quietly, just as he likes, for a bit. An when he's rested enough, I calls out, 'What's y' at there, you rascal?' And he wakes up, and he's all ready for his lesson again. They young things ben soon rested enough. It's just a bit of a change they wants. An then they's ready for their lesson again;—so long as they's not kept too long at it."

"I have often enjoyed seeing how you mingle pleasantry and amusement with your teaching."

"Yes; I jokes with 'em a bit now an then;—the little wagabonds! An they's pleased; and I'se pleased;—and we's all pleased together!"

"And when you sent those boys out to the pump with the bucket; with what glee they ran off with it!"

"Yes, the rascals! they likes it."

"When they were a little way off, they began to frolic and caper about, as if they could not be merry enough."

"That's what I sends 'em out for; to stretch their limbs, and have a breath of fresh air. It's a bit of a blow-off for their young spirits. An they comes in again all fresh, an ready for work again."

"I agree with you, Mr. Pounds. I think it a great mistake to keep children's attention applied too long at their lessons, without any relief."

"Yes!" the old man said with indignant warmth:—"for they poor little things to be kept hard at head work for two or three hours together, with nothing to freshen 'em up like;—its too much of it. They's not up to it; poor things!—No!—I lets 'em have their laugh, and their bits o' fun. And sometimes, I has a good laugh with 'em too! And they likes it; and I likes it!—But—not too much of it, ye knows, Sir. And they knows it;—the little rascals!—No; its only to freshen 'em up a bit. And then—to work again. And they falls to with fresh spirit; all the more pleased with it. I keeps 'em well to their work, I does; in right good arnest, I does. It's all for their good; an they knows it. But a good laugh now an then, brightens 'em up like. It helps on work.

"Sometimes, they says to me; 'Mr. Pounds, sing us a song.' So I sings 'em a song;—in my way. I'se not much of a musician." And the old man drooped his head, with a comical smile. 'But it pleases the little wagabonds; and if they's pleased, I'se pleased. Sometimes they says: —'Please, Mr. Pounds, tell us a nice story.' So I tells 'em a nice story. It's a bit of a change for 'em. And I goes on mending my shoe the while, just the same. And it's all to do 'em good,—the story I'se a-telling 'em. They's all a-larning something from it. Sometimes—when I'se telling 'em something funny, they all laughs outright; and I lets 'em; an I laughs too. But it's all what 'ill do 'em good, to think of again; and remember it for life. An when they's all had their good hearty laugh, I says;—'Now, for work again!'—And they all sets to; quick, an joyous like."

"I has a stick; I has. And they knows it;—the wagabonds! And sometimes I lays it on right well, I does. They doesn't like it at the time. But they loves me for it all the better after. They knows, it's all for their good."

"You managed differently with that poor little boy at tea-time; who had stayed away from school; and who seemed too sunk—and lifeless—to ask for any tea—or any bread-and-butter." "Ah,—poor little Rory!" "Yes, that's what you called him." "Poor little Rory! He'd not a-ben at school all day. And he steals slyly in at tea-time, whiles I'se a-gone to Lemmon's to boil my kettle. And when I comes back wi' my kettle, I'se not see him; he's a skulking behind t'others. Poor little Rory! He comes to school next morning; and's ben constant ever since."

"Your kind way of treating him answered."

"Yes, I likes to do it all by kindness, if I can. I keeps my eye upon him, without he's knowing it;—poor little thing! an when I sees him hungry, I'se a crust o' bread, or a taty ready, or something; and I feeds him; and that gives him fresh life and spirit; and he falls to his lessons again, an likes 'em. And he goes on very happy with us all.

"Sometimes I says to 'em on Monday morning:—'Now that one o' you all as bes best all the week I'se let him sweep my shop out on Saturday a'ternoon, and do it up ready for Sunday.' An they all tries an does their best all the week. For they knows, that one as sweeps out my shop on Saturday a'ternoon, stops an has some o' my tea wi' me, and a piece o' plum-cake; an we's very happy together."

"Some of your scholars read well, Mr. Pounds."

"I likes 'em to read well. It's a good thing all through life for 'em, to read well. Its a good thing in business. It makes a lad worth more to his employer, to read well."

"And I've noticed, as I've stood at your door, that while one of your better readers was reading to you, so simply and quietly, all the rest of the children were still, and listening, interested in what he was reading."

"Yes; I lets 'em all listen that likes, whiles one's a-reading; it's larning 'em all at a time like.

"I likes 'em to read well. It's a good thing for 'em at home. A little girl as reads clear and pleasant like, can read to 'em at home, whiles they's all at work round their candle, on a winter's night; and it makes work go on light an quick like; and all's cheerful and happy. And they lads; they's have to rough it in life, an work their way on, as they best can. And when their day's work's done, they likes to come home an read their book. And that's better than going to the ale-house, spending their wages, and making themselves worse than brutes; and coming home drunk, and making all miserable. And at night, when they's all enjoyed a peaceful evening together, they reads their Bible together; an goes to bed happy.

"An I tries to make 'em spell well too. That spelling's the hardest thing I has to larn 'em. But I makes 'em spell a good deal, I does. To blunder in spelling's a bad thing in business. It damages 'em with their employer. So we drills, and drills at it; and we does it at last. I gets 'em into it, before I'se done with 'em;—the little wagabonds!"

"I was very much pleased with the readiness and accuracy with which those boys answered my questions from the multiplication table."

"Why, ye sees, Sir, I tries to make 'em fit for business. That's what they's to get their living by. So I larns 'em all the rules in summing that's most wanted in business. And I says; No blunders, lads. Better slow, and no blundering. But I says; Quick, and no blundering's best of all."

"In looking over their sums on the slates you handed to me, I observed that the figures were clear and well formed, and neatly arranged. And the writing on the other slates that you showed me, was all good; the letters were well formed, the words clear, and pleasant to read."

"I says to 'em:—'Lads, whatever ye do, do it well.'" And the old man looked proud, and spoke with a tone of conscious self-respect.

"You keep their minds active."

"Yes, I questions 'em a good deal, I does; on all sorts o' things. This makes 'em think, and be ready and clear in answering; a good thing in business."

"And in all conditions of life;" I added.

"And I lets 'em question me. And I does my best to answer all their questions. And this keeps 'em lively to it; and they's always a-larning something from it."

"I have been much impressed with the good moral tone prevailing among your scholars."

"Yes. Whiles I wants 'em all to try and do their best; and some's eager and sharp to get a-head of t'others; I says, 'Let's have no unkindness among us. No. Let's have no jealousies; no ill-feeling. Love one another; be kind to one another; delight to help one another, and make one another happy. That's the way to be happy yourselves.' And we's all good friends together. Bless the Lord!

"If I catches any one telling a lie; I talks to him before all the others; very serious, I does. I shows 'em all how wicked it is to tell a lie. And then I gives him one blow with my stick. If it's a very bad lie; I tells 'em all so; and I gives him two blows wi' my stick. And I never catches 'em telling me a lie again."

"Those rambles, Mr. Pounds, that you take your scholars over the Hill, you seem to make, not only very amusing and an enjoyment, but the means of giving them useful instruction, and very various kinds. Our friend Mr. Lemmon interested me exceedingly with telling me about his going with you once; some years ago."

"Ah! that's in the spring-time!—in the merry month o' May!"—And the old man's face brightened; and there was a fine spring of enthusiasm in his voice.—"And a glorious day it was!—sun shining bright; fine fresh breeze; birds ben all a-singin, full o' life and joy; lambs playing about in the fields; trees an hedges fresh an green; buttercups and daisies everywhere; crab-trees in blossom;—so beautiful!—with their crimson, pink, and white. When we comes to Port's Bridge, tide's a-coming in strong. Thinks I;—We's have a grand sight, when we gets to the top o' the Hill!"—And the old man paused; and was silent a-while; his countenance deeply expressive with growing delight.—"The Book of Nature, Sir, 's a Divine Book, to larn 'em out of. I tells my wagabonds so. I'se have 'em live all their lives—as always with the great and good God, the Creator and Giver of all these beautiful things. I'se have 'em feel, that he's always with 'em; taking care of 'em; always doing 'em good; to make 'em happy; for this world, and the next."

"I felt deeply what you said to the children,—that keen frosty morning,—when a beautiful little boy came running jumping in, with his bright rosy cheeks;—and you asked him, How a little girl was; and he said:—'She's dead, Mr. Pounds.' 'Ah yes;—dear little Polly!—She died in the night.' Those few words that you spoke;—so simple and touching;—telling the children of heaven; and your hope, that they would all go to heaven, and meet her again there;—and be happy together for ever:—None can tell the influence you were exerting over them, in those few moments. They were rivetted, as they listened to you. They can never forget it. And who shall say, what influence that incident may have on them all through life?—Those few words, and their hope of meeting again in heaven, may be a blessing to them—never to die."

"Why, ye sees, Sir,—what's we all living here on earth for; but—

going to heaven?—If we's be ready.—The Lord grant us be ready, when he calls us.—And what's I a-giving 'em all this larning for;—but helping 'em on their way to heaven?—An if I'se not tell 'em something about heaven; some o' they poor little wagabonds—they's never hear of heaven at all;—poor things!"

"You said, Mr. Pounds, your Nephew was born with both his feet turned in, and overlapping one another. He shows no signs of it now."

"No! He's a fine young fellow now;—though I says it. And his feet's as straight as mine. But it's all along o' me."

"How so?"

"Why, Sir, ye sees, when I first takes him in hand;—that's when he's a little better than a year old;—to look at him then;—he's a poor little thing. Nobody's ever a' thought,—to look at him then,—he's ever a' made the fine young fellow he is now. Poor little thing!—to see him—trying to walk a bit,—an toddle like;—with both its little feet turned in, and overlapping;—and its ankles ben weak;—it's very sad—to look at. And Lemmon's children ben all so bright an sportive about him. An when neighbours begin bringing their children, and they's all a-playing together;—it makes me very sad, it does; to see my poor little Johnny cripple among 'em. Thinks I:—'I'se try an set they feet right.' But—how's I to begin? This puzzles me very much, it does, at first:—how I'se to set about it. But—I thinks,—and I thinks; and I can't sleep o' nights—for thinking about it. At last;—thinks I,—what's wanted is,—to turn its little feet—part round on the ankle, now its ankle joints ben soft an tender; and so bring 'em round to the right place; an keep 'em so:—till they grows strong on the ankle; an then—all's right. But—how's I do this? Thinks I: 'I'se make him a little pair o' boots of old-shoe-leather:—easy at first;—an put in another thickness o' leather,—where I wants to turn his little foot out a bit:—and so go on; a bit at a time; and I'se bring it all right in the end.' And so I makes him a little pair o' boots out of old-shoe-leather :—such little things,—to look at! They fits him easy at first. But I puts in another thickness of old-shoe-leather, where I wants to turn the foot out a bit; and I brings it round a bit, towards the right place. Poor little Johnny! He cries when I puts in t'other thickness o' leather, and pushes its little foot out a bit, on the ankle. But I lets it bide on. It's all for his good. And, by an by, Johnny gives over crying. And when it's ben on long enough, an gets easy like; I puts in another thickness of old-shoe-leather over that; an pushes the little foot out a bit more. Poor little Johnny cries again. But it's all for his good; an so I lets it bide on; and after a while, Johnny gives over crying. And then, when that's ben on long enough to get easy; I puts in another thickness o' leather over that, an pushes out its little foot a bit more. Johnny cries again; but I lets it bide on. An so I goes on; till I brings 'em both round into their right place. And I keeps 'em so; whiles Johnny's a-growing; an his bones ben a-hardening; and his ankle joints ben a-getting strong like. And they's all a-stiffening; and, in time, they grows firm; and all's right in the end. And that's how my Johnny's the fine young fellow he is now.—Bless the Lord for it!"

"How old is your Nephew, Mr. Pounds?"

"Why,—he's born in the year o' the battle o' Waterloo. That's eighteen year ago last June. And he's a good trade in his hands to live by. Ye sees, Sir; when my Johnny's growing a biggish lad; and he's well up in his summing; and reads well, and spells well;—thinks I,—I'se larn him my trade. It 'ill be something for him to live by. An so I larns him my trade. An when I'se larned him all I can in my trade; I puts him 'prentice, for the last year, to the best shoe-maker in Portsmouth;—a ladies' shoe-maker. That's beyond me. I'se not up to that. And when he's out of his time, he's good at his trade. And he's steady, and industrious. I'se say that for him. And he's arning a good living for himself."

"He still lives with you?"

"Yes;—dear Johnny!—I hopes—we's never part;—till death parts us, —please the Lord!"

"Have you ever done the same kind of cure for others?"

"Yes. When neighbours round sees my little Johnny's feet coming all right, they brings their poor little things to me;—first one, and then another; with their poor little feet crippled; some, with one foot turned in;—some, both; and overlapping, like my little Johnny's. And they says to me: 'Mr. Pounds, can y' cure these poor little feet o' my child's?' An the poor mother shows me her child's little feet,—turning in.—'Yes, Missus,' I says; 'I'se try.' And I takes it in hand; and I makes it a little pair o' boots out of old-shoe-leather; and I does for it, like I'se a-done for my little Johnny. They's a long time about. But I'se always make a good job of it for 'em in the end."

"What do you charge them for these cures, that you devote so much time and care to?"

"Charge?"—And the old man laughed.—"I charges 'em nothing!—Poor things!—they's nothing to pay with:—not they. No, poor souls!—it's hard enough for the like o' they—to buy a bit of victuals—to put into their poor little things' mouths. And I'se always glad to do 'em a good turn; when's I can. Bless the Lord, that I can!—I'se two in hand now."

"I'm told, Mr. Pounds, you'd a grand dinner at your house on Christmas day!"—The old man laughed heartily.—"And that you had a great many guests to partake of it!"—Again the old man laughed heartily.—"Ah, yes, Sir!—Ye sees, on Christmas day, I likes to have my plum-pudding;—an plenty of it! For all the neighbours round—knows they's welcome to come an taste o' my plum-pudding. I likes to see 'em enjoy themselves;—poor things!—They's have no plum-pudding all the year round besides." "May I ask, how many you had to taste your plum-pudding?" "I'se not know; I never counts. But they's not all there at a time. Some comes in, and has their taste like; an then they goes out, an makes room for others to come in, and have their taste. And so they keeps on going, and coming, as long's they like." "How long did your dinner-party last?" The old man laughed again.—"Why, ye sees, Sir; the last comer's not done a-coming, when we's a-getting our tea. But—there it is,—ready for 'em. And they all has their taste o' my plum-pudding."

XV.

Towards the close of the 1835, we opened a new Sunday-school in High Street; designed for girls and very little boys; to be conducted entirely by ladies of the Congregation; except that I, as Pastor, was privileged to take part in all their proceedings. The Sunday after its commencement, as the afternoon teaching was going quietly on, all seriously cheerful; there was a gentle tap at the door. A teacher went and opened it. It was the good old cobbler of St. Mary's Street; with three little children, two girls and a boy. "Yer sarvant, Ma'am!" he said, very respectfully. "I'se come to bring these scholars o' mine, if you's be so kind an enter 'em in your Sunday-school." "Yes, Mr. Pounds," the Teacher replied, with a very cordial welcome; "we shall be very happy to do so." "Ye knows, Ma'am, they's a-coming to your school o' Sundays, an they's be wi' me o' week-days." "Yes. But come in, Mr. Pounds." The old man entered—so gently, so respectfully; it was quite touching to see him. Several of the Teachers came forward to welcome him; some shook hands with him; all received him with great respect. And his aged countenance coloured; and his glistening eye—looked his thanks;—while, for a few moments, he stood silent;—looking gratefully up at them. When he spoke, his voice was gentle and rather tremulous, and his manner was subdued; but all he said was direct to the purpose; in few words; simple and very impressive; full of good feeling and benevolence. After a few minutes' pleasant conversation, he took his leave:—"Yer sarvant, ladies!"—looking round at all the Teachers,—gently bowing his head;—and quietly left the room;—his three little scholars that he left with us, looking lovingly after him as he went.

The next Sunday afternoon:—another gentle tap at the door. It was the good old cobbler again; bringing two little children, a boy and a girl; requesting to have them entered as scholars. As he entered the room, very gently, all the Teachers rose to welcome him; some coming and shaking hands with him. The two children, as they were kindly taken to their place, seemed quite happy, to find themselves seated beside their former companions; admitted the Sunday before. After a little friendly chat, the old man went quietly out; with—"Yer sarvant, ladies!"—gently bending his head forward.

These visits of the good old man became very frequent; bringing others of his scholars; and always with the same pleasing and grateful interest; the Teachers always happy to welcome him; and the old man looking happy, as he gave his scholars into their care. The Teachers remarked to one another, with a smile, that the children he brought, were always brought neatly dressed, with clean hands and face, their hair smooth; as if prepared with care for the occasion.

It was a very impressive sight, to see the old man striding along High Street so frequently on Sunday afternoons, so deformed and ungainly in his action, but with such earnest determination, taking scholars to the school. He had sometimes two children with him; sometimes, three; but more frequently, it was one;—led fondly by the hand; while the other hand grasped firmly his strong hazel stick,—for support;—which he struck forcibly down, as he strode along with his accustomed alacrity:—his head turning up with lively countenance.

When he wished to have a child entered, and could not come himself, he would send a note with it, addressed to the Teachers, expressing his request. Sometimes he would send the child alone, with such a note; but more frequently, children coming with such notes from him—came attended by their mother, or some other grown-up friend or relative. These notes were of the oddest sort. They were written on the merest scraps of paper, of no definable shape; always very little bits; torn, ragged, coarse, crumpled, as might happen; often very dingy; never quite white. They were sent open; or, now and then, one slightly doubled up. The writing was a rugged straggling scrawl; none of the letters well formed; with no attempt at straightness of lines, or parallel order. The writer seemed to have no thought of any thing of the kind being needed to make his meaning known. The words were few; scattered in any direction over the paper; just enough to tell what he meant, and nothing more; often uncouthly expressed. But we never thought this unseemliness or fewness of words implied hurry, or carelessness, or want of respect. They were touchingly respectful and considerate in making the request. And while their oddness of appearance and uncouthness of expression often excited a smile, as they were handed from Teacher to Teacher, it was always with pleasant esteem for the good old man.

Meeting me incidentally in the street, a day or two after one of his visits to the school, he stopped to talk about his scholars that he had brought to us. He spoke very gratefully of the satisfaction he felt in having them so taken care of; and said : "Ye knows, Sir, I never brings any o' my little wagabonds to your school till I'se made something of 'em myself. No! I'se not send any o' my unruly ons to plague your ladies. I sends they rough ons to the — school."

The following autumn we had a tea-party for the Sunday-scholars. It was intended simply as a little treat for the children; and was quietly provided in the Chapel library. But good old John Pounds had taken so much interest in the school from its commencement, and had been continually bringing so many of his best scholars; and he was so fond of Children, and was so happy to see them enjoy themselves; we all thought it would please him, if we were to invite him to the tea-party. He accepted the invitation with delight. It was Thursday, September 1st; a beautiful afternoon. The Teachers were all there early; to be in readiness to welcome the scholars, and receive any friends who might wish to be present; and especially, to receive and welcome the good old man John Pounds; who was to be their distinguished guest on this happy occasion.

The good old man arrived, as they were sure he would, before the time appointed for tea. As he turned the corner of the Chapel, and came in sight of the library, and saw the ladies within; for the door was open; he moderated his long ungainly strides,—so quick and energetic, —and struck down his strong hazel stick with less force and sound; and his head,—which turned up with such life,—he gently bent forward; and his countenance—softened to a mild glow of respectful expression. He was in full Sunday dress. He had his large broad-brimmed hat on;—

hands and face were well washed;—his ample frock-coat, dark brown, floated freely about him; his waistcoat was buttoned up to the top button; his shirt-collar was white, and fastened round the neck, and his black stock fitted neatly to it; his tight snuff-coloured knee-breeches and clean bluish-white stockings showed his long rather slender legs to advantage; his large shoes were very black and bright. When he drew near the open door, he paused, and took off his hat,—and gently bowed,—looking round at them all. Several of the ladies hastened to-meet him, and brought him in. He entered the room very gently; but with a countenance beaming with delight. All the ladies of the school shook hands with him very heartily; and others of the friends came about him, with deep interest, and marked respect. It was a very impressive sight, as the old cobbler stood in the midst of them, —resting with both hands on the top of his stick;—his long straight back—almost parallel with the floor;—and all eyes around were looking down to him as they spoke; and he looked up to them with radiant intelligence, as he replied. There was an air of triumph,—and pleasant assurance,—in the happy old man. He could not but feel, that he was there—the honoured guest! And his tremulous cheek, and sparkling eye, expressed it,—very feelingly.

The children were already seated at the table; and as he looked at them, many of his own scholars smiled in answer, to see their dear old master look at them, so pleased!

The Teachers had decided, that he should have the place of honour at the head of the table. As I led him up, through the party,—all eyes looking down upon him with smiles of congratulation,—to the vacant chair,—waiting for him; the old man was much moved with this mark of attention. And his eyes glistened—full of feeling, while he smiled, as if ready to cry, with gratefulness and joy.

Scarcely was he seated, when Lizzy Lemmon was on one knee, and another little girl, Georgiana Richmond, on the other. Both these little girls he had brought to the school some months before. They looked beautifully happy, as he put one arm fondly round one of them, and the other arm fondly round the other; and the old man looked brighter —and happier, as he looked lovingly down upon them, and they looked lovingly up at him. These two little girls he used to speak of—as—"My two little queens!"

And now it was time for tea. The Pastor implored a blessing upon it. And the little feast began. And all the children were busy, enjoying their bread-and-butter, and their plum-cake, and their nice warm tea;

—and the old man—as heartily as any of them! The Teachers were busy and happy—waiting upon them; and the other friends stood about, looking on with delight.

In the midst of this scene of enjoyment, the good old man—lifted up his face—from his own tea,—and looked down the table, so pleasantly lined with the children—on both sides,—enjoying themselves!—many of them—his own chosen scholars!—Then he turned his shining countenance,—and looked gratefully at the ladies of the school,—so busy,—waiting on them;—and the other friends,—looking so pleasantly on!—And he laughed—for very joy!—as if he could find no words to express what he felt;—clasping the two little girls on his knees—closer to him!

The Teachers looked at one another—with silent smiles;—delightfully impressed—with this simple utterance of a soul,—so full of joy!—and so benevolently—and gratefully happy!

The Teachers held frequent meetings, to deliberate on the interests of the school. In one of these meetings, the Pastor, in the Chair, having occasion to inquire of one of the ladies, what information she had to communicate relative to a scholar she undertook to go and ask John Pounds about:—"Really," she said, laughing,—"I'm very sorry;—but I've not been yet. For I was afraid to go. It is so difficult to get away again, when once we get into conversation with him."

"We've all found that!"—with a general laugh in response. "Whenever we stop to have a chat with him, it's no easy thing to get away again."—And Teacher after Teacher went on with rapid liveliness:—"No!—when once we begin talking with good John Pounds, he never seems to have done telling all he wants to tell! He goes on from one thing to another without stopping. And if we try to say Good bye; he's sure to have something else to tell us; something—that he very much wishes us to know!—So that it would seem unkind to go away."

"Yes!—Or there's a little boy he wants us to hear read!"

"Or he calls another—to spell to us!"

"Or say his verses!"

"Or he hands to us some slates, with writing or sums on, for us to look at!"

"And we must hear some boys say their multiplication-table!"

"Or he wants to tell us all about his cat, and his young birds in the corner, that she's nestling for him!"

"Or his poor little bird with a broken leg:—and he's put a splint on:

—and we must see how well it's getting on!"

"There's no end to it!—And the good old man's so thoroughly interested in all—in his own good heart:—that he wants us to know all about it too!"

So they went on,—Teacher after Teacher,—in lively succession:—all spontaneously testifying to the good old man:—every countenance bright:—every voice—cheerful and buoyant;—with a tone of beautiful, benevolent mirth—mingling with it all. The old man's spirit—kindled us all, to a host of happy remembrances, crowding instantly upon us, of his good deeds.

XVI.

The winter 1837-8 was unusually severe. The streets were covered with ice for weeks together. Birds of strong wing, accustomed to fly high, and not commonly seen in the neighbourhood of towns, were now seen flying low along the streets, in search of food. The hardships and sufferings of the poor were extreme. Great efforts were made to relieve them. A general meeting of the Borough was called, to consider how they might be the most efficiently assisted. The meeting was largely attended. An excellent spirit prevailed through all the proceedings. It was resolved, to give food, coals, warm clothing,or money, according to the various cases; that, for this purpose, soup kitchens, coal stores, stores for warm clothing, and other means for assisting, should be instituted in various parts of the Borough; that the whole Borough should be canvassed for donations of money; and, to carry out these arrangements, the Borough was divided into Districts, and a Committee appointed for each, to superintend and conduct the work in their own District.

One of these Districts was Portsmouth within the walls. I was requested to act on the Committee appointed for it; to which I very cordially acceded.

Our Committee promptly met, and were thoroughly in earnest, to do the work faithfully. That they might know how to give relief the most judiciously, they determined to visit the poor in their own homes, and inquire, as they might deem desirable, into the circumstances of each case. In order to this, they divided the District into Sections; and formed themselves into Groups of three or four, and apportioned one of these Sections to each Group, to visit the poor in it, house by house.

Standing in St. Mary's Street—where Warblington Street branches off from it to the wall and Landport Gate, on the right; and Crown Street to Quay Gate on the left:—that line, crossing St. Mary's Street;—with the connecting wall from Quay Gate to Landport Gate,—gives the Section which was apportioned to our Group:—that dense mass of profligacy and degradation, in the midst of which good John Pounds lived.

I felt it a great advantage, that the gentlemen with whom I had to act in our Group, were of long standing in the Borough, highly esteemed and trust-worthy for their sound judgment and good feeling, practically experienced in benevolent works of this kind, and well acquainted with the wretched neighbourhood, into the recesses of which we were now to go.

The morning sun was shining bright, as we began our visits to the suffering poor. It was an intense frost. The air glistened. The first alley that we entered was so narrow, that only one could go along it at a time. Its roof was very low; it was built over all its length. When we had gone in a few steps it was almost dark; and so continued till we came out at the other end. It brought us into a little square court; inclosed with very small houses; or rather—mere shells of houses;—so meagre and slight;—closely packed together on all four sides. The first door we knocked at, was opened by an old woman; pale and emaciated, feeble and tottering, as in a state of starvation. She seemed to have seen better days. "I would ask you to sit down, gentlemen," she said with mild tremulous voice, "if there were chairs for you; but that one in the corner is all I have; if one of you will please to take that. And there's my bed; for this is my only room to live in. If you will please to sit down upon that." We thanked her; but said, we would rather see her sit down in her own arm-chair. "Well, gentlemen; if it will please you." And she sat down. "You've no fire this cold morning." "No, I've had no fire for weeks." "Is that all the bed-clothing you have?" "Yes. I had more at the beginning of the winter. But when the cold weather came on so severe, I fell ill; and had to pawn some, to keep life in me. And I could not get the things out again; and so they're lost." As I glanced round the room, while others were conversing with her, I saw no signs of food:—nothing—to comfort her. All was bare, and utterly poverty-stricken. "Well, you shall soon hear from us again; and for your good;" one of them said; and gave her a shilling to buy some food with. "Thank you, gentlemen! The Lord bless you for your goodness. This will buy me a breakfast, and some dinner; and something for to-morrow, and next day. I've had nothing to eat yet to-day; and I'd only a bit of bread to eat yesterday. But—the Lord be thanked for his goodness in sending you. You'll find others worse off than I am."

The next house we went to, we heard heartrending sounds within, before we knocked at the door. A woman opened it, like a fury;—haggard,—passionate,—raving. There was a man, that we supposed was her husband:—his face was bleeding, and quivering with rage. They had been quarrelling. What little money they had, they had spent the night before—at the ale-house; and came back to their empty room,—desperate:—no fire:—no candle:—nothing to eat:—and they fell to quarrelling, in their desperation.

We asked them, gently and kindly:—Whether a good basin of hot soup—would not be better,—than that maddening drink? They both looked ashamed—at the thought. We told them, we would give them—some good hot soup,—every day:—to comfort them:—if they liked to come for it:—and they should have nothing to pay for it. They thanked us; and said they would come for it. And one or other of them came—regularly—to our soup-kitchen, every day,—for weeks after;—and gratefully received it, and carried it home, to eat it together.

We gave them coals, and wood for fuel; and they had every day a comfortable fire. The clothes they had on when first we came to them, were very scanty, dirty, and in rags. We gave them some good warm clothing. They were very grateful for it, and made good use of it; and they seemed to feel more self-respect. And we had the happiness, before the end of the winter, to see them reformed characters; habitually steady and sober, peaceable and well-conducted.

So we went into other dark alleys; leading us into other back courts; —scenes of want and suffering; too commonly—haunts of vice and infamy. Some were swarming with children;—many—dirty, ragged, squalid. Now and then, we came to a court—silent as death; with no sign of life,—till we entered some wretched abode:—where we found—life—but as a misery:—or a disgrace.

It was our duty—to visit Prospect Row:—one of the most disreputable and abandoned places in this garrison town. We had to take it, not only house by house, and floor by floor, but room by room. Children were scattered about;—chiefly outside;—most wretched to look at; dirty, neglected; with little clothing, and that little in rags; starving for want of food. We found the rooms very small; commonly, almost empty; with next to no furniture; and that little, of the most meagre sort:—the walls—bare and dirty; every thing—dirty:—the windows—cracked and broken,—patched up with paper,—or rags stuffed through, to keep out the weather:—here and there,—unhappy beings,—reckless,—fallen—fallen:—loathing life:—no appearance of self-respect in any:—save, perhaps,—some poor creature,—sorrowing alone;—deserted;—hopeless.

"There's the old cobbler!" one of the Group suddenly said, as we came out of the last house in Prospect Row. "Without hat or coat, as usual!" said another. "What's frost or cold to him?" said the third, in a hearty tone of admiration:—"his heart's warm enough!" I was the only one silent:—not from any want of most deep interest in the good old man. He was coming in through Quay Gate, and was leading a starved-looking little lad kindly by the hand. He crossed direct into Crown Street; the shortest way to his shop.

"And these are the scenes of infamy and wretchedness," I seemed to say to myself, "that the good old man is continually coming into, to pick up the little lost ones, that nobody cares for, and win them into his little shop, and feed them, and warm them; endearing them to him; and training them up, with all a parent's care, and patience, and love, to be good men and women!—happy and respected!—blessings to society!"

In the midst of that general beneficence, so largely exerted, and long continued, in such various ways, throughout the Borough, during that long and inclement winter;—by none was relief and comfort carried with more self-devoting assiduity and perseverance to poor sufferers, than by the good old cobbler John Pounds. Not that he was on any Committee. Such a thought—as John Pounds being on a Committee, would be altogether laughable to those who knew him; as utterly out of character. He never combined with any one, in his works of beneficence. He never seemed to seek counsel of any one, as to the best plans—for carrying on his usefulness. He did his own work, in his own way. He had no elaborate systematic arrangements to devise, for effecting his purpose. He simply acted from his own good heart. He saw his poor neighbours suffering, and in want; and he was all earnestness to help and comfort them.

It was no new thing for him, to be going about all parts of the day, early and late, and often in the night, carrying nice things, of his own preparing, to poor sufferers. But now—there was more for him to do; there were more in want, this inclement season; many about him—more severely suffering; and he was seen going out oftener, and striding along with quicker alacrity; carrying about his basins of hot broth, and his boiled potatoes, and plates of sprats—of his own cooking; and loaves of bread, and other good nourishing things; not thinking of himself; altogether bent on helping others;—happy in the work! Driving wind, keen biting frost, bitter snow-storms, cutting sleet;—all the same to him. Nothing stopped him in his rounds of beneficence.

Long before the day-break grew fervid:—in the deep darkness,—the early passer-by—might see him,—through his little window,—busy at his fire,—cooking hot breakfasts. And, soon, he would be going with them,—through the dark,—into back courts,—carrying them to the bed-sides of poor sufferers.

Notwithstanding all this large increase to his care and exertions,—demanding so much more of his time—all day long,—and often—far into the night;—continued, without diminution, as long as the hardships of this long, very trying winter lasted;—and—much longer—to him;—because of the painfully enduring consequences—long after afflicting his poor neighbours:—amid all these,—the good old man was as constant to his school as ever. There was no lessening of his attentions to his crowd of little scholars. His school went on with the same life and interest. Every morning, between eight and nine o'clock,—or earlier;—he was seen seated on his bench,—at his little tumble-down window,—cobbling; ready to welcome the first-comers; and with as much briskness and pleasantry, as if he had had nothing to do—more than usual; and as if he had enjoyed a good long night's rest. But his scholars saw him more busy—cooking; and he would oftener hear them say their lessons—while he was doing something at the fire. But still,—in the midst of all he was so busy doing,—he would talk to them just the same,—in his own pleasant instructive way. When, at times, something was cooking that did not require his close attention, he would turn round and look over their sums, and set them more work. Some of them he would send out with something nice and comforting, that he had just got ready, to some poor afflicted neighbour. Some he would, now and then, call to help him in cooking; first one, and then another; as a reward for their good conduct; and would hold out the same privilege to others, as an inducement for them to deserve it. And all aspired to it. For it was considered a high honour, to be allowed to help Mr. Pounds. Often, in the midst of school hours, he suddenly went out himself, with something he had cooked, and would leave the school to the care of one of the older scholars; and bid the rest

—"behave themselves"—while he was away. And the report of their conduct was generally satisfactory—when he came back.

XVII.

Mr. Thomas Sheppard, a boot and shoe maker of long standing in High Street, a member of my Flock, much respected for his sound good sense, his integrity, and general benevolence, called upon me one morning, and said: "There is a young man of the name of Sheaf, a journeyman shoe-maker, living in Landport, who has a taste for drawing and painting; he has done several Scripture pieces, which seem to me very creditable and promising, for so young an artist, entirely self-taught." And he asked me, if I would go and look at them. "For it may cheer and encourage him," he said, "to see that some take an interest in his efforts." I willingly consented; and we went in the afternoon. The young man showed us several oil-paintings that he had done. The subjects were all from Scripture. They showed considerable idea of design, and capability of effect in drawing, grouping, light and shade, and colouring; but all of a humble sort; though implying promising ability, if well cultured. I was much pleased with his earnestness as he showed us picture after picture, and the readiness and clearness with which he explained his design, as he pointed to various effects. As his choice was so decidedly for Scripture subjects, I offered to lend him a work on Jewish Antiquities; illustrating the institutions of the Jews, their observances, and their manners and costumes; which he expressed himself pleased in accepting.

Shortly after, Mr. Sheppard called on me again; and said: "I have advised Sheaf to try something more local in its interest; as more likely to help him forward, and bring him more into notice with his fellow townsmen. 'There's the old cobbler in St. Mary's Street,' I said, 'sitting at work on his bench, in the midst of his school:—try that.' And I took him to see the old man, with his host of little scholars about him;—all so busy, and happy. He took the hint, and has done the picture. And I want you to go, and give us your opinion of it." We went immediately. It was an oil-painting. On first seeing the picture, I felt:—-"There's the old cobbler!—done to the life!"—The likeness was excellent;—the coarseness of feature, well intimated, and not overdone. The action, just as he would turn sharp round from his work, to speak to a scholar; with his penetrating eye, and determined manner. The general form and appearance of the old man were well given. He was sitting on his bench, with a shoe in his hand—mending. A boy was standing beside him on his right, reading. Other boys were near him on the same side, some sitting, some standing, at their lessons. On the other side, several little girls were sitting close to the old man; one with her arms round the neck of another. His cat was brushing against him; as if pleased with all that was going on. Bird-cages were hanging on the wall.—All characteristic.—And we heartily congratulated the young man on his success.

But the hair of the old cobbler was painted of a dark colour;—not true to his grizzly gray head. And his hair was smooth; as if it had been recently combed and brushed. His face and hands looked clean. And he had his coat on. His shirt collar was fastened round his neck; and his black stock fitted neatly to it. All which looked as if he had been carefully prepared for the occasion.

The old man's arms were long, and very energetic; well proportioned to a strong man, six feet high, or more. This was not well intimated in the picture. And the more I looked at it,—I felt there was wanting—the expression of the superior intelligence, the tender benevolence, the power of love, the pure soul of piety, which,—with all his rough uncouthness,—I was accustomed to see when conversing with him.

In the foreground, there was an ample proportion of clear space; which, while it showed the rest of the picture off to advantage, gave no idea of the old man's crowding beneficence; for his scholars were close packed up to the very door. And the roomy appearance of the place made it look larger than his little shop :—little more than two yards wide:—where he so often had thirty or forty children at a time, busy and happy at their lessons.

Still, for a general view of the old cobbler at work on his bench, and teaching his scholars at the same time; it was happily hit off. And we very cordially renewed our congratulations, as we left the young artist.

On our way back, Mr. Sheppard, habitually thoughtful, and of few words, said: "I am in hopes, that this picture of the good old man, if it becomes much known, may be of service to him, in bringing him more into notice, and inducing others to help him. For he goes on working—in his never-ceasing usefulness,—year after year,—always the same:—no relaxing with him:—you always find him—sedulous,—thoroughly in earnest,—self-devoting to the good of others. And so few seem to take any notice of him. And very few indeed, he tells me, when I ask him;—for, otherwise, he would not touch on it:—so generous,—so contented,

—so unobtrusive,—and never complaining. But he told me the other day, when I asked him,—very few indeed rendered him any solid help: —in the way of money, or articles of clothing, or other things, for his poor children. For himself he would not accept any thing. For he has a high spirit of self-respect; and is very independent;—as you may have noticed."

"Yes, I soon saw that!"

"Friends, desiring to make him more comfortable, as they thought, have sometimes urged him to accept something for himself. But they could never succeed. But,—for his poor scholars,—he would always accept help; and always makes the best use of it for them.

"When I consider,"—Mr. Sheppard went on,—and warmed up to an unusual enthusiasm:—"how many years he has been carrying on that school of his:—in that poor little shop:—with such meagre materials for teaching:—and yet,—giving a solid, useful education—to hundreds of poor children:—and—in great measure—feeding and clothing many of them:—and many more years, before he began his school, he had been continually doing good among his poor neighbours—all round him: helping them in very various ways, according to their need; continually taking good substantial food to them, in their want and destitution; preparing nice things for them, in their illnesses:—and himself, the while,—with only his own poor cobbling to maintain himself:—I some-times find it difficult—to realize to myself,—how he can have been so long doing so much good,—with such small means."

Within a few weeks, Mr. Sheppard said to me: "Sheaf has taken his picture of John Pounds to Mr. Edward Carter, and requested his acceptance of it."

"What did Mr. Carter say?"

"He accepted the picture, and gave the young man a five-pound note."

Some highly esteemed benefactors of the good old cobbler, with a most friendly interest in him,—thinking it would give himself pleasure —to see himself in a picture,—managed to get him quietly into a room where his picture was, without letting him know their purpose. The picture was standing on the chimney-piece; a rather high one. And they gently led him on, till he found himself—in front of his own picture. They stood—silent—and still;—to see what effect it would produce upon him. He stood before it,—looking up at it,—quite still,— with fixed eye,—without speaking a word. There was no sign of his being at all interested in it. Not a feature of his countenance moved.

But he stood—looking up—fixedly—at the picture. All were still, and silent. And so—they stood—a considerable time:—when—suddenly—he said,—"There's my cat!"—and seemed pleased to see his cat there. This was all he said about the picture.

Conversing, a few days after, with the lady who was one of the friends who showed him his picture; he said, the two little girls close beside him, one clasping the other round the neck, were his "two little queens!"—as he used to call Lizzy Lemmon and Georgiana Richmond.

XVIII.

One bitterly cold night in December, an esteemed member of my Flock, Mr. Frank Faulkner, called upon me. He had driven the Rocket from London to Portsmouth that day, in the face of a cutting sleet; but he came in with a countenance and manner so full of generous interest, that there was no appearance of weariness or fatigue. He said, as he sat down by the fire: "I've been thinking a good deal of late—about that good old man, the old cobbler in St. Mary's Street; with his crowd of little scholars about him; working all the while at his trade for his own poor living; doing so much good, in such a quiet way, among his poor neighbours; so persevering, in that poor little bit of a shed of his; never tiring in his labours for others; and so little noticed, to cheer him. Scarcely any body seems to take much notice of him. I've been thinking, we ought to do something, to let the good old man know, how much we esteem and admire his self-devoting labours for others' good."

"I agree with you;" I said. "This can easily be done. What do you recommend?"

Mr. Faulkner replied: "I've been thinking, it would be a pleasant thing to present him with some testimonial of our sympathy and esteem for his unremitting labours;—so long continued;—going on so admirably in his humble works of goodness and benevolence;—with no show—or pretence; for so many years; always the same; as full of alacrity now—as ever!—In his old age;—more than seventy,—I'm told." "He is." "It would cheer his old heart,—to receive such a proof, that friends feel with him, and esteem, and admire—his disinterested perseverance for others' good."

"I heartily agree with you. What do you think would be the most suitable to present to him?"

"Oh, nothing very expensive;—simply—a mark of our esteem and friendly regard. I've been thinking,"—he said, with a look and tone of pleasantry, mingled with deep feeling and admiration;—and he paused: —as if silently dwelling on some pleasant thought. And he began again: gently, and hesitatingly; seemingly—as much in his own thoughts, as in external utterance:—"I've been thinking,—as he works—by the awl;"—and his eye sparkled with pleasantry;—"if we were to present him—with"—and he hesitated a little, and looked at me—rather inquiringly:—and then said, as if with renewed impulse of delight:—"A silver awl!—I was thinking of."—He said this with a look—and emphasis —of pleased imagination.

I hesitated. "Would that be in character? Do you think he would value it?"

"O yes!—as an expression of our regard and esteem."

"But don't you think—something solidly useful—would be more in character; and would be more valued by him? You know, he is a plain, practical man,—in all he says, and does;—with no show;—so thoroughly devoted, all through life, to the solidly useful;—altogether averse to any thing like superficial show. Would he value what he could make no use of?"

Still, our friend, while admitting somewhat the reasonableness of this, had evidently made up his mind—to—"the silver awl!"

I could not see any probability of John Pounds valuing it; except as an expression of our friendly esteem. "But this, you know, we might as fully express, and as pleasantly, by giving him something that might also be substantially useful to him; and which would add to his daily happiness."

"Well, what do you recommend?" Mr. Faulkner at length asked; but evidently clinging to his favourite idea—"the silver awl!"

"Don't you think, a nice quarto Bible—would be better?—with nice large print, and clear white paper;—to suit his old eyes? And you could have it as handsomely bound as you please."

Mr. Faulkner admitted that this would be a suitable present,—and acceptable to the good old man, and would be very highly valued by him. Still, he confessed, he rather clung to the idea—of—"the silver awl!—as—so in character with the old man's trade, that he lived by;—and—so beautiful a work of art,—as we would have it!"—he said, with a spring in his voice, and look of enthusiasm;—"for him to look at;—as a testimonial of our sympathy and admiration!—It would be something for his relatives to treasure up in memory of him,—after he was gone to his reward;—a sort of heir-loom—in the family;—a perpetual reminder for them, how much their good old relative was esteemed by us!"

"Well;—let us take time," I said; "and think about it."

And so—we parted—that night;—both agreeing, to give it our further consideration; and both agreed, that it was very desirable, to present him with something.

The next Sunday evening, Mr. Faulkner waited for me at the Chapel door, after worship, and, as I was coming out,—he said, with a pleasant smile, and a hearty shake of the hand : "I've been thinking of what you said, the other night, about the nice quarto Bible, with the nice large print, and the clear white paper;—so pleasant for the good old man's eyes!—And I think you were right. I quite agree with you, that this would be the best to present to him."

So we agreed upon it; and began at once to mention it to friends who were standing about the Chapel door. All were pleased with the idea as soon as they heard of it; and contributions began to come readily in. We did not attempt to urge it forward, nor did we wish to hasten it to completion; we rather left it to work its own quiet way, as friend mentioned it to friend, the interest kindling from one to another. And we suggested the desirability of the contributions being small; that the larger number might have the pleasure of joining in the testimonial; and, especially, that his poorer neighbours might have the privilege of giving their halfpennies and pennies, if they wished to contribute to this pleasant mark of esteem for their dear old Friend, and never-tiring Benefactor!

XIX.

Monday evening;—the last evening in the year:—meeting John Pounds in St. Mary's Street, as he was crossing over into Crown Street; —"Yer sarvant, Sir!—Sharp frost!" "Yes, Mr. Pounds; but you don't seem to feel it much; with your bare arms, and open chest, and no hat on!" "I likes it! It makes me feel fresh an brisk like! I'se been to the King's Bastion, to see the sun set:—the last sun, you knows, Sir, in the old year. He goes down very grand; all crimson and gold:—bright—to the last!"

"Yes, Mr. Pounds, we've had a glorious sunset, to close the old year; —full of splendour! And I am very glad you are so well and hearty to enjoy it."

"Never better in my life;—bless the Lord!—And I'se be up betimes i' the morning, to see the first sun o' the new year rise!—I'se now a-going to Mrs. More's, to give her little child's foot another bit of a push out like. It's the one in arms. You knows 'em;—the bigger ons come to your Sunday-school."

"Yes, I know them."

"Well;—one day I sees Mrs. More a-coming with her child in her arms. 'Missus,' I says, 'your child's foot turns in.' 'Yes, Mr. Pounds,' she says; 'it's born so.' 'I'se cure that child's foot,' I says; 'if you's let me try.' 'Yes, Mr. Pounds, an thank y';' she says. So I takes it in hand; an I makes it a little boot out o' old shoe-leather; like my little Johnny's. Poor little thing!—It cries very much, it does,—every time I gives it another bit of a push out. But I goes on with it; it's all for its good. It's a long time about; but I'se make a good job of it, before I'se done with it.

"An then—" and he paused;—and looked up at me with a comical smile;—resting with both hands on his strong hazel stick.—"Then, ye sees, Sir;—when I'se given Mrs. More's child's foot another bit of a push out,—I'se a-going to buy me a pint o' sprats for my dinner to-morrow!"—And he laughed at the thought. "I doesn't often cook a nice dinner for myself. But to-morrow's New Year's Day; an my Neffy's have a holiday;—poor lad!—an he's a-going to dine out wi' some friends of his. So,—thinks I to myself;—I'se be alone to-morrow;—I'se go an buy me a pint o' sprats for my dinner!—Yer sarvant, Sir!"—And he strode off, full of glee and energy; making the ice splinter—as he struck down his strong hazel stick.

"Good evening, Mr. Pounds. I hope you'll enjoy your sprats to-morrow!"

"No fear o' that!" he said, with a lively tone; looking back for a moment, and smiling. And he strode away with bright alacrity.

XX.

The New Year, 1839, opened with a glorious sun-rise; bright and clear. The frost was intense; but there was a dryness in the air which made it pleasant and refreshing. John Pounds was up long before the sun; cooking hot breakfasts; and taking them round to poor sufferers in the back courts and alleys. While he was out on his rounds of beneficence; some of his little scholars began to come into his shop,—although it was still very early,—and crowded to the fire. When he came in, they all ran to him; exclaiming with delight, "A happy New Year, Mr. Pounds!" "Thank y', dears! Same to you, an many on 'em!"

And he kissed them all. "Has y' had any breakfast?" "No, Mr. Pounds;"—several voices. "Mother's none to give us." "Well, here's some for y'." He had long had his own breakfast; but he quickly set out plentifully for them. And the hungry children set to eagerly. And the old man looked on with joy. He put fresh coals on the fire, and made it blaze up cheerfully; and they were all very happy.

Before nine o'clock, his little shop was filled with scholars; and he began setting them their lessons. "Dick, that slate o' yours?" "Here 'tis, Mr. Pounds." And he set the boy a sum. "Do that;—quick, lad;—an no blunders, mind." "I'se try, Mr. Pounds." "That's it, my lad! Try, an do your best. That's all I wants of you.

"Jenny, how's mother?" "Very bad, Mr. Pounds." "Sorry, for that, Jenny. Run and tell her, I'se bring her some hot dinner at twelve." "Yes, Mr. Pounds; and thank y'." "Mind you comes back again to school, Jenny." "Yes, Mr. Pounds." And she ran off, to tell her mother the good news; and was soon back again; and gave Mr. Pounds a look—and a smile, as she came in. "I sees ye, Jenny!—Good lass!—Here, larn these pretty verses. I knows you's like 'em; they's about the little busy bee!" "Yes, Mr. Pounds;"—with a happy springing voice, as he gave her a torn leaf with the verses on. "An you's be a busy bee, Jenny!" "Yes, Mr. Pounds!" And she stood beside the fire, learning her verses.

"Bill, my lad, come and read the first chapter of Genesis:—In the beginning God created the heaven and the earth." And a stoutish boy came and read that favourite chapter of his dear old master's with a clear voice, and as if he felt that his master was enjoying it. All the school were listening;—very still; and pleased.

About ten o'clock the old man rose from his bench, and said: —"Here, Ashton, you come along wi' me; an we's go to Mr. Carter's, an they's kindly gie you something to put on your bad heel; an I'se show 'em this sum o' yours;" taking up the boy's slate. "Now, you's all be good whiles I'se a-way." "Yes, Mr. Pounds!"—all at once,—gaily!—looking up at him with their bright loving faces. "I'se soon be back again." And he strode away with his accustomed alacrity.

They were soon in High Street; and at Mr. Carter's door. The slate was taken in, while the old cobbler remained standing in the hall. Almost immediately after, a noise was heard—as of some one falling down in the hall. Mr. Carter came out, and saw the old man stretched on the floor, and apparently endeavouring to get up, but not succeeding. "Stretch your leg out, and then you can get up;"—Mr. Carter said;—supposing he had accidentally slipped down, and was not exerting himself sufficiently, to get up again. "I can't, Sir;"—the old man said feebly,—and groaning. Mr. Carter then saw it was something serious. They lifted him up, and placed him in a chair. Mr. Carter went and brought a glass of wine. The old man took a little of it. Miss Carter put a smelling-bottle to his nose;—and he revived a little:—but only for a moment. The old man said: "I'm sorry this has happened here," "Say nothing of that;" Mr. Carter said kindly. Just then, Mr, Martell, the surgeon, happened to be passing on the other side of the street. Mr. Carter, seeing him, said to one of the servants, "There's Martell; call him in."

"As soon as I saw him," Mr. Martell said;—telling me of it after:—"I saw the old man was dying. In ten minutes—he was dead.

"Now came the question;—how the body was to be removed from the house, without disturbing the neighbourhood. I went and fetched a fly; and brought one of my pupils in it; L—; you know him." " Yes." "From the old man's extreme deformity, and stiffened joints, in consequence of his fall into the dry dock when a boy, we could only place him in the fly—in a sitting posture. So I told L—to get into the fly first, and take his seat in the farther corner. He didn't like it; but he couldn't help that. There was no time to choose. Then we lifted the poor old man in, and placed him on the seat,—as if he was sitting beside him. Then I got in, and took my place on this side; and shut the door. And so—we drove quietly away:—propping the body up between us. Anyone looking into the fly, as we passed along to the old man's shop, wouldn't suppose he was dead;—seeing him sitting upright between us.

"Meanwhile, the boy had run back to the scholars terrified; and told them, that Mr. Pounds had fallen down at Mr. Carter's; and they thought he was in a fit, or else dead; and they were bringing him home in a fly."

"The Nephew, who was in the house at the time, hearing this, came out and met us. Poor fellow!—It was a terrible blow for him. He fainted.

"When we came to the old man's shop, and lifted him out of the fly, —and carried the dead body in among the children:—no words can describe the scene of terror and confusion. The children ran out screaming in all directions. It flew like wild-fire. The whole neighbourhood felt the shock. People came out of their houses—crowding towards us—all along the street. Poor creatures came pouring out from the back courts and alleys. It was one scene of excitement and loud lamentation. All had lost a Friend.

"We carried the body up-stairs, and laid him on his bed. And I went to tell Lemmon what had happened. Poor Lemmon!—You'd have thought—his heart was broken. They had been friends from childhood. They were play-fellows together as little children."

A Coroner's inquest was held in the afternoon. The jury gave it as their verdict, that the death was caused by "an affection of the heart."

XXI.

In the evening of the following day, the Nephew called at my lodgings to arrange for the funeral. He wished it to be on Saturday afternoon; and we appointed three o'clock. And his desire was, that the grave should be as near where his Uncle used to sit in Chapel as could be. We therefore chose the spot just beyond the north-west corner of the Chapel; as it was near the north-west end of the gallery that his Uncle used to sit; and where he was so constantly seen,—to the very last Sunday evening.

"Ah, Sir!" he said, with a full heart:—"who'd ever have thought it?—Poor dear old Uncle!—that he was so near his end?—So happy, and hearty,—as he was—yesterday morning;—and here we are,—arranging to bury him. He got up yesterday before the gun fired; and lighted his fire, and busied himself—with getting nice hot breakfasts ready—for his poor sick neighbours; and was happy in taking them round to them. And he enjoyed his own breakfast heartily. His little scholars began to come in long before school-time; merrily wishing him—a Happy New Year! And he thanked them, fondly; and wished them the same; and kissed the little ones; and gathered them about the fire; and gave those a breakfast—that hadn't any breakfast at home. And the shop was soon filled; and he was all life and joy among them; setting them their lessons. And about ten o'clock, when he went out to Mr. Carter's—with the boy Ashton; he started off in high spirits, and full of vigour; pleased to take the boy's sum—and show them, and get something for his sore heel. Very soon after, the boy came running back in a fright, and said, Uncle had fallen down in a fit at Mr. Carter's, and they thought he was dead; and were bringing him back in a fly. I went out—and met them—bringing him in the fly—quite dead. He was sitting up in the fly—between George Martell and somebody else.—Oh! to see him!—My heart—sunk within me. When they lifted him out of the fly—and took him in among the children—such a scene!—I seem to recollect nothing else—what they did. A blank came over me. They say,

I fainted.

"When next—I seem to remember any thing, I was very faint;—and didn't know—where I was;—or—what had happened.—All—seemed confused—But—as I gradually came to,—I found myself—up in the bed-room;—and sitting in Uncle's old arm-chair;—and a kind neighbour was doing all she could—to bring me round again.—I saw some friends —busy—about dear old Uncle's bed:—and—the dead body—lying upon it.—Then—the reality came full upon me.—Uncle—was dead.—And fell into a fit of crying—that I couldn't stop."

I told the Nephew, I should feel it my duty to preach a funeral sermon for his Uncle, next Sunday evening. "I am in the midst of a Course of Sunday-evening lectures; and the subject for next Sunday's lecture was announced last Sunday. But that must now be postponed. Your Uncle was at Chapel, and heard it announced. How little did any of us think, that,—before the next Sunday,—he would be dead—and buried!"

The young man asked me, if I would take tea with him on Sunday afternoon. I thanked him, and cordially accepted his invitation.

When we had completed the arrangements relative to the funeral, he seemed to feel it a comfort to sit and go on talking about his Uncle, and every thing connected with him. "Uncle's poor cat," he said, "was noticed yesterday, sitting in the middle of the street, in front of the house;—as if taking no notice of any thing."

"I saw it so; it was in the afternoon. She seemed quite unconscious of the cold; though so intense; and seemed not to notice anything that was passing."

"She sat so till after the gun fired. And then I took her in. Poor thing!—as I lifted her up, it was like taking up a dead cat in my hands; she was so lifeless. As I took her in, I heard some persons who were passing say:—'Mr. Pounds' poor cat!'—in a tone of pity.—So lively before; taking an interest in every thing that was going on:—she now takes no interest in any thing. She walks about the house, as if without an object. She takes no food. She does not settle herself down to sleep, as she used to do. She seems to find no place of rest any where.—She has been sitting again outside in the street, in front of the house, to-day;—for hours;—only walking slowly about a little, at times; but with no object.

"Others have spoken to me of it;—sitting among the snow and ice, in front of the house;—as if disconsolate. 'His poor cat!'—they say, with tender commiseration."

"She's the common talk of all the neighbourhood :—'Mr. Pounds' poor cat!'—Nobody disturbs her. Every body pities her. She seems to grieve:—as if she had nothing to live for. If we might say so of a cat."

"I think we may."

"Oh, how different from what she was on Christmas day!—

"On Christmas day, Sir, Uncle was in his glory!—To see dear old Uncle then! It was a bright day, you know, Sir."

"It was;—a brilliant day!"

"Uncle was all in his best!—Every thing looked bright and happy! He had all those of his scholars to dine with him, who were not likely to have any plum-pudding at home;—some, perhaps,—no dinner at all. First came a big piece of roast beef. And when the children had eaten heartily of that:—Uncle brought out his great Christmas plum-pudding!—And a general shout, and laugh of joy, burst forth from all the children, to welcome it. And he joyfully gave every one of them a good big piece. While they were eating it, neighbours began to come in, to taste Uncle's Christmas plum-pudding! And all afternoon, neighbour after neighbour kept on coming in, to have a taste of the plum-pudding!—and then going out,—to make room for others to come in, and have a taste!—The many that came!—It seemed as if they would never have done coming in!—And Uncle was so glad to welcome them! —He shook hands with every one of them; and blessed them. And they were all so pleased!—and said, it was so good!"

"Your Cousin Miss Jamieson told me, it was always her privilege to make your Uncle's Christmas plum-pudding."

"Yes. He used to go out the day before, and buy all the things to make it of; and he took them to her; and she was sure to have it ready the next day for dinner."

"It must have been a large plum-pudding, for so many to eat of it."

"Yes!" the young man said emphatically, "And I never knew it fail lasting out to the last comer."

"How large was it?"

He looked about the room, for something to tell its size by. There was an old sofa in the room, with straight back and front, and square ends, a long way from front to back;—large enough to have served occasionally as a bed; which probably it did, in case of emergency, in the war time; when Portsmouth was often crowded to overflowing. At each end of the sofa there was a large bolster, reaching from front to back, and thick in proportion. Suddenly fixing his eyes on one end of the sofa, he said with hearty emphasis:—" About two-thirds the size of that bolster!"

Then,—with altered tone and countenance,—he said : "When his scholars had feasted enough, and were now amusing themselves with playthings that Uncle had in readiness for them; he stirred the fire, and put on more coals, and made it blaze up and look cheerful. And then he sat down in his old arm-chair; and his cat came brushing against him, pleased with every thing!—And Uncle was so happy!—welcoming his neighbours, as they kept coming in, and wishing him—a merry Christmas!—And he looked up,—with a bright smiling face,—and said:—'I'm as happy as happy can be!—I haven't a wish on earth unfulfilled!—And now,—if it please God—to take me—before I can no longer help myself—No!'—he said, very earnestly: 'I would not live so long—as be a burden to any one. No!—when I can no longer do for myself;—I should like to die—like a bird dropping from its perch.'

"Oh, Sir!—it seems as if God had answered his prayer." "It does."

He paused;—deeply moved. We both remained silent for a while. Then he said, with a tremulous voice:—"Yesterday was New Year's Day; and I was to have a holiday; and was going out to dine with some friends of mine. And Uncle said to me, the day before:—'Johnny, you're going to dine out tomorrow; I shall be alone; I think I'll cook a nice dinner for myself for once!' And he laughed at the thought of cooking a nice dinner for himself.—'I'll go and buy me a pint of sprats, he said; 'and I'll cook them for my dinner tomorrow!'—And he laughed again merrily at the thought.—Poor dear Uncle! Nobody ever knew him do such a thing before. He would cook nice dinners for me; for he used to say, I worked hard at my trade; and he liked to encourage honest industry. And he was continually cooking nice dinners for poor sick neighbours;—and taking them to them himself:—Oh!—so kindly, Sir!—So tenderly—he would talk to them!—They'll miss him."—And the young man wept.

"Yes," I said;—"many,—many, will miss him."

After a while, he went on:—"No, Sir:—for himself;—as for Uncle's cooking any thing,—it wasn't to be called cooking. A crust of bread and cheese;—or a bit of cold meat;—any thing that was wholesome,—would do for Uncle. His eating—was of the very plainest. And he enjoyed it heartily;—with a thankful heart.

"Poor dear Uncle!—There are the sprats now,—on the shelf;—just as he left them."

XXII.

Saturday was a bitterly cold day; dark and gloomy; blowing a gale, with a cutting north-east wind. The frost was intense. The streets were sheeted with ice and frozen snow. But this did not prevent large crowds attending the poor old cobbler to his grave. As the funeral came out of White Horse Street into High Street, and turned to the left towards the Chapel, it seemed as if all St. Mary's Street were passing after it. The Nephew, and Mr. Lemmon and his family, and others of his near friends and relatives, walked after the coffin as mourners; but hundreds more came crowding along,—one mass of bereavement and lamentation.

The Pastor met the coffin at the Chapel door:—solemnly repeating those words :—"I am the Resurrection and the Life, saith the Lord. He that believeth in me, though he were dead, yet shall he live: and whosoever liveth and believeth in me shall never die."—And he led the coffin into the Chapel:—the chief mourners following:—and all the rest crowded in after. Presently, and all was still. And the solemn service proceeded.

The Pastor spoke of the transitiveness of life.

"As for man, his days are as grass: as a flower of the field, so he flourisheth. For the wind passeth over it, and it is gone; and the place shall know it no more."

He spoke of the Departed, as a fellow-worshipper in their brotherhood; and most constant among them. "Last Sabbath evening, my friends, he was here with us; joining happily in our devotions:—How little thinking, that,—when next he entered this place,—he should be borne in by other hands;—for his funeral!

"We mourn the loss of our Brother from amongst us.

"But, my friends, we sorrow not as those who are without hope. For now is Christ risen from the dead, and become the firstfruits of them that slept. For since by man came death, by man came also the resurrection of the dead. For as in Adam all die, even so in Christ shall all be made alive.

"But every man in his own order: Christ the firstfruits; afterward they that are Christ's, at his coming. Then cometh the end; when he shall have delivered up the Kingdom to God, even the Father; when he shall have put down all rule and all authority and power. For he must reign, till he hath put all enemies under his feet. The last enemy shall be destroyed, Death. For he hath put all things under him.

"But when he saith all things are put under him, it is manifest that he is excepted, who did put all things under him.

"And when all things shall be subdued unto him, then shall the Son also himself be subject unto him that put all things under him; that God may be all in all.

"But some man will say, How are the dead raised up? and with what body do they come?

"Inconsiderate man!—That which thou sowest is not quickened, except it die. And that which thou sowest, thou sowest not that body that shall be, but bare grain; it may chance of wheat, or of some other grain. But God giveth it a body as it hath pleased him, and to every seed its own body. All flesh is not the same flesh: but there is one kind of flesh of men, another flesh of beasts, another of fishes, and another of birds. There are also celestial bodies, and bodies terrestrial: but the glory of the celestial is one, and the glory of the terrestrial is another. There is one glory of the sun, and another glory of the moon, and another glory of the stars: for one star differeth from another star in glory.

"So also is the resurrection of the dead. It is sown in corruption; it is raised in incorruption. It is sown in dishonour; it is raised in glory. It is sown in weakness; it is raised in power. It is sown a natural body; it is raised a spiritual body.

"There is a natural body, and there is a spiritual body. And so it is written: The first man, Adam, was made a living soul; the last Adam was made a quickening spirit. Howbeit that was not first which is spiritual, but that which is natural: and afterward that which is spiritual. The first man is of the earth, earthy : the second man is the Lord from heaven. As is the earthy, such are they also that are earthy; and as is the heavenly, such are they also that are heavenly. And as we have borne the image of the earthy, we shall also bear the image of the heavenly.

"Now this I say, brethren, that flesh and blood cannot inherit the Kingdom of God: neither doth corruption inherit incorruption.

"Behold, I show you a mystery: we shall not all sleep; but we shall all be changed; in a moment, in the twinkling of an eye, at the last trump. For the trumpet shall sound, and the dead shall be raised incorruptible; and we shall be changed. For this corruptible must put on incorruption, and this mortal must put on immortality.

"So when this corruptible shall have put on incorruption, and this mortal shall have put on immortality, then shall be brought to pass the saying that is written, Death is swallowed up in victory.

"O Death, where is thy sting? O Grave, where is thy victory?

"The sting of death is sin: and the strength of sin is the law. But thanks be to God, who giveth us the victory, through our Lord Jesus Christ.

"Therefore, my beloved brethren, be ye steadfast, immoveable, always abounding in the work of the Lord: forasmuch as ye know that your labour is not in vain in the Lord."

When that part of the service which was solemnized in the Chapel was completed; and they carried the coffin out, and placed it beside the grave:—it was a very solemn sight,—deeply affecting,—to look upon that large thronging crowd;—hundreds of sorrowing countenances,—pressing towards the grave;—largely, a mass of poverty and suffering destitution:—mothers, with their babes in their arms; poor sickly invalids; aged cripples, leaning on their sticks and their crutches; respectable young men and women, formerly the old man's scholars;—wretched creatures, crouching among the crowd,—forlorn and desolate:—all deeply sorrowing. And there were many little children, huddling together in groups;—many of them his scholars,—who were in the shop,—when the dead body was lifted in among them,—and they flew off—screaming and affrighted, in all directions;—now gathered together,—sorrowing at his grave.

When all was still; and they were lowering the coffin into the grave:—the Pastor said, with a clear voice, heard through all the crowd:—"The dust returneth to the earth as it was: the spirit returneth unto God who gave it."

As he drew near the close of the service; he addressed himself direct to the crowd. He spoke of the awful suddenness of the death. "The last evening of the Old Year," he said, "our departed Friend was bright in spirit; and full of bright expectations for the morrow:—very happy!—going about among you doing good. The first morning of the New Year, he rose before the sun; full of life and vigour; and joyfully set to work at his accustomed usefulness:—happy—in making others happy!—That morning,—in the very midst of his usefulness;—he dropped down,—and died.

"Our Friend was ready.

"Are you ready?

"None of you can be more confident in life than he was last Monday evening. The next morning—he suddenly dropped down—and died.

"If it please God to call you suddenly; with little warning:—are you ready to render in your last account?

"Our Friend lived a long life—continually doing good. He loved his neighbour as himself. He loved God; and blessed him for all his mercies and loving-kindness; and lived ever as in his presence; and did all he could—to fulfil his will.

"And I seem to see our Saviour—welcome him into heaven:—Well done, thou good and faithful servant. Enter into the joy of thy Lord.

"You have lost your dear old Friend; and you are full of sorrow. But God is with you; your almighty Friend. Live—as with him. Remember that he is always with you; that he sees all you do; and hears all you say; and knows all you think, and intend, and desire. Put your trust in him. Live faithful to him.

"Live,—as about to meet your dear departed Friend in heaven.

"Let us pray."—And the Pastor prayed for them all; and for all dear to them:—That they might live on earth—as preparing for a happy home in heaven.

When he had finished praying;—he opened his eyes, and looked round upon them all, and said :—"May the blessing of our Heavenly Father be with you all, and with all dear to you, now—and evermore. Amen."

XXIII.

A few minutes before five o'clock on Sunday afternoon, I tapped at the little door in St. Mary's Street. The Nephew came to let me in. There was nobody else in the house. As he opened the door, all was dark and still in the little shop. We crossed the shop, and went up-stairs into the bedroom, where we were to take tea. All looked bright and cheerful there. There was a blazing fire. The furniture, what little there was, looked bright and well dusted, and all put in proper order. The little tea-table was set out beside the fire; all in readiness. The kettle was singing on the hob.

There were two beds in the little room. "That—was Uncle's bed;" the young man said, pointing to the bed beside the window at the other end of the room. "He would lie—and read his book-in that bed,—with the window open,—by the hour together,—on a fine summer's morning;—before it was time to get up. And, sometimes,—long into the night;—holding his book in one hand, and a candle in the other.

"It was on that bed—they laid him; when they brought him up—dead.—Poor dear old Uncle!—To see him—lying there—dead:—when,—

but a few hours before,—he got up—so fresh and hearty:—for another day's happiness and usefulness:—as he thought."

The young man motioned me to a bright old arm-chair beside the fire; saying, "That was Uncle's arm-chair. He always sat in that chair, when we were in this room." As soon as I sat down in the old man's arm-chair, the cat jumped up on my knee, and tucked herself comfortably up, and began purring. And so she sat all tea-time.

During tea, the young man was all assiduity and kind attention. Not much was said by either of us. But there was no want of interchange of thought and feeling. Everything was full of feeling;—deep,—tender feeling;—mutually felt—and understood. Soon after tea I took my leave; wishing to have a little quiet retirement before the evening service.

XXIV.

Notwithstanding the inclemency of the weather, our venerable old Chapel was crowded for the evening service. The remembrance of our departed Friend pervaded the whole service.

The hymns were chosen in tone with his cheerful piety. The Pastor read the sixth chapter of the Gospel of Matthew; explaining and illustrating as he went on. Our Saviour, he said, was sitting on a mountain, discoursing to his disciples, and a mixed multitude. He bade them not do their good deeds before men, to be seen of them: otherwise they would have no reward of their Father who is in heaven. "But when thou doest alms, let not thy left hand know what thy right hand doeth: that thine alms may be in secret: and thy Father who seeth in secret himself shall reward thee openly.

"Lay not up for yourselves treasures upon earth, where moth and rust doth corrupt, and where thieves break through and steal: but lay up for yourselves treasures in heaven, where neither moth nor rust doth corrupt, and where thieves do not break through nor steal: for where your treasure is, there will your heart be also.

"The light of the body is the eye: if therefore thine eye be single, thy whole body shall be full of light. But if thine eye be evil, thy whole shall be full of darkness. If therefore the light that is in thee be darkness, how great is that darkness!

"No man can serve two masters: for either he will hate the one, and love the other; or else he will hold to the one, and despise the other. Ye cannot serve God and mammon.

"Therefore I say unto you, Be not anxious for your life, what ye shall eat, or what ye shall drink; nor yet for your body, what ye shall put on. Is not the life more than meat, and the body than raiment?

"Behold the birds of the air: for they sow not, neither do they reap, nor gather into barns; yet your Heavenly Father feedeth them. Will he not much more provide for you, his children?

"Which of you by anxious thought can add one cubit unto his stature? And why are ye anxious about raiment? Consider the lilies of the field, how they grow; they toil not, neither do they spin: and yet I say unto you, That even Solomon in all his glory was not arrayed like one of these. Wherefore, if God so clothe the grass of the field, which to-day is, and to-morrow is cast into the oven, shall he not much more clothe you, O ye of little faith? Therefore be not anxious, saying, What shall we eat? or, What shall we drink? or, Wherewithal shall we be clothed? For your Heavenly Father knoweth that ye have need of all these things. But seek ye first the Kingdom of God, and fulfil the duties which he hath given you to do; and you shall have all things needful for you.

"Be not anxious therefore for the morrow: for, so living, the morrow shall find you prepared for it."

Prayer was offered up for the bereaved relatives and friends; and for the whole neighbourhood, in the midst of which the Departed had lived continually doing good; and where so many sufferers were now sorrowing for his loss.

When the Pastor rose to address the Congregation, he said: "Probably some present have come with the expectation of hearing the Lecture which was announced last Sabbath for this evening. But, my friends, an event has occurred since then, which must now take place of it. There was one amongst us then, a constant fellow-worshipper in this place, who heard that announcement; but who was not to be present with us, to hear the subject illustrated." And the Pastor dwelt on the awful suddenness of the death:—so awful a warning for every one of us. "Boast not thyself of tomorrow; for thou knowest not what a day may bring forth."

But this, he said, was not the chief subject he was now desirous to bring before them. "The life that has been so suddenly closed, was a remarkable one. Spent in quiet and almost unnoticed obscurity; with very scanty means, and labouring under great bodily disadvantages; it was a life of constant, persevering usefulness; and even extraordinary beneficence. And it has fervently brought home to heart and mind those words of our Saviour: 'When thou doest alms, let not thy left hand know what thy right hand doeth,' that thine alms may be in secret: and thy Father who seeth in secret himself shall reward thee openly.

"So beautiful was our Saviour's own spirit; so purely beneficent; the same in the most retired scenes of his ministry;—all love and tenderness for the suffering and the poor; unseen of world:—as in the most public and magnificent works of his Divine power and majesty.

"Sent by the Universal Father, in his love for the world, to be the Saviour of the world; our Saviour reveals, that the soul of this salvation was to leaven the whole world.

"But while this soul of salvation was gradually to penetrate and imbue the whole world:—all social institutions; all nations and governments; all international emulations and influences;—with its purifying, generous, loving, ennobling, happy spirit:—this life and growth of salvation was to be continually going on in the heart and conduct of every individual disciple:—in the most retired scenes of life, the most gentle and silent of social influences, as thoroughly imbuing and life-giving,—as in the most public, the most vast, and mighty of Human enterprises and achievements:—inspiring through all, to ever finer excellence and happiness.

"And this heavenward soul of salvation, our Saviour reveals, might live and flourish in the hearts and lives of the humblest and most obscure of his followers;—unseen of men;—or looked down upon with contempt; despised in their lowliness:—but seen of God, and blessed."

The Pastor enlarged upon this view of our Saviour's revealings:—bringing forward many and various examples from our Saviour's own words and ministrations. "And the number of these examples," he said, "might easily be increased.

"Who was the man that went down from the temple to his home justified?—The despised and lowly publican; who would not so much as lift up his eyes to heaven; but stood afar off, and smote on his breast, saying,'God, be merciful to me a sinner.'

"Who was it, that was carried by the angels into Abraham's bosom?—The poor beggar; who was laid at the rich man's gate, full of sores; desiring to be fed with the crumbs that fell from the rich man's table: and the dogs came and licked his sores.

"Who was it, that cast the most precious gift into the treasury for the service of God?—The poor widow; who cast in two mites, Jesus called to him his disciples, and said: 'Verily I say unto you, that this poor widow hath cast more in, than all they who have cast into the treasury. For all they cast in of their abundance; but she, of her want, cast in all that she had; all her living.'

"'God seeth not as man seeth; for man looketh on the outward appearance, but God looketh on the heart.' And in many a rough casket, he seeth a precious jewel. Where the world looks with scorn, God may be looking down with approving smile—and cherishing love. In the lowly habitation—that men pass by from day to day with indifference, the Eye that seeth in secret—may have long seen, with Fatherly approval, the humble—persevering usefulness—of a faithful friend of the poor and needy.

"But in examples of usefulness in the midst of poverty and obscurity, we are in danger of looking upon them through a false medium; and therefore, of estimating them by an erroneous standard. Too easily dazzled by show, and led away in our opinions by what is popular, and commands general admiration; charmed with what is pleasant, and beautiful, and refined; we are in danger, however unintentionally, of forming low ideas of what has no external comeliness to recommend it. Even when we are rejoiced to have found a truly useful, disinterested, exemplary Christian—in the lowly recesses of obscurity: with his little means—dispensing morsels of food to the hungry; a pittance of clothing—to the almost naked; and a little useful knowledge—to the children of penury and neglect:—though we may dwell on such kind-hearted goodness with admiration, and speak of it with heart-felt praise; still, the external unseemliness—pressing painfully, and perhaps repulsively, on our daily observation, may obscure to us the real worth of the character. We may esteem the humble benefactor, dispensing his little kindnesses—to those more needy than himself; but, at the same time, there may be a conflicting feeling of distaste excited within us, by the lowly mode of life, the uncouth way of conducting his well-meant efforts, and numberless nameless circumstances continually disfiguring the scene.

"Not so—with God. God seeth worth itself. He looks through the external circumstances, into the goodness of the heart. He can divest such disinterested beneficence—of a garb unworthy of it; and look upon it in its true nature; its pure benevolence; worthy a child of the Supreme Source of all good.

"Accustomed, as we may be, to contemplate the lowly benefactor—in the midst of those to whom he directs his kind care and assistance; many of them little deserving, by their own conduct, of his persevering assiduity;—sunk in sin and profligacy:—the general impression from the wretched, debased, self-abandoned objects—to which his kind efforts are directed, may imperceptibly degrade the work to our estimation.

"Not so—with God. God sees the kind care directed to his own children. However fallen;—however gone astray:—the recipient of such goodness—is not so lost, but the Father who sent his Son to seek—and to save—all that were lost,—can reclaim—the poor out-cast;—can touch the self-abandoned—to a sense of remorse;—to the poignancy of self-condemnation:—and he will weep.—The penitent—will return; and seek a Father's forgiveness;—with full—heart-felt confession of his unworthiness. And our Saviour says:—'There is joy in heaven over one sinner that repenteth,'

"Familiarized, as we may be, with all his own personal disadvantages, that this benefactor in humble life may have had to contend with:—but little educated himself; his knowledge—desultory, partial, fragmentary; his views but little expanded; his ideas of human capabilities and interests never drawn forth beyond the confines of his own little lowly sphere of action; his own habits and conduct—uncultured, coarse, uncouth:—these disadvantages, strongly apparent, may lower the idea of his worth to our estimation.

"Not so—with God. The kind of excellence, not the extent of it, is the standard—which our Saviour reveals—for the Divine approval and acceptance. 'My son, give me thy heart;' is the voice from heaven.

"So viewed:—think my friends, of the life, so suddenly passed from amongst us.

"I need not repeat to you the circumstances of the case. For, however unnoticed he may have lived for so many years, his sudden loss has excited general attention to his worth.

"You know where he dwelt. On first choosing his abode in that contentious neighbourhood; he made a resolution, that he would not suffer himself to be drawn into any of their broils; and he kept it steadfastly through a long life.

"Fond of peace, and brotherly kindness; he had another motive to this resolution. With no family of his own to provide for; his good heart led him to look abroad for objects for his fostering care. And this, he said to me, near the close of his good old age, would be enough for him to attend to; without meddling with other people's strifes and quarrels.

"You know the little humble abode in which he lived. In that little shop he would gather the children of the poorest about him; even to numbers that astonished us to hear tell of. And there, from morning to evening, he would take care of them; and, to the best of his ability, would instruct them. Some—he would feed. Some—he would clothe. In their illnesses—he would tend them with kind cherishing tenderness. He grounded them well—in some of the more useful parts of a plain education. He trained them to the active use of their minds. He watched their dispositions; correcting their faults, and cherishing their better feelings. With little offers of reward, he would lead them, of their own free choice, to accompany him to the House of God. And—the only day in the seven—that he reserved to himself—as his day of rest, he watchfully procured their admission—where they might still be kindly taught and cherished. His habitual kindness to so many children, may be best inferred from the testimony, that they were all attached to him. They all loved him.

"This school—he continued for more than twenty years. So that many hundreds of children were taught and cherished by him. And he has told me himself, that he never had one—that had been long with him—who turned out ill in after life:—while many of his scholars have become highly esteemed and valuable members of society.

"This school of his was a charge of no small labour, and of no slight personal privations. He devoted himself to it with constant and penetrating attention. He was watchful and considerate in his care and treatment of each scholar, according to their several dispositions and capabilities. There was no negligence in his teaching and managing his scholars; no superficial hastiness. He was always thoroughly in earnest with them.

"When we consider—the mental effort, and the bodily endurance, requisite—to sustain the assiduous care of so many children,—so many hours in the day,—crowded in so small a place; and think of his continuing this,—day after day,—and week after week,—for more than twenty years:—a stranger might ask:—What remuneration he received—for all this work;—so unremitting;—so long continued? He would never receive any remuneration for it. He would accept gifts for the benefit of the poor children; but never any thing for himself. And what was given him for his scholars—was very little, compared with the good he was continually doing for them. His object was—to do good. He diligently sought out those children that were most destitute, and the most neglected. And his remuneration was in his own satisfaction; in seeing those happy—that he made so:—in seeing the children that he taught and trained—grow up—good men and women; useful and respected in life.

"It was this that encouraged him to persevere in so laborious a work, while all along he had to toil at his own humble trade for his own scanty maintenance. It was this generous satisfaction that enabled him to bear up against the ungenerous remarks and heartless pleasantries that often wounded his ear from passers-by. Cheered with this satisfaction, he willingly submitted to the often wearisome labour; persevering, when there was no novelty, no sound of popularity, to excite him; nothing, but the consciousness of doing good. And with this to sustain him; his labours were continued, with undiminished interest and assiduity, to the very last.

"He lived to a good old age; more than threescore years and ten; with no apparent diminution of mental or bodily energy:—cherishing those poor children in the spirit of Him who said, 'Suffer little children to come unto me; for of such is the Kingdom of Heaven.' And, like his Saviour, he would take them up in his arms, and bless them.

"But his teaching and taking care of so many poor children—was only part of his usefulness; so constant, and untiring. He was continually going about among his poor neighbours doing good; carrying food to the hungering; and—for the sick, taking suitable nourishing things, carefully prepared by his own hands. He would sit with them, and comfort them in their afflictions. He was always willing and ready to do any good service in his power for any one. And all this, with his very meagre means;—hard earned;—working daily at his trade; and labouring under great bodily disadvantages, all through life from his boyhood, from his extreme lameness and deformity. No inclemencies of weather stopped him. Early and late, he was all assiduity; often far into the night, when some poor sufferer needed his aid. And many are now sorrowing for his loss.

"You have seen him striding along the street, with his eager alacrity;—rough and uncouth in appearance;—lame—and deformed, to extreme unsightliness;—distressing to look upon. That Form—is now hallowed to our remembrance, by the Spirit that animated it.

"He lived contented and happy. In the evening of Christmas day, as he sat, pleased to see some of his little scholars, who had shared his dinner with him, amusing themselves with play-things that he had provided for them;—and welcoming neighbours coming in, with their grateful good wishes of the season, to partake of his little bounties:—he said,—looking up with bright beaming countenance:—He was as happy as happy could be!—That he hadn't a wish on earth unfulfilled!—And now,—if it please God—to take him—before he could no longer help himself—No!—he said; very earnestly:—he did not wish to live so long—as to be a burden to any one.

"His last wish was fulfilled. That day week,—in the very midst of his active usefulness,—he dropped down,—and died.

"Our Saviour said:—'When thou makest a feast; call the poor, the maimed, the lame, the blind : and thou shalt be blessed; for they cannot recompense thee: for thou shalt be recompensed at the resurrection of the just.'

"And our Saviour says:—'Inasmuch as thou hast done it unto one of the least of these, thou hast done it unto me.'

"My friends, does this Example of humble—persevering Beneficence—awaken in your hearts—no whispers of self-accusation? Have you done your utmost—to benefit others? Have you never relaxed too readily in your good endeavours? Have you never,—from personal annoyances,—or want of the charm of novelty—or popularity—to incite you,—grown weary in well doing; and suffered the good work to languish; and given yourselves up to more alluring pursuits?

"God grant, that it may not be laid to our charge—at the last,—that,—with more means,—we were less useful. Amen."

XXV.

The next morning, a rather ample Obituary Notice appeared in the Hampshire Telegraph; a weekly newspaper, published at Portsmouth. It was headed, "Philanthropy and real Charity in Humble Life." There were inaccuracies in it, showing a want of sufficient knowledge of facts; some statements, contrary to fact. But it was written in a good spirit; and gave a characteristic and very interesting sketch of the good old cobbler, and his usefulness:—terminated so awfully, by his sudden death. The Hampshire Telegraph was a paper of long standing, in good repute, and with a large circulation, both at home and abroad.

XXVI.

Mr. Martell the surgeon, commonly called George Martell, called upon me in the evening: and with a subdued voice and colouring countenance,—rather tremulous,—said;—-hesitatingly,—and looking at me—as if with an uncertain, inquiring eye:—"I hope you will write some little narrative—of the good old man, on behalf of the family?—It may do good." In making this request, he spoke in a very different manner from his accustomed firm manly assurance. He seemed unnerved, and indecisive. He seemed to fear, lest he might be thought to be making too much of it;—to request, that any thing like a memoir for publication—should be written about a poor old cobbler. When I promised him I would, he seemed relieved; and smiled;—thanking me fervently. "You probably know," he said, "I was somewhat related to the old man?"

"First cousin once removed, I believe." "Yes." And he sat down; inclined for further conversation.

George Martell was for many years, till his death, by far the first surgeon, for skill and extent and excellence of practice, throughout the Borough, and many miles beyond. He was a man of strong mind, sound judgment, enlarged views; with great bodily strength and energy; large-boned and muscular;—well formed for great surgical operations. And he delighted in the work;—but with a feeling and generous benevolence, tenderly considerate for the sufferers; conscious that he was doing it for the good of those he was operating upon:—still, confident, and resolute; glorying in his skill. He was a favourite pupil of Abernethy's. When Abernethy heard that he had commenced practice at Portsmouth, he said: "Is Martell at Portsmouth? If Portsmouth has two such men, it has more than its share."

He told me, he had to use the knife, before they could straighten the limbs of the old man sufficiently to lay him in the coffin; because of his extreme deformity, and the stiffened joints, from the fall into the dry dock when a boy.

"Poor old man!—How much he must have had to contend with through life!"

"And how good and happy that life!" Mr. Martell said.—"So cheerful and contented!—No complaining, or discontent, with John Pounds!" "He must have lived well, to have lived so long in such a neighbourhood—without having an enemy."

"Nay,—all friends!"—Mr. Martell said, with instant enthusiasm, "Not one has ever been known to speak of him but in a friendly spirit."

"This sudden outburst of lamentation throughout that whole neighbourhood, in which he lived all his life, is a strong testimony to how much good he must have been doing among them."

"And while there are such general demonstrations of grief and mourning in public," Mr. Martell said,—"seen of every one;—how many are sorrowing in secret; bowed down by suffering and want!—their dear old friend no longer coming in to cheer and help them.

"And those poor little children," Mr. Martell went on, with warmth: —"such a crowd of them—in the old man's shop!—so happy, and busy, when he left them that morning!—Oh, the scene—when we brought him back; and lifted the dead body in among them!—Poor things!—Every one of his scholars has lost a friend. They all loved him; and he loved them. They'll sorely miss him. In their illnesses:—he will no more come to them, and bring them nice things, and sit with them, comforting them. And in the cold weather, there will no longer be his fire-side for them to come in and warm themselves, when they have no fire at home. When their shoes let in the wintry weather; who will mend them now—for nothing; when they can't pay for them? Who will store up for them nice clothes, to go to Chapel in on Sundays;—and take care of them all the week; ready for them to go to Chapel in the next Sunday?"

"And we shall miss him," I said, "in the Sunday-school. It was very pleasant to see him coming in on Sunday afternoons, bringing his chosen scholars, neat and clean, to have them entered as Sunday-scholars. There will be no more of those interesting notes, to be received from him, when he could not come himself:—which often made us smile;—while we reverenced the spirit that sent them. And the Teachers will miss him; in their inquiries after absent scholars; and about poor suffering invalids."

"And in the House of God," Mr. Martell said with deep earnestness; "he will be missed. His presence there was exemplary:—so constant;—so simple-hearted, and humble;—but always manly,—with a proper self-respect,—in his humble way." "Yes," I said; "we might almost say—dignified." "It was dignified!" Mr. Martell said very emphatically. "There was dignity; sterling dignity:—the dignity of plain unaffected goodness:—thoroughly in earnest, worshipping his Maker. The dear—good old man!—God bless him!"—And George Martell's manly voice—faltered—with emotion. "But," he went on, after a pause; with subdued voice:—"his example—will live; and will be felt—in remembrance. It cannot die;—to those who have been accustomed to see him there:—constant,—to the last!"

Both felt it deeply; and there was an interval of silence. Presently: —"Sailors and soldiers," Mr. Martell said:—"formerly his scholars;—now—gone abroad:—when their ship comes up to Spit-head, or their regiment is marched in;—they will come to the old place in St. Mary's

Street, to see their dear old master; and bless him for all the good he has done for them.—What will be their feelings,—to find him—gone?

"No John Pounds will now be seen going along Warblington Street, and Crown Street, and Town Quay,—looking about for little starving children—that nobody cares for; and winning them into his shop, by giving them something to eat; and taking such kind care of them, and making them happy."

"It was his kindness and love that won those children to him, and made them so fond of being with him."

"Yes!"—Mr. Martell said, with a smile:—"It could not be any thing in the poor old man's appearance, or roughness of manner; or that dark, and, I must say, dirty-looking shop,—that could win them into it, and make them so fond of coming to school, and so happy in learning their lessons. It would have been altogether dismal,—repulsive;—but for the dear old friend they loved so—in it. There was a charm in the old man's loving kindness—that made all pleasant and endearing. They felt that he loved them; and they loved him; and liked to be with him.

"But while his love and kindness might win the children to him, and make them so fond of being with him; there were other causes that combined for the success of his school."

"What do you consider the chief?" "Among the chief, I would rank—his sound good sense. In every thing he said and did for them; even in his fun and drollery, there was no nonsense. He had an object in it all: —to relieve their weariness; or quicken their attention; or enliven them with happy feelings; or to impress some useful lesson, that he gave in this comical way. In his most child-like playfulness with them, it would always bear reflecting upon. And the more you reflected upon it, the more you saw its good intention, and its suitableness for his purpose. And that purpose was always for their good. In his more serious treatment of his scholars, none could ever doubt his sound good sense. It was always apparent; strongly decisive."

"His readiness to perceive character and capability, must also have conduced largely to his success with his scholars."

"He had that," Mr, Martell said, "to an extraordinary degree. It seemed intuitive with him. It was instant. And I never knew him to err in his estimate."

"And his power to concentrate his attention."

"Yes;" Mr. Martell said. "He was remarkable for his power of concentration when a child. In their sports, I have heard Lemmon tell, there was always that fixedness of purpose; whatever the game was they were playing at. And it characterized him all through life. Whatever he applied himself to:—thought, feeling, his whole soul, was given to it, for the time.

"And this power of concentrating his attention seemed as instant, and ever ready, as his readiness to discriminate character, and estimate capability."

"It was;" Mr. Martell said:—"and probably no where exerted more constantly than in his school. The readiness with which he would turn from one child, that he had been thoroughly interested in teaching, to another;—perhaps of very different disposition:—has astonished me. Instantly—thought, feeling, interest,—were as thoroughly with this other. And the child felt it so; and was happy in saying its lesson. In a moment, he would turn to another; of very different disposition and capability; and was all heart and soul with. And the child felt he was. And they all loved him for it. Every one felt, in turn, that he was interested in its own lesson,—then going on; and they had confidence in him; and were happy. And so—the good old man went on—all day;—never tiring:—and day after day,—and week after week:—terminating only with his death."

"His graphic way of bringing subjects before them," I said, "made it a pleasure to the children to listen. It was more like looking at a picture, than learning a lesson."

"He had great graphic power. He was a strong thinker."

"And a clear thinker;" I said.

"Yes. And he spoke as he thought."

"There were no hazy goings about and about it with him."

"No; he went direct to the mark. A few words, and it was done;—to the life."

"His being so thoroughly in earnest, no doubt gave the more intense clearness and strength to what he wished the children to understand and feel."

"He was always in earnest;" Mr. Martell said, very feelingly. "And this earnestness of thought, feeling, purpose, gave the more life and strength to his expression. There was no languor of manner, as if not quite up to the mark; no coolness; no dulness; as if he was not heartily interested in it himself; or as if his thoughts were elsewhere. All was life and earnestness. Thoroughly interested himself, he interested all the rest."

"And what patience he had!"

"His patience was inexhaustible;" Mr. Martell said. "I never knew it to fail him."

"And yet it must often have been very much tried."

"It must. So thoroughly in earnest himself; so desiring that they should receive, and value, and be benefitted by what he would teach them:—the slowness of some, the dulness of others; and, at times, with the rougher ones, and more wilful, there must have been more painful causes for dissatisfaction:—yet I never heard of his patience giving way. His good heart, bent only on doing them good, bore it all with kindness and love; and persevered untiringly:—happy, in his self-devotedness."

"Probably, his intermingling so much of fun and pleasantry in his teaching—did not lessen its effectiveness."

"Very much the contrary;" Mr. Martell said, heartily. "No! I consider his intermingling so much of pleasantry and amusement with his teaching one of the chief causes of his success. Children require frequent relief, to relish the continuance of graver instruction."

"And not only to relish. I would say, to derive the best influence from it."

"I agree with you;" Mr. Martell said. "A mind refreshed—is more likely to receive instruction well, and derive the best influence from it; than when applying to it—wearied—and depressed. The abundance and frequency of relief that he mixed with their application to their lessons; his fun with them; his now and then singing them a song, or telling them an entertaining story:—all tended to enliven their work. There was a prevailing life and pleasantness in his school. Their work was a delight; not a drudgery. That touch of fun, continually breaking out at intervals, gave more acceptableness to his more serious instructions. He was perpetually enlivening their attention,—by some kind word,—or comical playfulness. But, with all his fun and drollery, he never lost his self-respect."

"I have been deeply impressed with that;" I said; "as I have stood at his open half-door, listening, and looking on. When telling them some funny story to make them laugh; and he laughed heartily with them:—his own good spirit hallowed it all."

"His own good spirit imbued every thing he did and said;" Mr. Martell said, in subdued tone of deep feeling. "In every thing they saw him do, or heard him say; all—was in the same good spirit. It was all a work of love. He was not doing it—as a trade; to make money by it. And very little children could appreciate this self-devoting kindness,—done for them:—his only desire, and endeavour,—to do them good;—and make them happy. They saw him working every day at his trade, for his own maintenance; while he was teaching them for nothing; and doing them so many kindnesses. And they loved him for it; and trusted him; and delighted to do whatever he bade them do."

"This good influence," I said, "he exerted—as if unconsciously to himself."

"Yes; there was no studied method in it; no systematic design. It came—as if spontaneously;—continually;—and without an effort. He lived it—among them:—to the blessing of so many of God's children!"

"There was another cause for the success of his school:—the general respect and esteem felt for him in all the surrounding neighbourhood."

"Yes;" Mr. Martell said, "Out of school-hours,—when playing in the streets and back courts and alleys; they would see with what respect and gratefulness he was met by poor sufferers he had been kind to;—they would see how kindly he would stop, and listen to all they wished to tell him;—and, as he passed along, they would see, that he had a kind word for every one.—In their homes; they heard their parents and friends tell of the good deeds he was continually doing, all round, among their neighbours.—And they would love him the more!—and delight to come and be taught by so good a man!

"But there's no end to it!" Mr. Martell exclaimed; partly in pleasantry; but deeply in earnest:—as thought after thought went on suggesting other happy influences. "No wonder those poor children were so fond of coming to school, and so happy in learning the lessons he gave them."

"The lessons he gave them," I said, "were very various in kind and subject."

"Yes. Besides grounding them solidly in the rules of arithmetic commonly used in business, and teaching them to read well, and write well:—on slates, you know:—he had no means, or room, to teach them writing with pen and ink:—he taught them many other things. John Pounds was a great reader, in a desultory way. He had a capacious and very retentive memory. He thus got together a large amount of miscellaneous knowledge. And his stores of information were continually increasing by his quickness and penetration to observe and estimate whatever he heard or saw. His memory was also ready and clear, to reproduce at will what he wished to tell the children. I never knew him hesitate for a moment to recollect any thing, or at all inaccurate in telling it. Whatever he thought might be useful to them, either at the time, or in after life; he was always desirous to tell his scholars. For his teaching was thoroughly practical; all, designed to be useful to them. He was thus continually giving them a great variety of information;—scattered, as it were, throughout their more regular work;—if we may use such a term!"—with a smile. "He would tell them, in a lively way, about plants, and animals, and ships;—Merchant shipping, and the Royal Navy, and trading vessels, and the Channel Islands, that such vessels as come to our Town Quay and into the Camber trade with;—and a sailor's life and duties.—Some of them might become sailors.—And he would tell them about the Dockyard, and Gun Wharf, and the Custom House, and the Royal Clarence Yard, for victualling the navy; in all which some of them might find employment:—and a great deal more:—different kinds of business; local employment in our own towns and neighbourhood:—desultory scatterings of knowledge:—but all tending to give them useful information; and putting them in the way of earning a respectable livelihood. And those pleasant rambles that he took them, into the fields and copses, and over the Hill, a whole day together;—he made them a succession of instruction;—on a great variety of subjects;—while, all the time, the children felt it to be more a day of amusements, than any thing like learning lessons!"

"And giving them knowledge was not the only good work he was constantly doing for his scholars.

"There was the culture of themselves;—in his humble way. He was constantly cherishing their own native powers and capabilities into vigorous growth and activity."

"True;"—Mr. Martell said, thoughtfully.

"There was the culture of their minds."

"Yes;" Mr. Martell said;—"he practised them diligently to quick and accurate observations;—both in his shop, and in their rambles."

"And their memory—he practised quite as diligently."

"John knew the value of a good memory in business."

"And in all the affairs of life."

"Right. And he knew that this power of their minds might be rendered more and more capacious by practising it."

"And more retentive," I said; "and more ready."

"Yes. And he was continually storing it with good things; worth remembering."

"And, in their little beginnings," I said, "he was watchful, all along to train his scholars to soundness of judgment."

"He was. John never thought it too early to begin to train them to sound and just judgment. He would have them judge right from the beginning. In training those little children, he felt that he was training the future men and women they were to become. And he knew the clearness and the permanency through life of impressions received in childhood. He never made light of their early impressions."

"Besides this culture of their minds, there was moral culture, in his training his scholars."

"His moral culture," Mr. Martell said, "was all-pervading. In his school; in their rambles; in their homes; even in his fun and playfulness with them:—all his influences had a sound healthy moral tone. Much of his teaching was intended to be direct moral teaching:—the hymns, for example, that he gave them to learn; and in his explaining what they read to him; and in his conversing with them."

"His chief moral instructions," I remarked, "were very short and simple."

"The more likely to be remembered;" Mr. Martell replied, with an emphatic smile. "And his so often repeating them; and so emphatically; would impress them the more. 'Do to others,' he would say, 'as you would have others do to you. Love one another. Delight to help one another. Try to make one another happy. Never tell a lie. Always speak the truth.' He sedulously taught them to be industrious. 'Hate idleness;' he would say. 'Idleness is the way to get into mischief; and to get put in jail. Never get drunk:'—and he would point to some wretched drunkard, passing by at the time; or lounging near; and show them the horrors of self-degradation:—so terribly abounding in that dissolute neighbourhood; with the depraved language the children had so often to hear from those self-despoiled victims of wickedness.

"In their rambles, he enjoined it upon them,—in all their eagerness and sport,—never to do mischief. 'Never break through fences;' he would say. 'Never break down young plantation trees. Never trample down corn, or meadow grass. Always be kind to dumb animals. Never do a cruel thing.'

"While they were with their dear old friend, whatever they were doing, they were always receiving good moral influence. His example among them was always a good moral influence. They saw him doing, what he taught them to do."

"I have been deeply impressed," I said, "with his simple, touching remarks to the children on their own conduct:—so affectionately cherishing them in what was good; and guarding them against what tended to evil."

"Yes; and quite as kind and affectionate in his censurings; when he had to reprove any of them for misconduct. They saw he was sorry to have to speak severely to them. They saw it gave him pain to be displeased with them.

"His punishments consisted chiefly in his own displeasure. He talked to them very seriously:—showing them how wrong their conduct had been. He very seldom inflicted bodily punishment. And when he did, it was more in the fear of it:—not that he caused them much bodily pain. But he frightened them in the anticipation. His punishments,—even the severest,—were so administered, that the children,—the punished themselves,—saw that it was all meant for their good. There was nothing like vindictiveness; no angry passion; no hasty temper,—as if he had lost his self-control; no undue severity." "Still," I said, "he was firm." "O yes; he was not afraid to be severe, when their conduct required it. Severity might be the truest kindness then. But he was never too severe. He was always ready, and glad, to relent,—and smile upon them,—as soon as they showed themselves sorry for what they had done amiss, and desiring to do better."

"And there was spiritual culture," I said,—"in a simple way."

"Simple indeed;" Mr. Martell replied; "but genuine:—child-like in its simplicity; but true to a good heart, and a pure spirit. He delighted to impress his scholars with the presence and goodness of God—their Heavenly Father!—all love for them!—And he would often say to them, with loving earnestness:—'Always live as in the sight of God. You can't see him; but he sees you; and knows all you do, and all you think and feel; and hears all you say. Never say or do any thing you would not like God to know. For he's sure to know it. Always try and do what will please him. This,' he would say, 'is the way to be happy.'

"When his birds were singing, in full voice; some in his shop, some hanging outside in the street; vying with one another; while his scholars were busy at their lessons:—he would say: 'Isn't it good of God, to make those pretty birds sing so merrily for us?' And the hearty —'Yes! Mr. Pounds!'—from many voices,—showed that the children felt it happily.

"In their rambles;—when in the midst of beautiful scenery; and the birds were singing in the trees, and lambs sporting about on the grass; and every thing looked bright and full of life and joy;—he would sit down; and his scholars would gather round him to listen:—and he would tell them of God, who created them all; and say:—'Isn't it very kind of Almighty God, to make all these birds and pretty lambs, to enjoy themselves?—and all this beautiful world, for his children to be happy in?' And then he would say: 'Love God; and be thankful for all his loving kindness!' And he was often doing this;—bringing the children—feelingly near to God; and happily training them to live mindful of God; as always in his presence.

"John Pounds had a fervent spirit of piety himself; and his scholars were continually feeling this in his ordinary conversations with them. His piety was of a very happy and cheerful kind; and it always influenced his own feelings and conduct. It imbued his presence. He loved it. It was the soul of all he did and said. And the children were happy in feeling its cherishing influence."

"And we have seen happy examples," I said, "of the good results of this humble nurture;—mental, moral, spiritual;—in excellent men and women; now respected members of society, heads of well-ordered families;—formerly his scholars."

"We have;"—Mr. Martell said, with deep feeling.

"When I consider the room available in that little shop for his keeping his school; with himself sitting on his bench at the window, working at his trade, with his tools and materials about him; it seems astonishing he could have done so much in it."

"From front to back," Mr. Martell said, "not quite five yards; from side to side, about two yards; as to height, a man six feet high could only just stand straight up in it.

"Scarcely anything for the children to sit on:—some old broken boxes; a little form or two; and the lower steps of the very little stairs."

"That was all."

"Not a desk, or a table:—and such poor meagre means for teaching with."

"In his earlier years of school-keeping," Mr. Martell said, "he had little but stray leaves out of old worn-out books to teach his scholars to read with. He had to use hand-bills, and scraps of newspapers,—any thing he happened to meet with. As for teaching them writing; nothing but bits of broken slates; and sometimes hard put to it to find sufficient of those for so many scholars. But he never lost heart. He would talk to them, when he had no other means for giving them lessons.

"More than twenty years," Mr. Martell went on with enthusiasm, "the good old man carried on his school in that little shop; with his thirty or forty scholars about him at a time! And during all those years,

I never heard of his closing his school a day, or half a day, or shortening the time of teaching in the least, from any feeling of weariness, or disinclination, or any plea of illness, or any consideration for himself. For his scholars, you know, he would sometimes close it for a day, to take them out for the enjoyment of a day's excursion. But never on his own account."

"The poor old cobbler has shown what may be done with very small means, and in very lowly life."

"Where the heart's in it!" Mr. Martell said with bright emphasis.

"Yes; there's the secret!"

"The main-spring of it all!"

"What a fondness for birds he had, and other animals!"

"And he had the way," Mr. Martell said, "of making others as fond of them as himself. His friend Lemmon, for instance. Though Lemmon does not keep them in his house. Lemmon's house, you know, is a small one; and, with his children and grandchildren, he may think it full enough without. But he has the same lively interest in them."

"I have observed it, with pleasure." "And not only for animals. The fresh air, the open downs, magnificent trees, wild plants, beautiful flowers,—all the delights of Nature;—green fields, fine landscape scenery:—Johnny rejoiced in them all! And he delighted to go out among them; and take others with him, to enjoy them together.

"He and his friend Lemmon would go out on a fine summer's evening, when the old man's school was over, and they had both had their tea; and would walk hours together; along the green lanes, bordered with hedge-rows; and into the fields; and out beyond, into the woodland scenery; and up Portsdown:—and come home by moonlight, ready for a good night's rest." "Their's—was a beautiful friendship." "It was;" Mr. Martell said; "in a humble way. They were like brothers. They were play-fellows as children; and firm friends through life. There could not have been a friendship more faithful, or more affectionate:—unclouded—to the last." "But in some things they were different." "Yes; of minor importance;" Mr. Martell said: —"strikingly different. Poor old Johnny,"—with a touch of pleasantry, —"had a rough outside. Not so—Lemmon. Johnny was coarse in appearance; sometimes, in manner and conduct. Lemmon, never."

"I have, from the first, looked upon our good friend Mr. Lemmon— as one of Nature's gentlemen!"

"Yes; there is a native propriety,—we may almost say—gracefulness, —in every thing he says and does. There is a native air of gentlemanly appearance and bearing about him. And the great charm is, he seems quite unconscious of it himself!

"The poor old man," Mr. Martell went on, "was sadly negligent about his own person and dress. We all had to lament this. He was sadly deficient in cleanliness. It was never so with Lemmon. Nor Johnny,—on a Sunday!" he added with a smile. "On Sundays, all was clean and proper; and pleasant to look at. Lemmon,—meet him when you might,—in the house, or out of it,—was always pleasant to look at: —dress, person, every thing,—becoming and pleasant:—and never with any appearance of thinking about it. There is a pleasing absence of self-consciousness habitual to him.

"Wherever you saw the old man in the streets, he was striding along in haste; as if he hadn't a minute to spare:—unless he happened to stop to attend to some poor suffering creature;—or listen to some tale of woe. He was never in haste then. Lemmon—never seemed in haste. Not that there was any want of life and attention:—but he always seemed to be self-possessed, and at ease; with a mild manly dignity; as if conscious, that he had his time and actions entirely at his own control.

"But while they were so different in some things, of secondary importance;—in the most important, and the best,—they were One!"

"Yes!" Mr. Martell said, very emphatically. "They were, both of them, incapable of an untruth. They were, both of them, incapable of an ungenerous action. With all his roughness of appearance and manner;—John Pounds—was incapable of saying or doing a rude thing. Lemmon,—nobody could ever doubt. Both—were alike gentlemanly in spirit."

"And both were truly Christian in spirit."

"They were!" Mr. Martell said, with deep full tone of admiration. "All through life," he said, "their spirit has been truly Christian. And their conduct, all through life,—has been the simple, true-hearted life of their happy religion."

"They were both constant in the House of God;" I said. "Mr. Lemmon once told me;—regretting what he thought the too easy absence of some on rainy Sundays:—One very wet stormy Sunday, as he was getting ready to go to Chapel; they said to him at home; 'Grandfather, you'll not go out to day; so wet and stormy. I replied:' he said, 'My Pastor will be there. And if my Pastor can be there, I can be there.'"

"No;" Mr. Martell said; "No storminess of weather ever prevented Lemmon, or his friend Johnny, from being in their place on the Lord's

Day. I can only speak of the evening service; because, you know, I must be with my patients in the morning. But in the evening, I have never missed John Pounds in his place;—till last night.

"It was very touching,"—Mr. Martell went on, with subdued voice, and colouring countenance;—"to see those two plain old men,—homely as they looked,—side by side,—devoutly singing the hymns; looking over the same book. Poor Lemmon!—He'll feel the difference—next Sunday."

Mr. Martell was much moved.—After a while;—"It is to the good old man," he said, with an affectionate smile of remembrance, "that I owe my own taste for Natural History. When I was a boy, he would take me over the Hill, and carry me on his back,—lame as he was,—miles and miles in the day. And we went along the hedge-rows, looking at the birds' nests; and into the copses, and among the wild bushes; and he would sometimes bring young birds home with him. But he had a way of doing it, that he never gave me any idea of cruelty. He always seemed to have a nice feeling about it. There was something very kind and gentle in the impression it left."

"I have been told, he had sometimes a strange variety of birds at the same time in his shop; before he began keeping his school."

"Yes; and other animals too;"—with a smile. "While he had half a dozen cages hanging about the walls, and some outside in the street, with canaries, and linnets, and goldfinches, and other singing birds, all singing together; he would have a crow, or a raven, or magpie, hopping about the floor; and some young pewits; perhaps, running about. And on the hearth you might see the cat and some kittens sleeping before the fire; and a bird asleep on the cat's back; and two or three young birds nestling with the kittens; and some young guinea pigs in a basket in the corner." "Is it true, that he once made a wooden leg for a little bird, that had lost a leg?"

"O yes!" Mr. Martell said. "He did that for several!" And he laughed heartily. "When he saw a bird that had lost a leg, he took a bit of a match, and made it another leg, and fitted it on; and left it to go about amongst the others.

"While he was in the shop with them, he could keep them all right and safe; but when he was going out, he used to put the large birds down into a hole under the floor, and shut them down with a trap-door; so that they should not hurt the little ones. But sometimes he found a little bird with a toe off, or a leg gone; and he could not account for it:—till, one day, standing awhile at the door, before he came in,—he saw something catch at one of the little birds, as it was hopping over the crevice, where the trap-door did not fit quite close to the edge of the hole. Then he saw how it was. The great birds down below were on the watch, to snap at the little ones as they came near the crevice."

"But could the birds make use of the wooden leg?"

"O yes! He made it light; and measured the other leg, and made it the right length, and fitted it on nicely; and they hopped about with the other birds, and didn't seem to know the difference. But when he found out the cause why the little birds lost their legs and their toes, he got rid of all the great birds, and after that, kept only little ones.

"He was fond of taking morning walks. One of his favourite walks was along the Portsmouth walls;—that part between the Mill-dam and the Colewort-barracks, crossing the end of St. Mary's Street. Many a time, before sun-rise,—sometimes before the day-break gun fired,—the sentries along that part of the walls—have seen him striding along, enjoying the bracing air;—commonly without hat or coat on!—Whatever the weather, hot or cold, wet or dry; no matter to Johnny!—he must have his morning's walk. His cat was commonly his companion in these morning walks. And when he saw the cat looking tired;—he didn't stop for her;—but just set his arm a-kimbo, resting the back of his hand on that hip that bulged out,—with the open palm turned upwards:—and puss jumped up, and sat down in it; and so they went on together!"

XXVII.

No sooner was it heard, that the old man was dead, than the rumour seemed to be instantly all over the Borough. Every where was heard—"The old cobbler in St. Mary's Street 's dead." So little noticed before, while living:—as soon as it was known that he was dead, the whole Borough seemed to wake up to his worth. Every body had something to say about him:—some anecdote to tell;—some kindness they had heard of his doing—to some poor creature—that nobody cared for;—some characteristic oddity,—with a good-natured smile! It was so in all ranks of society; throughout all religious Denominations, —all political parties. All felt, that a Benefactor was gone;—the poor had lost a Friend. Persons who jeered at him before,—now spoke of him seriously, and with kindly respect; while they might still smile at his peculiarities. All spoke of him with respect and esteem. The peculiarities seemed only subject for good-natured pleasantry now; while the good he had been doing,—so quietly,—in such obscure life,—so perseveringly,—with such small means;—rose into admiration!—and went on rising in generous praise and esteem.

In the midst of this sudden awakening of interest, Mr. Charpentier, a respected engraver and stationer in High Street, stopped me in the street and said: "There seems a good deal of interest excited about this old man;—the old cobbler, I mean, in St. Mary's Street. The London papers are taking it up. I've been thinking, it might answer, to lithograph Sheaf's picture of him. What do you think?" "That the interest in him is fast extending," I said, "we have proofs from greater and greater distances. If it is done well, I feel sure such a lithograph would sell readily." "I think I'll do it," he said; and bid me Good morning.

Very soon after, the lithograph was announced as published. It gives a good idea of Sheaf's painting. Under it is inscribed:—"John Pounds, late of St. Mary's Street, Portsmouth; who while earning an honest subsistence by mending shoes, was also School-Master, gratuitously, to some hundreds of the Children of his poor Neighbours. Born 17, June, 1766—Died 1, January, 1839; aged 72—'They cannot recompense thee; for thou shalt be recompensed at the resurrection of the Just.' Luke Ch. xiv; v. 14."

Immediately on the publication of Charpentier's lithograph, Mr. Price, a printer and bookseller in the same street, published a small anonymous pamphlet of a few pages, entitled, "A Memoir of the late Mr. John Pounds of Portsmouth, Shoe-mender and gratuitous Teacher of poor Children." It opens thus: "It has been the lot of many a one, who has through life pursued a course of usefulness towards his fellow-creatures, that his good deeds have been scarcely known, except to those immediately benefitted, until death has placed him beyond the reach of earthly praise. This is no reason why, when brought to light, they should not be placed on record for the imitation of survivors. To preserve the memory of a man, whose good and useful deeds were thus performed within a very humble sphere of life, the following brief Memoir was penned. It will also serve," the writer goes on, "to explain a point, representing the same individual in the midst of the pursuits for which he was remarkable, published by Mr. Charpentier, of this town, from a painting taken"—"before his death, by Mr. Sheaf, of Landport, by trade also a shoe-maker, a self-taught artist of excellent promise."

The primary purpose of the writer in publishing this Memoir, seemed to be, to help forward the sale of his neighbour's lithograph; but it also gave an interesting narrative of the good old man's life and chief kinds of usefulness; especially his conducting his school in his little shop, and gratuitously; while working at his trade for his own homely subsistence. There were inaccuracies of statement and deficiencies in it similar to those in the Obituary Notice; but it was written in an excellent spirit, and gave a graphic and characteristic picture of the old cobbler and his doings. Though published anonymously, it soon became known, that it was written by the publisher himself. Nearly the whole Memoir re-appeared as an Obituary Notice in the March number of the Christian Reformer; a monthly magazine, published in London; with a highly estimable circulation.

The lithograph had a ready and rapidly extending sale. And more frequent letters soon began to come to us from friends at a distance, and from persons unknown to us;—desiring more information about "the philanthropic old cobbler!"—as he now began to be very commonly called. Beside the London papers, other periodicals, in very various parts of the kingdom, and in fast increasing numbers, dwelt with enthusiasm on what they described as this fine Example of Philanthropy in Humble Life!

XXVIII.

The Nephew, having occasion to call upon me a few days after the funeral, said as he was going out, "Now that the old man's gone, I think I'll spirt up the old house a bit." And the next time I passed the house, which was but a few days after, I was startled at the change. The little tumble-down window, where we had been accustomed to see the old man at work, cobbling;—was gone. The little half-door, where we had stood so often, looking in upon his school, and listening to the busy scene, all happy at their lessons;—was gone. The whole front was gone; —so weather-worn, and covered thick with dust. And a new front was up;—painted all over a light yellow-ochre; except the window frames; which were painted white. The wood-work was neat and good. The whole front, from near the ground to the level of the chamber-floor, was one large window; leaving only a narrow strip to the left, for the door. The window consisted of nine oblong panes of glass; three above three, length-ways upwards. The frames were very light, and well put together; looking quite smart. The chamber had a neat sash-window; from near the floor up to the eaves. The shop inside,—so dark before,—was now painted white, and looked very bright and clean; and, so abundantly lighted by the large window, showed to advantage—the walls—plentifully stocked with ready-made articles for sale, arranged in business-like order. The windows were well cleaned and bright. At the shop-window were displayed a good assortment of ladies' shoes, set out tastefully for effect. Every thing, within and without, looked bright and cheerful. The Nephew was sitting near the window, at work; with the air of a good man of business, consciously master of his trade; and thoroughly in earnest; with an ample provision of tools and materials about him. He was alone in the shop.—No crowd of little children now.—All was silent and still:—save the sound of his hammer, at intervals.

XXIX.

When the shock—from the so awfully sudden death of our good old friend—had somewhat subsided; and we had buried him:—friends began to speak with regret of the testimonial, which they had been looking forward with so much pleasure to their presenting to him. Nearly sufficient had been received for the purchase of the quarto Bible. What was now to be done with the money? We called a general meeting of the friends who had contributed; and a very interesting meeting it was; full of feeling; deeply impressive. All felt that it would not be desirable to return to the contributors what they had so happily given; but none seemed to have come with any idea to propose, as to what might be the best to do with it. I had thought of our adding a little to it, and putting up a plain, simple marble tablet in the Chapel to his memory. But when I suggested this to the meeting, none were ready to concur in it. Some were startled at the idea; and showed it by their look and manner. Others,—and excellent friends of the good old man,—highly esteemed amongst us,—seriously hesitated. Some,—while desiring to pay proper respect to his memory,—decidedly opposed it; as out of character. The rest seemed to doubt, whether it could be in character: a marble tablet—for a poor old cobbler. I did not urge it; but left it—quietly and gently to work its own way. The meeting separated, without coming to any decision.

By degrees, friend after friend, as they had time to reflect upon it, and converse leisurely with one another about it, came into the idea.

And, after a moderate interval, we called another meeting of the contributors. At length, all approved of it. And it was unanimously decided; that a small, plain, simple marble tablet should be put up in the Chapel to the memory of John Pounds. And a Committee was appointed, empowered to carry it into effect.

The meetings of this Committee were very pleasant. We were all of one mind, that, while everything was to be plain and simple, all should be thoroughly good. But on other points, there was considerable variety of opinion, to begin with. But by patiently deliberating upon point after point, and mutually allowing every one perfect freedom of discussion, we became unanimous on every final decision.

The design adopted for the tablet, was a plain white slab, with a plain black border, gently oblong, to be placed lengthways horizontally:—the following inscription to be put upon it, in plain Roman letters:—"Erected by Friends as a Memorial of their Esteem and Respect for John Pounds; who, while earning his livelihood by mending shoes, gratuitously educated, and in part clothed and fed some hundreds of poor children. He died suddenly on the 1st of January, 1839; aged 72 years. 'Thou shalt be blessed: for they cannot recompense thee.'"

The tablet was affixed to the wall under the left gallery, going into the Chapel; the gallery in which the Old Man had for so many years been seen, a constant worshipper. When it was up, all were pleased with it; and regarded it with sacred satisfaction.

XXX.

No longer having the good John Pounds to help us, in going to look after the scholars he had brought to the Sunday School, from the back courts and alleys about St. Mary's Street, and Warblington Street, and all that crowded neighbourhood; our excellent Teachers went into those scenes of degradation and infamy. The alleys were all narrow; some of them, dark. In going along one of these, where we could go only one at a time, I felt my elbows touching the wall on one side or the other all along. We sometimes found ourselves in the midst of sad scenes of abandoned wretchedness. But the poor creatures always received us very respectfully, and expressed themselves grateful for the care taken of their children. Other scenes—were very touching:—poor sickly creatures—on scanty beds,—with scarcely any clothing:—others,—starving for want of food,—clad in rags,—with no fire in their little grate this severe winter. But wherever we went, however severe the distress and destitution; we everywhere met with testimonies of gratefulness, and respect, and affection, for "good Mr. Pounds!"—the good deeds he had done for them;—tenderly touching tales of his kindness and consideration:—the good friend they had lost.

In one of those courts, which looked cleaner and brighter than most of them, more quiet and orderly; as we entered it and crossed over to the further corner, where the house was we were going to call at; the mother, a decent looking woman, but very poor, came and met us at the door, and asked us in. I was struck with the neatness and cleanliness of everything. All was of the poorest sort, and there was not much of anything; but what there was, showed good management. The furniture was bright; some plain little shelves had a nice set out of shiny plate and cups and saucers; the window was clean and bright; and along the sill was a row of flower-pots with plants growing in them. In one, a little clump of snow-drops, beautifully in blossom; in another, some crocus leaves were peeping up; in another, a rose-tree, waiting for spring to open its buds. Everything had an air of comfort, though of a very homely sort. She soon began to speak of—"dear old Mr. Pounds!"—"He comes to me one day, and says,'Missus, your Jem's not been to school this three days.' 'No,' I says, 'Mr. Pounds; it's 'cause it's a-ben so rainy; and his boots ben full of holes, and lets in the water.' 'Boots full of holes?' he says. 'Let me look at 'em.' 'Jemmy,' says I, 'show Mr. Pounds your boots.' So Jemmy takes off his boots; and he takes 'em,—so kind like,—dear old soul!—and he turns 'em about and about, and looks at 'em; so careful, he does! And he says; 'Missus, anybody else 'ill charge you sixpence; I'se mend 'em for three-pence; and, you knows, that other three-pence 'ill buy you a loaf of bread.' Dear old soul!—So kind and thoughtful! We's all miss him very much."

In many of these poor houses we saw signs of that interest in plants and animals, which John Pounds, so fond of them himself, had the happy way of cherishing in others. Most of them had a plant or two growing; some, several; and showing good care and management. Some were enlivened by both plants and animals. In one house, a cat and kittens were comfortably asleep before the fire, and a bird nestling with them. In another,—a magpie, at some cunning trick; making the children laugh merrily. In another,—a little dog and a kitten, playing with one another. All, giving a charm—to the abodes of poverty;—some,—enlivening the bed-side of long-enduring suffering;—or entertaining some aged cripple,—sitting,—helpless,—laughing heartily,

—in his quiet corner.

Going into another court, of a much less pleasing sort, we tapped gently at the door of a very poor shed; and a slender voice faintly said from within; "Come in." As we entered, we saw an emaciated frame,—small and fragile, and very old,—sitting alone, beside a very little bit of a fire. Reaching out her arm to get her crutch;—"Dear old Mr. Pounds made me this crutch!" she said, with a glow of enthusiasm. "And he's not have anything for it,—when I'se a-going to pay him. 'No;' he says; 'you's enough to do to get you a bit of wittles. I'se be able to work for my living:—bless the Lord!'—And he goes out so quick like, and kind!

"Dolly, here's the ladies." And a decent motherly woman, her daughter, came in. As soon as she had replied to what we came to inquire about, she began talking about—"Dear old Mr. Pounds!"

"This little old guy's my Billy's. Mr. Pounds cut it out for him out of a carrot, last fifth of November. And, now he's dead and gone, my Billy treasures it up dearly. They's some acorns in that cup;" pointing to a tea-cup on the table, "My Donnie makes much on 'em. Mr. Pounds helped him get 'em off the tree, last time they goes over the Hill with him.—Dear old soul!—They's never go over the Hill again with him.—Ye sees, the branch is too high for my little Donnie to reach. And so Mr. Pounds comes, and pulls it down for him with his hook stick; and holds it down, whiles my Donnie pulls off the acorns, and puts 'em into his pocket. He says, he's keep 'em as long as he lives, for dear Mr. Pounds' sake.

"My Donnie gets very tired that day, when they's a-coming home; for they's ben miles and miles over the Hill. So Mr. Pounds takes him up on his back, and carries him:—dear old soul!—When they gets back as far as Cosham, Mr. Pounds takes 'em all to a pump; and they all gets a good drink o' water; and then the bigger lads starts off again fresh, and runs all about, as lively as ever. But Mr. Pounds takes up my Donnie again, and puts him on his back,—dear old soul!—and carries him as far as Kingston Cross. And then he puts him down gently, and lets him walk a bit; and takes up another little one, and carries him on his back; and so they goes on, till they comes home into his shop in St. Mary's Street:—where there's a good tea ready for 'em all; before they goes home to bed. Nothing's too good for dear old Mr. Pounds to be doing for any one. He's always doing somebody a good turn.

"There's poor old Sally—there, in next court. When she's ill o' the fever, and like to die; and nobody won't go to her, for fear o' catching the fever:—dear Mr. Pounds comes, and brings her some nice warm gruel;—he's made it himself for her;—and he sits down beside her;—all so kind and comforting; with his pleasant talk. And he's in no hurry to go. Another time, he brings her some nice roasted apples, he's ben and roasted for her;—so nicely done! But there's an end to all that—now. God bless him!"

"What have you in this flower-pot?" "That's dear little Polly's daisy; pink and white. Mr. Pounds got it up for her. He was taking his scholars over the Hill. The little ones, you know, Sir, couldn't go so far as that. Some of them went part way. My Polly went as far as Tipnor Lane. And there she saw this pretty daisy; pink and white, full in flower. And she was so pleased with it, Mr. Pounds digs it up for her with his stick;—his stick had a bit of iron at the end. And he said, 'Here, Polly!'—and gave her a kiss; and said,'There; take it home to mother!' And she brought it home, and set it in this pot; and made much of it. She often watered it; and was looking forward with such delight to see the flowers come out again the next spring. 'If it please God, Polly, to let you live so long;'—Mr. Pounds once said to her. 'Yes, Mr. Pounds;'—she says. Dear little Polly! She often talked about the pretty flowers; pink and white; and how glad she should be when they came out again in the spring. But she was not to see them. It pleased the Lord to take her. We have taken good care of it ever since; for dear Polly's sake; she was so fond of it. And dear Mr. Pounds—would stand—and look at it:—so still—and silent;—after dear Polly was dead. He loved Polly; and Polly loved him."

"Let us hope," I said, "she is gone to a better land; where the flowers do not wither."

"Ah yes!—That's what dear Mr. Pounds used to say to us; to comfort us. Bless his soul!

"Poor little Polly!—She died in the winter:—one very cold night:—and we'd no fire in the house:—no coal:—to get her any thing warm."

And the mother wept.

As we were returning along St. Mary's Street from one of these rounds of calling, Mrs. More met us at the end of Crown Street, just as the sun-set gun fired, with her child in her arms; looking very sorrowful. At once she began deploring dear old Mr. Pounds. "Who's cure my child's foot now?" And she showed us the child's foot, turned inward. "It's born so. And when Mr. Pounds sees it, he says, 'Missus, I'se cure that child's foot, if you's let me try.' 'Yes, Mr. Pounds,' I says, and thank y'.' And he takes it in hand. Look; here's the little boot he makes for it, out of old-shoe leather. But I'se take it off; it makes my child cry so. 'It's a long time about, Missus,' he says; but I'se make a good job of it, before I'se done with it.' And he drops down dead, before it's done. Nobody's cure it now. We's never have another Mr. Pounds like him."

XXXI.

As weeks and months went on, the interest in the good old man did not seem to abate or cool down. Wherever we went, wherever we called, whomever we met to speak to; almost every one began speaking of John Pounds. Even strangers,—persons that I had never spoken to before,—knowing that he was one of our Congregation, and that I buried him,—would stop me in the street to talk about John Pounds; seeming to think themselves at liberty to speak to his Pastor about him; desiring to express their esteem and admiration for the poor old cobbler; and would stand talking, as if not wishing to end the conversation. New anecdotes were continually crowding upon us; told with lively enthusiasm; commonly a cluster at a time; one suggesting another with eager rapidity.

One evening, being invited to take tea with a much respected lady, a widow, advanced in life:—as I sat down, she began to talk about John Pounds. She said, she remembered him living in the same poor shed before he began to keep his school. "He was living alone then. His little shop was just the same dark, dirty looking place. The upper half-door was open; and the old man was sitting at work cobbling at his open window;—the same dark dingy-looking man, as if with no thought of his own personal appearance. And all about him were his birds, and cats and dogs, and an old raven walking about, and some guinea-pigs, and a litter of young puppies playing on the floor." She said, she was a perfect stranger to him; and that, one day, as she was walking by his shop, with one of her little nieces, a girl of six years old; the child suddenly pulled her back; "O, stop, Aunt! Look at the pretty 'ittle puppies!"—"Mr. Pounds, hearing it, looked up from bis work, and said; 'Do you like puppies, Miss? I'll give you one.' However, it did not suit the Aunt's convenience to let her accept it. We thanked him, and passed on. I merely mention this, to show how ready he was to do a kindness; even to a child, and a stranger."

A wine-merchant, who, during a long life, had been all along making money, by steady, close habits of business;—a dull-looking man, of few words, with little expression of countenance; as if he had scarcely a thought or a sympathy beyond his money-getting;—now, a wealthy man;—but as closely devoted to business as ever; as if money-getting was the only thing worth living for:—stopped to speak to me in High Street:—at which I was rather surprised; for he had never done so before, though we had been acquainted some years. He said:—"And so the poor old cobbler in St. Mary Street's dead:"—and went on with scarcely a pause:—"I once heard of a woman who brought her son to him, requesting that he might be admitted into his school; and, as a great recommendation,—to show how little trouble he would give him, —she said, 'He's the very best boy in all Portsmouth.' 'Well, then,' Mr. Pounds replied, 'I'll have nothing to do with him; for I want the very worst boys in all Portsmouth!'"—And the wine-merchant laughed benevolently;—and went on:—

"A private, in a regiment that had just come into the town, brought his boys to have them received as scholars.—And looking among the crowd of children, he said; very respectfully, and rather subdued:—'I see you've our sergeant-major's sons there.' 'What?' says John Pounds sharply, as if in wrath. The soldier repeated; 'I see our sergeant-major's two boys there.'—'Which be they?' 'Yonder, in that corner.'—And the old man called them to him, and said: 'Now, you go home; and tell your father, you're not coming here any more. He can afford to pay for your schooling: I want those that can't pay.'"

I could not help observing, that the wealthy wine-merchant showed a feeling and generous delight in telling these anecdotes, that I had never seen in him before. His heart seemed to warm, and his countenance brightened to a pleasing intelligence.

Calling on Mr. and Mrs. F—, esteemed for their plain sound sense and good feeling, Members of my Flock; the father and mother of a numerous family:—as I was sitting conversing with them by their fire-side; some of their children listening to our conversation:—Mrs. F said, with fervent feeling; her countenance very expressive with the remembrance of past goodness:—"And so, Mr. Hawkes, we have lost one of our good friends;—poor old John Pounds.—He was a good man!"

Mr. F— mentioned an anecdote, that Mr. Pounds, he said, told him himself. "One day, a fine young man, a sergeant, stopped at the door, and leaning over the lower half, and looking in upon the little crowd, said, 'Well, Mr. Pounds!' Mr. Pounds looked up from his work, and said, 'You know me; but I don't know you.' 'Yes, but you do know me!' 'Why, what's your name?' The sergeant mentioned his name. 'What, you?' the old man exclaimed with admiration. 'Oh, I know you now! And you

—a sergeant!' 'Yes, but I should never have been a sergeant, if it hadn't been for you!' And he threw him in some money, to lay out for the children.

"As I was once talking with him," Mr. F—went on, "about his school; Mr. Pounds said, he wanted all the worst of the off-scouring of the earth. He sometimes refused to receive the good children, for fear the poor little things should be contaminated by mixing with such a set of reprobates. He used to boast, that he never had one hanged!"

Mrs. F— spoke of a married sister, living in a distant part of the country, who, when she was over here, used to like to go and see poor old Mr. Pounds in his school. "The first time we took her to see him, she was so delighted, that when she went home again, she bought a great many children's books, and sent him. She and her husband were great admirers of John Howard. And they were accustomed to call Mr. Pounds—'the Howard of his day!'—They had a portrait of John Howard hanging up in their house; and as soon as they heard of Mr. Pounds' death; and that a likeness of him was published; they sent for one of the pictures, and hung it up with John Howard's!"

Mr. S—, a respectable armourer in the Gun Wharf, who had been a Member of my Flock ever since I came to Portsmouth, was uniformly mild and gentle; altogether unobtrusive; never in haste to speak first. As I was approaching the Chapel on Sunday morning, I saw a cluster of friends standing at the gate, in earnest conversation. Mr. S— was among them; quiet and placid as usual. I found they were talking about John Pounds. When I had shaken hands with each of them, and exchanged a few friendly words, I moved forward, to go to the vestry. Just as I turned round the corner of the Chapel, Mr. S— came running after me, to my surprise; for he had never done any thing of the kind before; and, with an eagerness quite unusual to him, he said; "I've something to tell you! I've often meant to tell it you. A fine, tall, handsome young man came up to John Pounds as he was standing talking with some persons in the street, and said; 'You taught me to read!' 'Did I?' said John Pounds; 'I don't remember you.' 'Yes, you did; and God bless you for it!' And the young man stooped down, and suddenly took him up on his back, and ran off with him a considerable distance; twenty yards, or more!—and then ran back with him; and put him gently down!—Now, I know that to be true!" Mr. S— said, with ardour and enthusiasm; "for the friend saw it himself, who told me of it!"

Another friend told of a hearty young corporal, that belonged to a regiment that had marched into the town from Winchester that day, who stopped at his open half-door, and looked savagely in at the old man, and said in a loud threatening voice;—"Ha, you old villain!—There you are on the old bench!"—And he doubled his fist, and shook it at him. "You once thrashed me;" he said. "I could now thrash you." The children were all terrified.

"Who's you?" the old man said.

"Don't you know me?" the young man said, in a softened voice.

"No. Who bes you?"

"Don't you remember Jack Woods?"—and the young fellow's voice quivered.

"Yes; but you's not he." "But I am though."

"And you—a corporal!"—looking at him with pride and admiration.

"Yes; but it's all along of you. I should never have been a corporal, but for the schooling you gave me. I can't stop now; but I wanted just to come and see you;—and thank you;—and see the dear old place again! Here's half-a-crown to lay out for your scholars. And God bless you!" The young man said this with a colouring countenance, and a trembling voice; and turned hastily away.

"And God bless you, my lad!" the old man said very fervently. "And thank you, my lad!"—And he looked after him, ready to weep for joy,—as the fine young corporal went away hastily.

In a meeting of the Sunday School Teachers, one of the ladies said, with an earnest, bright interest, in the midst of a general conversation about their old friend John Pounds:—"I met him one day, coming out of Warblington Street, just as I was passing the end of it, going along St. Mary's Street into Portsea; and I said; 'Mr. Pounds, I've often wished it had pleased God to make you rich.' 'Pleased God to make me rich? Why so?' I said: 'Because I think you would have done so much good with it.' 'I don't know that;' he said. 'If it had pleased God to make me rich; perhaps I shouldn't have done more good with it, than other rich folks. No!' he said, with great emphasis; 'God has given me the will; and that's better than riches! And John Pounds' as happy as the day's long. Good morning to you!' And he passed on to his little shop with quick and lively step!"

XXXII.

In several parts of the Borough, schools were enthusiastically instituted—as Memorials of John Pounds;—designed to carry forward gratuitously the same good work. These Memorial Schools became centres of generous emulation; where benevolent persons met from different ranks in life, from opposite political parties, and from very various religious Denominations, and worked earnestly and happily together; teaching and cherishing the poorest and most neglected children they could gather in.

Proofs continued to come, from other parts of England and Scotland, from our most distant Colonies, and from other nations, that the interest in the poor old cobbler was still extending; and from all directions, however distant, as lively and enthusiastic as ever. From America, surprisingly soon, publications came over, not only with warm eulogies of "the philanthropic old cobbler of Portsmouth!"—but illustrated with woodcuts from Charpentier's lithograph of Sheaf's picture of him; cheap periodicals, designed for the masses of the people. Presently, other periodicals, both in Great Britain and America, had woodcuts from other pictures, by other artists; chiefly designed to represent the old man's kindnesses towards children. Some of these fancy sketches, we could not but regret, were strikingly out of character, for want of the artist's knowing more accurately the appearance,—especially his great deformity,—and the winning manner of the good old man in approaching poor starving children. The artist seemed to have caught some one excellence; probably from some anecdote, heard repeated, or met with in some periodical;—for anecdotes about this "Philanthropist in humble life!"—became frequent in newspapers and other periodicals;—and this one excellence he expressed strongly; but with little or nothing of the characteristic personal appearance and manner of the Benefactor himself:—unlike all others;—himself, emphatically, in every thing he said and did. Not that there was any affectation of singularity. There was no affectation with him. All was genuine simplicity;—but strongly characteristic:—unconsciously thus marked out from all others.

XXXIII.

When Dr. Guthrie, in 1847, threw himself with all his ardour and energy into what came to be called "The Ragged School Movement," this generous Movement went on with increased vigour and expansiveness. Kindred spirits gathered to him. Powerful speakers, strong-minded writers, large-hearted philanthropists, hastened to help forward the great work.

In the spring of that year, Dr. Guthrie published a "Plea for Ragged Schools:"—so powerful, that, though only a sixpenny pamphlet, it was reviewed in the Edinburgh Review, with high esteem and admiration; and letters of congratulation and encouragement, and gifts of money for carrying on the good work, both from his own friends, and from persons unknown to him, came pouring in far beyond any thing he had dared to hope; even to his astonishment. And he and his friends in the summer commenced their Ragged School in Edinburgh, and brought it into excellent and permanent effectiveness.

Rather more than two years after publishing his first "Plea for Ragged Schools," Dr. Guthrie published a second; full of the same grieving benevolence; setting forth,—as in a long gallery of dark pictures,—the neglect, the want, and miseries, steeping such large numbers of children in wretchedness and crime:—and then, in bright contrast, a succession of cheerful pictures, from their own Ragged School; showing beautiful results already achieved in many of their scholars;—their wretchedness, crime, starvation,—changed into comfort, and virtue, and happiness.

Towards the close, he enlarges on the vast amount of ignorance and crime in the lowest orders;—dangerous to society; undermining the social fabric; fearfully on the increase; threatening a terrible wreck, if not checked. "To attempt to avert such a fate," he says, "is every man's duty; and, more than he dreams of, is within every man's doing. This is no idle saying. Were we to make a pilgrimage;—as soon as to the lonely heath where martyrs repose, we would direct our steps to the busy streets of Portsmouth; and would turn from the proud array of Old England's floating bulwarks to seek out the humble shop where John Pounds achieved works of mercy, and earned an imperishable fame. There is no poetry in his name, and none in his profession; but there was more than poetry in his life,—the noblest benevolence. Within the shop where he cobbled shoes, he might be seen surrounded by some score or two of ragged urchins, whom he was educating and converting into valuable members of society. Honour to the memory of him, beneath whose leathern apron there beat the kindest heart,—there glowed a bosom fired with the noblest ambition. Without fee or reward from man, while he toiled for his hard-earned bread with the sweat of his brow, this poor cobbler educated not less than five hundred outcasts, before they laid him in his lowly grave! Honour, we say again, to the memory of this illustrious patriot! Nor is there any sight we would have travelled so far to see, as that self-same man, when he followed some ragged boy along the quays of Portsmouth, keeping his kind, keen eye upon him, and tempting the young savage to his school with the bribe of a smoking potato. Princes and peers, judges and divines, might have stood uncovered in his presence; and marble monuments might be removed from the venerable walls of Westminster to make room for his.

"His history proves what a single-handed but right-hearted man may do; what,—would the reader address himself in earnest to the work,—he himself might do. Animated by his example, and encouraged by his success, we entreat you to turn an eye of piety and of pity on these unhappy children. These are the children of our Common Father. Man, they are thy brothers and sisters." The Ragged School Movement had now grown into large dimensions. The whole nation seemed to have wakened up to the wants and claims of the most destitute and neglected children; left a prey to every vilest corruption from the cradle; too commonly outcast, till in the hands of the police; the prison their home. The duty, the sacred, the alarming responsibility, seemed more and more felt among the better educated, and those with ample means, to do their utmost for the gathering up these lost ones:—to rescue them while little children, and the most easily influenced to better things; to take them into their cherishing care; and provide for their comfort; and train them to virtue and happiness; and let them grow up valuable members of society,—blessings to their fellow-creatures. Hundreds of Ragged Schools rapidly sprung up in our large towns; and were fast-increasing in numbers. The Movement was spreading with growing strength and power throughout the length and breadth of the land; commanding the esteem of all ranks of society. Leading statesmen, illustrious noblemen, deemed themselves honoured in taking part in public meetings, pleading for these poor children.

Something had been done; but far more remained to do. From the platform, not only in Edinburgh, but in London, in Birmingham, and other great centres of philanthropic co-operation, Dr. Guthrie, addressing large and influential meetings, called aloud, with all his vehemence and power of appeal, for all possible help for the rescuing these thousands upon thousands of poor neglected children, swarming in our large towns, ready to perish.

Considering the magnitude of the work, and what they considered the inadequacy of voluntary means to cope with it; Dr. Guthrie and his friends determined to apply to Government for State aid. And in 1852, a Committee of the House of Commons was appointed, to inquire into the condition of "criminal and destitute juveniles in this country, and what changes are desirable in their present treatment, in order to supply industrial training, and to combine reformation with the due correction of juvenile crime."

XXXIV.

1852. A lady who held in very high esteem the memory of "the philanthropic old cobbler," and his disinterested usefulness, visited Portsmouth this spring, and requested me to show her his grave. I took her to it. After standing awhile beside it, silent and very serious, she expressed her desire, that a laurel might be planted on the grave; and placed money in my hand to buy the laurel. I assured her it should be done.

That we might render the planting the laurel on the good man's grave the more useful in its influence, I reserved it for an occasion when we were likely to have a good attendance of Sunday-scholars, and Teachers, and other friends.

Earlier in the year we had instituted a Flower Show for the Sunday-scholars, to be held annually. We had now a Sunday-School for boys, as well as that for girls. The competition for the prizes at the Flower Show was alike for the scholars of both schools. One of our chief objects in this little institution was, to train the children to the good management of their plants; considering this would be putting them in the way of adding pleasantness and beauty to their homes; and would give them desirable amusement for their leisure hours; and might perhaps lead some to become gardeners, as a means of earning their livelihood. To make sure of their having their plants under their own care for at least two months before the Show, we appointed an Inspection, to be held rather more than two months before it; at which all the scholars who intended to compete were to bring their plants; that we might see them, and make a list of them, with the names of the competitors. And no other plants were to compete for the prizes at the Show.

The first of these Scholars' Flower Shows was to be in the following June; and the Inspection, preparatory for it, was announced for Monday, the 5th of the preceding April; to commence at six o'clock in the evening, in the Upper Schoolroom; a pleasant cheerful room; our largest available for such a purpose. We had mentioned it to the scholars a month before, to give them time to provide themselves with plants. Before six o'clock, on the evening appointed for the Inspection, the room was comfortably filled with a good attendance of scholars and Teachers, and other friends; all looking very happy. Nearly eighty of the children had brought plants. They were all in flower-pots, and were arranged on a long table down the centre of the room, and added delightfully to the characteristic interest of the scene.

As we were making the list, and child after child brought up its plant, with happy face, to the cross table at the head of the room, to have it entered; passing along in the midst of friends, smiling congratulation and encouragement:—I paused;—and explained to them, that a lady had expressed a desire, that a laurel might be planted on the grave of good John Pounds; and had left money with me to buy the laurel. I told them, I had bought a fine healthy laurel, and that we would now go down into the Chapel yard, and plant the laurel on the good man's grave. All became tenderly solemn on this announcement. The change from the preceding liveliness, and the stillness, was very impressive. Even the very little ones showed by their tender seriousness, that they felt it. I had previously explained to the Teachers what I was going to do. They all entered feelingly into the solemn interest; and, as we went down stairs, they mingled with the scholars. The other friends came down with us. It was a beautiful evening; clear and bright. The sun was set; but bright beams of golden light spread up into the heavens, as we gathered about the good man's grave. As I stood beside the grave:—before planting the laurel, I spoke a few words to the children. Why were we going to plant a laurel on the grave of a poor old cobbler? I told them of the goodness and kindness of the old man; that he was continually doing good among his poor neighbours; though he was very poor himself, and had to work hard for his own living; that while he was working at his trade, mending shoes, he kept a school in his little shop; that he kept this school more than twenty years; and taught hundreds of children like themselves; and would never have any thing for it. He did it all for the love of doing good. And we bless his memory for it.—With a few more such words:—and all were very still; deeply interested:—I said:—"We will now plant the laurel on his grave." I planted the laurel at the head of the grave. I then said:—"Let us pray."—And we prayed for the blessing of God, on what we had now done.

None were in haste to leave the grave. There was a most impressive quiet—of deep,—sacred interest. After a while, we went up into the school-room, and completed the Inspection of the children's plants.

Having occasion to write about this time to my friend the Rev. William Didler, the highly esteemed Secretary of the London Sunday School Association, I told him how happy we had been in these simple proceedings relative to the Sunday Scholars' Flower Show; and the solemn interest all felt, in our going down to the grave of John Pounds, and planting a laurel upon it. He extracted that part of the letter, and it was included in their Annual Report.

XXXV.

In the autumn of the same year, a gentleman called upon me, and introduced himself as a Universalist Minister from America. He said, he had just crossed the Atlantic; and that he had come to Portsmouth for the purpose of seeing the grave of John Pounds. And he requested me to take him to it. As soon as we came to the grave;—"And what!" he exclaimed;—"No grave-stone upon it?"

I mentioned this to our Sunday-School Teachers at their next meeting. All felt it. The subject was at once taken into earnest consideration. After deliberating awhile; all were of opinion, that,—not a grave-stone,—but a suitable monument should be erected on the grave:—and that as many as might wish should have an opportunity of contributing to it. With this desire, we determined not to hasten it forward to completion, but give it plenty of time. We were desirous that the very poor should have the privilege of giving their halfpennies and pennies, without feeling any painful difference as to the smallness of their gift; and that little children should have the pleasure of giving; which they might remember happily in after life. We therefore started it as for penny contributions. We did not issue any public announcement; but simply began—mentioning it—friend to friend; feeling sure that the interest would work its own way throughout our own neighbourhood; and so—beyond, in all directions,—farther and farther;—never doubting that the good work would be eventually done; and happily. And we felt, that this quiet way of doing it, would be the more in character with the unostentatious spirit and usefulness of the good old man. And there was another reason, why we were desirous not to hasten it to completion. We felt, that wherever it was working its way forward, it would be doing good the while; cherishing others in the same spirit.

Wherever we mentioned it, it was welcomed with delight. And little contributions began to come freely and happily in. We laid great stress on the desire that the contributions should be small; and requested friends to explain the reason for it, as they mentioned it to others.

1853; March 1st. This evening we held our Annual Meeting of the Sunday-School Teachers; taking tea together in the Upper School-room. After tea, on proceeding to business, lists of contributions for the intended monument were handed in; and all bore testimony to the delight with which the idea was welcomed, wherever they mentioned it. Little children and very poor persons were happy in giving their halfpennies and pennies; and wealthy friends regarded our wish, and gave only small contributions.

April 18th. In another meeting of the Teachers, specially called for deliberating on the proposed monument:—after we had been conversing very happily on the subject for about an hour;—I asked them, whether it might not be desirable, if there should be any surplus remaining after we had completed the monument, to devote it to the instituting a Memorial Library, specially designed and suitable for poor children, to carry forward as extensively as practicable, the useful and healthy kind of instruction that John Pounds was so self-devoting to impart,—so long,—and to so many? All were delighted with the idea. And after earnestly deliberating upon it, the suggestion was unanimously and very heartily adopted; and the whole subject was referred to the Sunday-School Committee for further maturing. This Committee consisted entirely of Teachers; elected annually by the whole body of Teachers; with the Pastor, a member ex-officio.

1854; February 14th. A desire having become gradually prevalent among the Teachers, that the intention to erect a monument on the grave of John Pounds shall now be made more extensively known; so that others, living at greater distances, might have the privilege of contributing, if they wished; the Committee requested me to write a letter on their behalf, for insertion in the Christian Reformer, and other periodicals, stating what had been already done. I readily acceded; and the letter appeared in the April number of the Christian Reformer. It was also inserted, about the same time, in the Sunday School Magazine, and in the Inquirer, a weekly newspaper; both published in London.

XXXVI.

The letter appearing in the periodicals seemed to give a fresh start to the movement. Pennies and other small contributions soon began to come in with alacrity; and, by degrees, from places more and more remote; till, at length, we received some from the Far West of America, and from our Antipodes.

When the contributions amounted to nearly sufficient for what would probably be required to complete the monument, the Teachers thought themselves justified in taking immediate steps for its erection.

We all felt the delicacy and the difficulty of the work we were now entering upon:—to erect on that hallowed spot—a monument—of sufficient dignity and beauty; and yet—not out of character with the poor old cobbler.

A Sub-Committee was appointed; to consider, what would be a desirable kind of monument; and to report upon it to the Committee. The Sub-Committee met at the grave; and, after lengthened deliberation, became unanimous in their choice. The design which they resolved to recommend was, that the monument should be of good stone, square at the base, three feet each way; with four plane sides, narrowing gently upward, about six feet high; moderately relieved about the base, and near the summit, with a little plain ornamental work; the general appearance—modest, substantial, and quietly dignified. And they requested the Committee to meet them at the grave, to receive their report.

The Committee and Sub-Committee met at the grave; and on receiving the report, the Committee unanimously approved of the kind of monument recommended; and decided to call a General Meeting of the Teachers, to lay the design before them, for their determination. At the time appointed, all the Teachers were present; and all very cordially approved of the kind of monument recommended.

Thus far, the Teachers had had the whole management of these very interesting proceedings. But now that they were ready to set the mason to work, they were desirous that the Congregation should co-operate with them in completing the Memorial; and they unanimously resolved, to invite the Congregation to a tea-party; for the purpose of laying the whole proceedings before them; that they might all rejoice together in completing the work.

1855. The Teachers' tea-party was appointed for the first Wednesday in February; to be in the Upper School-room. And a most delightful evening it was. About ninety sat down to tea; but more friends came in later in the evening, till the room was filled.

The room was beautifully decorated with evergreens. The original painting of John Pounds, teaching his scholars, while working at his trade, which had been kindly lent for the occasion, was placed at the upper end of the room; wreathed with laurel. At the opposite end, a large model of the intended monument was suspended, so as to be seen to advantage.

At the desire of the Teachers several friends from a distance were invited; highly esteemed by us all, as fellow-workers in the Lord's vineyard, and personally as friends; and some of them were able to accept our invitation, and added to our happiness by being present with us, and taking part in the proceedings.

The lady who had acceded to the request of the Teachers to preside during tea, had been a constant and highly esteemed Teacher all the time John Pounds had taken so constant and earnest an interest in the school; and had been a good friend to him long before. It was in her Father's house that he died; and she was with him in his last moments. When the Pastor had shown this lady to the head of the table, he said, —addressing the Meeting:—

"And now, my friends, your Pastor has another very happy duty to fulfil on your behalf; one that will delight you all. You see a place vacant to the right of the Chair. This is for one—who, as a little boy, played with John Pounds, himself a little boy. They grew up friends together. They constantly worshipped together in the House of God. And he will this evening sing the hymns with you from the very Hymn-book that he and his friend John Pounds used to sing from together in Chapel;—side by side; to the very last Sunday evening of his friend's life." He then went down to the other end of the room, and offered his arm to an old man of more than eighty; and, in the midst of most enthusiastic cheering from all sides, led Mr. Lemmon up to the seat of honour for the evening.

The Pastor then took his own place at the left of the Chair; and gave out a Hymn of Praise. All sang it, Congregationally; the organist accompanying us on a piano. After tea, all joined in singing a Hymn of Thanksgiving.

The Pastor now changed places with the lady who had presided to the gratification of all during tea; and opened the rest of the proceedings for the evening, by giving a statement of what had been done by the Teachers preparatory to the erection of the intended monument on the grave of John Pounds. The Teachers, he said, had expressed their desire that the contributions should be small, that the very poor, and that little children, might have the happiness of giving their halfpennies and pennies. And they left the appeal very much to itself, to work its own peaceful way, by its own soul-felt interest, as friend mentioned it to friend; never doubting its final success;—giving it time. And the peaceful movement had gone on,—farther and farther; till, at length, we received small contributions from some of the most distant parts of the world; from the Far West of America, and from our Antipodes.

The Meeting received these glad tidings with enthusiastic expressions of congratulation; all faces bright with sacred joy!

The Chairman then called on the Rev. Edmund Kell, of Southampton, to address the Meeting.

Mr. Kell said; the sentiment entrusted to him was:—"We bless the Memory of John Pounds as the Friend of the Poor." He observed, that it was the custom of all nations to erect monuments of honour to the exalted in rank and station; to kings and emperors; to great conquerors, military and naval; to great statesmen and great lawyers, and others high in public fame. But where will you find the like honour for the faithful instructor of youth?—A function of the highest importance for the well-being of society? He congratulated the Teachers and the other friends present, that they were now met to do honour to a poor man; in obscure life; who, while working at his lowly trade for his own poor livelihood, had educated hundreds of the poorest, most neglected children he could meet with. He said, that some of the most excellent principles of education were strikingly illustrated in the poor old cobbler's manner of teaching and cherishing those poor children:—his using the interrogative system; his stimulating them to exertion by love, rather than fear; endearing them to him by many little kindnesses; entering into their sports, and making them playthings. But there was one feature in the conduct of his school which deserved most to be noticed, as that which distinguished it above all others. Other gratuitous Teachers who have the choice, are apt to select the cleanest and best clad children. John Pounds, who had many competitors for admission into his school, preferred the most ragged and wretched; those neglected by every one else; those who most needed instruction. "It is this," Mr. Kell said, "which has entitled him to be called—'The Founder of Ragged Schools:'—those admirable Institutions which are rapidly springing up in all the large towns throughout the Kingdom. In choosing this class of scholars, it cannot but bring to remembrance, that he seems to have imbibed the very spirit, as he closely followed the example, of Him who said, he came 'not to call the righteous, but sinners to repentance.' A deep spiritual lesson may be learned from it by all; to devote their sympathies and labours to those who most need them. And especially may Ministers of religion take a valuable hint from this trait in John Pounds' character.

"'We bless the Memory of John Pounds as the Friend of the Poor.' We bless him for what he did during his life; for the happy fruit of his labours in the instruction he afforded to very many children of the poor. And we bless him for the precious example he has bequeathed to future generations, of what may be done by one earnest, faithful labourer for the good of his fellow-creatures. His simple disinterestedness and benevolence shall be one of the happy influences to instruct and stimulate mankind. When the names of a Howard, a Clarkson, a Wilberforce, a Raikes, are mentioned with grateful reverence; when such names as Mrs. Fry are honoured, and Miss Nightingale;—then shall the name of John Pounds be remembered also."

The Rev. John Crawford Woods, of Newport, Isle of Wight, spoke to the sentiment; "We bless the Memory of John Pounds, as having shown to all the world, while not working for fame, that, with very little house-room, with very little leisure, with very little money, and with not much mental attainment,—a man with a heart for the work—may do great and constant good—for many years,—in educating hundreds of the children of his neighbours, and may help to make many homes about him happy."

In the year 1841, an incident had occurred in a small sea-port town in Scotland, Anstruther, situated on the borders of the Firth of Forth, which led to great results.

After giving us several other illustrations of his subject, Mr. Woods said, he had brought a newspaper, to read to the Meeting an extract from a speech delivered at a public meeting in Edinburgh last month, by Dr. Guthrie, the great promoter of Ragged Schools. Dr. Guthrie was speaking of Ragged Schools; and said:—"It was by a picture I was at first led to take an interest in Ragged Schools;—by a picture in an old, obscure, decaying burgh that stands on the shores of the Firth of Forth. I had gone thither with a companion on a pilgrimage:—not that there was any beauty about the place; for it has no beauty. It has little trade. Its deserted harbour, and silent streets, and old houses, some of them nodding to their fall, bore all the marks of decay. But one circumstance has redeemed it from obscurity, and will preserve its name to the latest ages;—it was the birthplace of Thomas Chalmers. I went to see this place many years ago; and going into an inn for refreshment, I found the room covered with pictures of shepherdesses with their crooks, and sailors in holiday attire; not particularly interesting. But above the chimney-piece there stood a large print, more respectable than its neighbours, which some skipper,—the captain of one of the few ships which now trade between that once busy port and England,—had probably brought to the town. It represented a cobbler's room. The cobbler was there himself, spectacles on nose, an old shoe between his knees;—that massive forehead, and firm mouth, indicating great determination of character; and from beneath his bushy eyebrows benevolence gleamed on a number of poor ragged boys and girls who stood at their lessons around the busy cobbler. My curiosity was awakened; and in the inscription I read how this man, John Pounds, a cobbler in Portsmouth, taking pity on the multitude of poor ragged children left by Minister and Magistrates, and ladies and gentlemen, to go to ruin on the streets; —how like a good shepherd he gathered in these wretched outcasts;— how he had trained them to God, and to the world;—and how, while earning his daily bread by the sweat of his brow, he had rescued from misery, and saved to society, not less than five hundred of these children. I felt ashamed of myself. I felt reproved for the little I had done. My feelings were touched. I was astonished at this man's achievements; and I well remember, in the enthusiasm of the moment, saying to my companion;—and I have seen in my calmer and cooler moments no reason for unsaying the saying:—'That man's an honour to humanity; and deserves the tallest monument ever raised within the shores of Britain!'"

The Chairman called on a senior Teacher of the Boys' School to give out the next hymn; which had been chosen in harmony with the soul of the Commemoration. The Teacher rose in the midst of the Meeting, and read the hymn with a clear voice, and pleasant expressiveness. And all the Meeting sang it heartily.

Other friends spoke; some, copiously; some, saying but a few words: but all feelingly imbued with the remembrance of the good old man. Even good old Mr. Lemmon became so excited by the interest of the evening, that, toward the close, he rose, somewhat tottering, and said, in a tremulous and faint voice, he had something he wished to say. All were still in a moment. The attention of the whole Meeting was fixed reverently upon him; listening most respectfully all the time he was speaking; though most of what he said was scarcely intelligible, even to those near him, from the faintness of his voice and his tremulous utterance. But there was one simultaneous deep feeling of reverence and tender regard manifested for the old friend and play-fellow of John Pounds!

The Pastor gave out the closing hymn with thankful aspiration; and the whole Meeting sung it in full voice; solemnly happy. When the hymn ceased; the Pastor offered up prayer and thanksgiving; and implored the Divine blessing on all that had been said and done.

Though it was late when the Meeting broke up, none seemed in haste to go. In all parts of the room there were animated groups; friends earnestly talking together. All were highly delighted.

Mr. Kell sent an interesting Report of the Meeting to the Inquirer; in which paper it appeared the following week. He afterwards published it in a separate form.

XXXVII.

February 13th. Invited Mr. Lemmon to take tea with me, that we might have all the evening to talk about his old friend John Pounds. As we were at tea, I told him, that when the Nephew had taken down the old front of the house, and put up the new one, and so completely changed the appearance of the place; the thought occurred to me, that it might be interesting to some of his friends that used to see him so often at work at his little tumble-down window, and used to stop chatting with him at his open half-door, to have some reminder—of what it was—in the old time; and that I had made a sketch of it from memory, with pen and ink;—"rough enough;" I said; "for I'm not much of a draughtsman; but it may serve to bring to mind—what it used to be." When the tea-things were removed, I laid the sketch down on the table before him. He stood looking at it intently,—and in silence,—for some time; and then said, with deep, tender feeling;—"Ah, that's it!"—and his eyes filled with tears. "This brings back old times!"—Still looking fixedly at it; and in silence; for a considerable time; he suddenly said:—"Ah, Johnny never thought of all this. To be so talked about; and so much thought of;—and have a monument raised to him! —The Founder of Ragged Schools!—Johnny never thought of that!"

"No," I said; "he only thought of doing all the good he could,—in his own quiet way, among his poor neighbours.

"I've made some other sketches," I said, "of the same rough sort, that may perhaps be interesting to you." And I laid them on the table. "They may bring to your remembrance some of the many interesting, characteristic incidents, that so often happened at his open half-door." In one of the sketches he saw the cat. "Johnny had another cat before this," he said, full of life and animation, as he looked fervently at it: —"a black cat. It would do anything for him. It would bring any thing up;—young birds,—young rabbits,—any thing that wanted to be kept nice and warm! He kept them all together in an old salmon-kit. When he brought any young birds home, he put them in to puss; and she curled herself round them, and kept them warm. She'd suckle young rabbits; and any thing else that wanted suckling. I've seen her many a time with the birds—before the fire—in winter. They were all good friends together. They would peck her nose; and if they pecked too hard, she'd give them a good pat with her paw; but, law, Sir! she'd never hurt them. He lost that black cat, before he got this. A neighbour was tormented with a rat in his house; and he borrowed Johnny's black cat, to try and catch it; and she got into the cellar; and was missing. She never came back again."

"I think I may perhaps give you some clue as to what became of the black cat. Soon after I came to Portsmouth, a Member of the Philosophical Society was taking me round the Museum; and, among many other interesting things, I was struck with what appeared, at first glance, two skeletons; the one—of a cat, and the other—of a rat. On looking at them more closely, the bones seemed to have the skin stretched over them; with a coating of shining varnish all over them. They were both laid down on their side,—on the full stretch,—as if running; the cat after the rat; but the cat not quite touching the rat. In this relative position, they were imbedded about half their depth in cement; which had hardened about them, and kept them firm. They were both entirely shrivelled. I mentioned them to our late friend George Martell. And he said, they were found so, in a crevice of a dry wall; when they were taking down some rubbishy old houses, to clear the ground, for building the Philosophical Society's place. It was in a crevice narrowing inward. The cat was evidently pursuing the rat; the rat had run into the crevice, till it stuck fast, by its narrowing inward; the cat, rushing in after it,—also stuck fast;—but just before it caught the rat. Both were jambed in; and seemed to have remained so till they dried up to skin and bone. When they were found, they were as dry as dust. The Committee had them imbedded in cement, George Martell said, in the relative position in which they were found; and covered them over with a thick coating of varnish, to preserve them from the action of the air."

"Ah! That's Johnny's black cat!" Mr. Lemmon exclaimed,—with a colouring countenance of feeling remembrance. "It was just at that corner where the neighbour's house stood, that was pestered with the rat."

"Friends have sometimes thought, Mr. Lemmon, when we have been talking about our dear old friend, that he must have had something more to live upon, than what little he could earn by his trade; some little property of his own; to enable him to do so much good."

"No; nothing, but what he earned by his trade; and that, latterly, was very little."

"How much do you think he commonly earned?"

"During the war-time he worked as journeyman to a good respectable shoe-maker, and made his guinea a week. But when the battle of Waterloo put an end to the war, trade in Portsmouth became very much depressed. There was an end to John's earning his guinea a week. From that time he had to depend altogether on what little business of his own he could do; and that was chiefly for his poor neighbours. And very often he could scarcely make both ends meet."

"Then he did not lay any thing by when he was in better work?"

"No; it all went in buying dinners, or something or other to give away. Law, Sir!—the sprats!—When sprats were in season;—the quantities he would buy, and give away in dinners!"

"It is commonly said, that he could never make a shoe; that he was only a mender of shoes."

"I've heard it said so; but that's not true. He could make a good shoe; and did; for officers, as well as men; while the war lasted. All was hurry then. All must be done directly; they didn't care how much they paid for it. But when peace came, it was very different. He had very little work then, of any sort. That's how it was he had so much spare time latterly."

"Did he ever work at any thing else beside his trade as a shoe-maker?"

"Yes;"—with a comical smile. "One summer he went to sea, with a trading vessel, plying between Portsmouth and Swanage; to bring stone for the Ordnance works. It was when the press-gang was so much about. Law, Sir, what times those were! I can remember when soldiers were placed at every gate; and every good-looking man,—no matter who,—gentleman or poor man,—it made no difference;—they laid hold of him, and took him off to the Main Guard:—where they overhauled him, to see whether he would do. In High Street, the constables would lay hold of any one by night, and put him in gaol, to be overhauled next morning. I've seen hundreds of young men about Point, who had been 'pressed. So that trading vessels could hardly get any hands at all to work them, at any price. And the master of a small craft asked Johnny if he would go with him to Swanage; and he would give him a guinea a week. So Johnny went with him. He liked the change; it seemed like a pleasure trip to him. And there was no danger of his being 'pressed, because of his lameness. But he always took his kit of tools with him; for the master of the vessel was a drunken dog; and he did not know but—in one of his drunken fits—he might put him on shore, and leave him. But Johnny was not afraid of that. He knew, if he had his tools with him, he was safe to work his way home again."

"How often did he make the trip to Swanage?"

"About twice a week; there and back. But it was only for that one summer. He didn't try it again."

"This, I suppose, was before he began his school."

"Yes. He was not living in that house then. He worked then in a room in his father's house; nearly opposite to where I live; near the sally-port at the end of St. Mary's Street."

"Did he ever keep his school in any place but that small wooden house?"

"No, nowhere."

"I suppose, Mr. Lemmon, you remember our old friend's beginning his school?"

"As clear as if it was yesterday. But, law, Sir! it was no school, to begin with. Johnny never thought of having a school, to begin with; not he. It came upon him—all unawares. It was all owing to that little child, his Nephew. The child was born with both feet turning in, and overlapping one another. And his mother took him to the first surgeon in the place, when it was in arms; to see if any thing could be done for it. The Doctor said: 'The child's too young yet'—its ankles were too soft yet to do any thing with them. But he told her to keep it about a year longer, and then bring it to him; and he would break its ankle-bones for her, and set its feet right. So she kept it nearly a year; and was taking it to the Doctor's again; and she met John. 'What's you a-going to do with that child?' John says. You know, Sir, Johnny used to talk so." "Yes, broad Portsmouth!" "She said, she was going to take it to the Doctor's, to have its ankles, broken, and the feet set right. 'Why, you savage old brute!' John says to her; 'You's not a-going to do that 'ere?—Give me the child. You's not fit to have the care of a child.'—And he took the child out of her arms; and brought it home with him, to his own little wooden house. And there it lived with him ever after.

"And Johnny comes to me, and says; 'Lemmon, my little Johnny wants a play-fellow to play with him; let your little ones come and play with my little Johnny; and they shall lose none of their schooling by it.' For, he said, he would teach them their reading and spelling, and verses; and when they were old enough, he would teach them to do sums, and write; and they should lose nothing by coming to play with his little Johnny. I gladly agreed to it. And they went. You know his shop is only a few doors off from my house; and on the same side. Our Dick was one of them. You remember our Dick? You attended him on his death-bed; when he was a man grown."

"I remember him well; and with deep interest."

"The children didn't think it going to school. They used to say after breakfast,'Come, let's go and play with little Johnny.' Sometimes they said; 'Let's go and play with Mr. Pounds!' For he played with them. And he made them playthings. Sometimes they brought home a ball that he had made for them; sometimes, a bat; or a shuttle-cock and battle-dore. And he made them all very nicely; no signs of haste or carelessness. Sometimes they brought home marbles, that he had bought for them. He was always doing something to please them. And they were fond of going to him.

"But while there was plenty of play and amusement, he mingled useful lessons with it all. My children were rather older than little Johnny, and knew their letters already; and the elder ones could read a little. But he soon brought on Johnny, to say his letters, and read with them. But, law, Sir! the reading he gave them! He'd next to no books, of any sort, for them to read out of. He'd take a hand-bill, with large letters, and let them read that; or a bit of a newspaper; anything he happened to have ready; sometimes, a stray leaf out of an old worn-out book, that he happened to pick up. But he talked about it all so nicely, he made it pleasant and interesting to them. And he never kept them at it too long, so as to weary them. He would always let them play again as soon as he thought they'd had enough. If any one seemed sleepy, he'd let it lie down, and go to sleep. 'Nature's the best judge;' he used to say. He often told them pretty stories; all to do them good. Johnny was always good at telling interesting stories. And they were eager to listen to them. By and bye, he got them some little slates, to write on; and began to teach them how to do little sums. And neighbours would stop and look in, and listen to them reading, and saying their verses; and all seemed so pleasant and happy, first one neighbour would say, 'Mr. Pounds, will you kindly let my little ones come and say lessons with your's?'—and then another. And he always said, 'Yes; bring 'em:'—till his shop was full. And when once his shop was full, it never slackened. So it went on to the end.

"On Coronation-day, he was asked to go to the public dinner, and take all his scholars with him, like the other schools; and share in the public rejoicings. But he thought it better not to take the little ones. The bigger ones went; but he stayed at home, to take care of the little ones. Oh, the dinner he got for them!—There was plum-pudding, and roast beef, and I don't know what!"

"And did they all dine with him in that little shop?"

"All the little ones. And when they'd enjoyed a good dinner, he took them out on the Common. It was a bright fine day, you may remember." "Yes; in June." "And he walked about with those little things on the Common all the afternoon; that they might enjoy themselves, and see the sports.

"But Johnny did not need public rejoicings, or any unusual excitement, to do a kindness. Poor widows would bring their little children to him in the morning; and he took care of them all day; and they never came again for them, till nine o'clock at night. They couldn't; they were out working all day; and they'd often find them asleep beside the fire. They'd have had no food, but what he gave them."

"I have often been struck with the fact," I said, "that new kinds of his usefulness have been continually opening upon us, since his death, that we had not heard of before."

Mr. Lemmon replied with ardour; "He would do any thing for any body. All the neighbours round would come to him when they wanted any thing doing; it did not matter what. 'Mr. Pounds,' one would say, 'will you come and tap my beer for me?' 'Yes;' he would say; and he goes down into their cellar, and taps their beer for them. 'Mr. Pounds,' another would say, 'will you come and put up our bed-stead for us?' 'Yes,' he says; and he goes up-stairs and puts up their bed-stead for them. And all for nothing. Nothing came amiss to him, if he could help a poor neighbour.

"There was another shoe-maker lived near him. They began business about the same time. The other made money very fast; nobody quite knew how. It was in the war-time. He soon made a fortune; and gave up business; and set up for a gentleman; while Johnny went on working as hard as ever; and laying by nothing. One day, the other, after his fortune was made, came and called on John; and said: 'Well, John, here you are, working yet.' 'Yes,' says John; 'and you's made your fortune. How is it? We both began together. I'se not been a drunkard; I'se not been extravagant; I'se always worked hard.' 'It's here;—it's here, John:' he said, tapping his forehead. And yet—that man's forgotten; though he had made a fortune: and John Pounds is talked of, and blessed, to the other side of the world!

"He often swore at him. For his chamber window looked into John's chamber window. And he could see Johnny lying in bed, holding a candle in one hand, and his book in the other, reading; and he was afraid he'd set the house on fire.

"Johnny was a terrible one for a book. So was his mother before him. The books he would read, to be sure! Whenever a book fell in his way; if it interested him, he'd read it through before he'd done with it. Whatever it was; book, or hand-bill, or play-bill;—no matter what;—he'd read it through, before he laid it down. That's how it was he got such a heap of learning."

"What sort of a woman was his mother? I mean, as to character and disposition."

"She was a good sort of woman; a pleasant kind of respectable woman. But she'd always be reading.

"Nothing was too little for Johnny to take interest in, if he could do good by it. I'd a young thrush once, that fell down and broke its leg. And Johnny took a match, and broke a bit off, and cut a little splint, neat and light, and tied it on;—so nicely and tenderly he did it!—And it got well."

"How he enjoyed rambling out into the country!"

"Yes! Johnny dearly loved the fields and the hedge-rows and the copses, and to hear the birds sing, and see the lambs sporting about, and the sheep feeding so peacefully; and every thing enjoying itself!—and to get on the top of the Hill;—and look down over Portsmouth, and the Harbour, and the Isle of Wight, and Spithead!—That—was his great delight!—At high water; when the tide filled Langston Harbour on one side, and our Port on the other, up to the foot of Ports-down;—four or five miles!—he would stand—on the top of the Hill,—leaning with both hands on his stick,—looking down over it all,—with unutterable delight. I've seen his eyes fill with tears of joy,—as he stood looking at it—in silence. His heart seemed too full for utterance:—save—now and then—a short ejaculation—that would break from him—in subdued voice,—'The goodness of God!'—'This beautiful world!'—as if speaking to himself."

"Is not it surprising, that, with such a fondness for the fields and beautiful scenery, and the refreshing enjoyments of Nature, he should have chosen to live all his life in so different a place?"

"Ah! Johnny did that, to be the more useful to others."

"A finer spirit!—Truly Christ-like."

"He'd a favourite old raven, that he was very fond of. It would go all about the neighbourhood. It was a great pet; and—a great pest, some thought it,—for the mischief it did!"—And the old man laughed, and chuckled, as at some comical remembrances. "It was the terror of the children, that swarmed all round;—this was before he began his school:—but the amusement of the older folks; who forgave the mischief it did, for the sake of its odd tricks. To ladies and gentlemen walking along the street, it was sometimes a serious annoyance, by pecking at their heels and dresses, with its strong beak. It once picked a hole through the door of the house opposite. But it was safe among the neighbours, and protected by all, because of their respect for its owner:—till, one day, being on the walls near the sallyport at the end of the street, it got on one of the guns. The sentry had orders to drive it off the guns. But the raven turned again, and there was a fierce fight, for some time. But at last—the sentry beat it down with the butt-end of his musket, and killed it. Johnny never had another raven after that."

"Did he teach any of his scholars his trade?" "None but his Nephew:—and that, not all himself. For the last year he sent him, for the cutting-out, to a good shoe-maker; a ladies' shoemaker. He could not teach him that himself. And he paid three guineas with him."

"The Nephew seems to be getting on well with his business."

"Yes. He is a good workman, and keeps steadily at it. It is astonishing how ladies and gentlemen began to come to him, from far and near, soon after the Uncle's death. They wanted to see the place where the old man lived, and worked at his trade, and kept his school. They were surprised to find it such a smart-looking shop! So bright and cheerful, with that large window! They expected to find it a mean-looking little place; dark and dull; such as it was in the old man's time. The Nephew explained, that he had had it fresh done up, since his Uncle's death.

"Ladies and gentlemen kept on coming more and more; till John, the Nephew, began to think, it would look more respectable for him to get into a larger shop; and so he removed into that next door towards the sally-port. And he did it up, and made a good shop of it. And there his business has gone on increasing ever since. And ladies and gentlemen keep on coming; some, from great distances; and they often stand talking with him a long time in his shop; inquiring all about 'the old cobbler;'—as some speak it; but others will say,—'the philanthropic old cobbler!'"—And a smile gleamed over the face of his old friend. "And the ladies buy shoes of him, to show their respect for his Uncle.

"On first coming, they always express their wonder, that he could have kept so large a school in so small a place. And we might have felt the same, if we had not so often seen it."

"Yes, Mr. Lemmon. And as I have stood chatting with him, and looking in at the full little shop; I could scarcely have fancied sometimes that there were so many in it; they were all so comfortable and pleasant together. It was a beautiful sight, to stand looking at them, over the little half-door.

"Ah!—that little half-door!—How often have I stood leaning over it, —talking with him!"—His voice faltered; and the old man's head drooped; and we were both silent, for a considerable time:—till, at length,—as if making an effort—to resume conversation:—"Old Lilly-white"—he said—"Did you know old Lillywhite?—Sexton of Colly Garden."—"I've heard of him."—"Well;—old Lillywhite would come and talk with John sometimes. Well; one day old Lillywhite comes and says; 'John, I don't feel all right in my stomach.' 'Don't you?' says John. 'No;' he says; 'I think I'll go over the way, and get a glass of hot gin-and-water. 'Well, I would, if I'se you;' John says; 'if you think it'll do you good. 'So he goes across the street to get his glass of hot gin-and-water. Ten minutes after, somebody comes, inquiring for Lillywhite. 'No, he's not here;' John says; 'he's gone over the way to get a glass of hot gin-and-water; he's not all right in his stomach, he says.' So he goes over the way to see for him. But—No, he's not there. After a while, John goes to Lillywhite's house, to inquire after him. And there was poor old Lillywhite—sitting straight up in his arm-chair—dead.—Ah!— John's often talked of that since. He often said; he should like to die— just like old Lilly-white."

Again, both were silent. We could not but feel,—the death was quite as sudden,—and as unlocked for.

After a few moments, I said: "How thoroughly our dear old friend lived for others!"

"He did. And it made him happy. He was always giving something, or doing something, for somebody."

"With the smallness of his means, it seems wonderful that he could give away so much."

"His means for giving away," Mr. Lemmon replied, "must not be measured by his small earnings of money. His own never-tiring assiduities, his thoughtfulness, his good management of what little he had, his indefatigable industry, making things that others needed;—all he could do—to bless and comfort others,—was continually adding largely to his stores for charity and beneficence."

"Our Saviour said:—'Thou shalt love thy neighbour as thyself.'"

"Johnny's life was very much like that!"

"So bountiful to others; how sparing he was to himself!"

"Yes;" Mr. Lemmon said. "Even that pint of sprats—which he bought for his New Year's Day dinner:—and which he did not live to taste:—Even that—he seemed to think—an extraordinary extravagance —to lay out for himself."

"Our Saviour said:—'When thou doest alms, let not thy left hand know what thy right hand doeth.'"

"That was dear Johnny. He never did his good deeds before men, to be seen of them. No; Johnny never sought the praises of men. His eye was single:—as our Saviour says. He did good—for the sake of doing good."

"That thine alms may be in secret."

"That, again, was dear old Johnny!"

"We found it so; when, after his death, we had to go into the back courts and dark alleys to inquire about scholars that he used to look after for us. We were perpetually hearing of different sorts of kindness that we had not heard of before; and seeing proofs of good that he had done,—which probably none knew any thing of—but the poor creatures that received it, and their immediate neighbours.

"With all his roughness and coarseness of appearance and manner; our friend had a beautiful spirit. And he was continually exerting, in his plain way, a pure and elevating influence on others."

"Yes!" Mr. Lemmon said, with a fervour of feeling—deeply impressive. "He showed that, not only in training up boys, so that they became respectable, trustworthy men, and faithful friends; but, I think, most of all, in his way of teaching and cherishing the little girls. His way was very simple; but always—so pleasant and endearing; always—so good. Many's the good mother,—he's trained—and taught—when a child. And her husband and children have had to bless his memory—for their happy Christian home!

" You'll put it on his monument,—won't you,"—Mr. Lemmon said suddenly, as he was rising to get his hat,—"that he was Founder of Ragged Schools?"

"I don't know, Mr. Lemmon. We must see what the Teachers say. You know, our good old friend was very quiet and unpretending in his way of doing good. He had no idea of founding Ragged Schools. All he thought of was—just the good he was himself doing—from day to day—in his own homely way of usefulness."

"That's true,—you're right.—So he did.—No, I see,—it wouldn't do."—But this he said—rather in a tone of yielding,—reluctantly;—not that he felt satisfied.

XXXVIII.

The next evening one of the Teachers of the Girl's School called upon me, and after speaking with enthusiasm of the delight they all felt at the tea-party for the monument, she said, she came to tell me of a respectable policeman, now serving in the Dockyard; mentioning his name. She had told him some time before of our intention to erect a monument to the memory of John Pounds, by penny subscriptions; and at once he said he should be glad to give fourpence; adding, that John Pounds was the first person he spoke to, when he came—a youth—to Portsmouth, to seek work. He knew nobody here. He was perfectly a stranger in Portsmouth. He had never heard of John Pounds. But, meeting him accidentally in the street, he was struck with his manner, and pleased with his kindness. He wanted to go to some place near the Quay; and he asked Mr. Pounds if he could tell him the way. "Yes, my child! " he said; and went with him, and showed him the place. A while after, seeing his boots wanted mending, he went to Mr. Pounds to have them mended; and took them off, and sat with him, an hour or more, while he was mending them. And he said;—"It was so delightful! There were all his birds about him! And his cat! And every thing seemed so pleasant;—so interesting! And he talked to me so kindly!—I would give ever so much," he said, "to have another such a happy hour with him!"

XXXIX.

One of our District Societies in the South of England, for promoting the knowledge and diffusion of the Truth as we believe it to be in Jesus, held their Annual Meeting at Portsmouth in the spring of the present year. We had a good gathering of Ministers and other friends from a distance; the weather was fine, and every thing favourable for a most happy Meeting. The District Committee had invited my beloved relative the Revd. Edward Higginson, of Wakefield, to be the morning preacher; who came, to the delight of us all.

On Thursday evening before Good Friday, he solemnized for us the Lord's Supper; our Anniversary Commemoration of our Saviour's instituting the Memorial, the evening before his crucifixion:—a solemnly delightful evening!

The next morning he preached for us. After service, the visitors from a distance and other friends went to the grave of John Pounds. As we stood beside it, not much was said; and what was said—was in a gentle—subdued tone;—all very simple; but all was fervently solemn,—deeply impressive. In that humble grave,—we felt,—the remains of a great Benefactor reposed.

Mr. Higginson having expressed a desire to see the house in which John Pounds lived, and kept his school; I took him the next morning. As we were walking along St. Mary's Street, "What is that white building," he said, "with the four columns in front?" "The Philosophical Society," I replied, "built it some years since for their use. It contains a good museum. When Lord Brougham was making—what the Times called 'his Tour of the Provinces'"—"I remember. It was when he was Lord Chancellor." "Yes. He came to Portsmouth. And we had a spontaneous muster of the Society to receive him. As we took him round the museum, he seemed much interested at some points. From the museum we went to the lecture-room; and the President showed him up to the bench: from which he addressed us. Speaking of the museum, he said, it was the third best he had seen out of London."

"How completely the character and appearance of the street alters from this point!"

"Yes. Terribly for the worse. We are now going into the midst of intemperance, profligacy, and their miserably degrading consequences. And in the midst of this wretchedness and degradation, the good old man chose to live; perpetually doing good; a friend to all.

"Through this narrow opening we are passing on our right, you see a Church; St. Mary's. There was no Church there in the old man's time. It was building at the time of his death. And a few steps farther on, we come to his house. Here it is."

"What!—that little bit of a thing?" And he laughed aloud. "How wide is it?" I lent him a foot measure which I had in my pocket. "Not quite seven feet,—from outside to outside!"

"And the shop inside," I said, "from front to back, is little more than twice its breadth."

"How ever did he get them all in?" "It does seem astonishing. And himself too, sitting on his bench, working at his trade; with his tools and materials about him."

"But I did not expect to find the poor old cobbler's shop such a smart affair."

"It was not so in the old man's time; very much the contrary. Soon after the old man's death, the Nephew had the old front taken down, and this new one put up; and had it all painted bright, inside and out; and made a dashing little shop of it. He is a ladies' shoe-maker; and a good workman. After the old man's death, so many came to see the place where the philanthropic old cobbler lived,—as he now began to be commonly called!—and the Nephew's trade went on prospering so fast; that he thought it would look more respectable, if he got into a larger shop; and he removed to that shop next door; where he is doing a good business. There are some ladies going in now. And there's the Nephew, standing behind the counter." "A good looking man of business." "Yes; he's steady and industrious, and goes on respectably. He is now about forty years of age. He was born with both feet turning in, and overlapping one another. And that little cripple was the cause of the old man's school!—But, come, we'll move forward. We can go on talking as we walk.

"As we came into St. Mary's Street from High Street, we will go out at the other end, through that sally-port. That will enable me to show you some other characteristic points of this fortified place." "Thank you; that will interest me. But I want to hear more about this extraordinary old man; how he gathered all these poor children about him; and how he did so much good with such small means." "I shall be glad to go on telling you more, as we walk along.

"This house we are now passing on our right is the house in which John Pounds was born. His friend Mr. Lemmon now lives in it; with his children and grand-children. John Pounds and Mr. Lemmon were play-fellows as children, and firm friends all through life."

We went through the sally-port, and crossed the moat, and turned the corner to our left, and went along between the moat and the Gun Wharf wall to the Town Quay, crossed the entrance of the Camber by the swing-bridge, went along East Street into Broad Street, turned to our left, and went through King James's Gate into High Street. "And now I have shown you," I said, "about the extent of the old cobbler's range; his little sphere of practical usefulness; within the limits of which he lived and laboured, pretty nearly all his life; continually going about doing good:—a mass of crowded small old houses, intersected with small narrow streets and alleys, and abounding in little back courts."

"Soon compassed in extent;" Mr. Higginson said:—"but incalculable in growing influence."

After a pause—of deep thoughtfulness:—"Is it true, that he would entice poor starving children into his school by giving them a potato, or some other eatable, that he carried about with him for the purpose?"

"He told me so himself, when sitting by my fire-side one winter's evening. But Dr. Guthrie was wrong, when, in his now famous eulogy of John Pounds, in his Edinburgh speech, he said:—'He was sometimes seen hunting down a ragged urchin on the quays of Portsmouth, and compelling him to come to school,—not by the power of a policeman,—but a potato.' This was not his manner of approach. John Pounds was never seen hunting down poor children. His manner was much more gentle and winning. As he went about all the lowest and most degraded places in that wretched neighbourhood, seeking for poor children—'that nobody cared for;'—(to use his own words;)—when he saw a poor starving little thing—'poking in the gutter;'—(again to use his own words;)—'That's the one for me!'—he said with enthusiasm!—And his old countenance brightened, and softened, as he was telling me; and his eye kindled to a fine eager benevolence and desire!—'An I goes—gently—towards it,'—he said, with a voice all gentleness and tender fervency; and he leaned lovingly forward in his arm-chair, and seemed to see the child,—as he drew near:—'And I says to it, Will y' have a taty?—And I has a boiled taty ready in my pocket. And I pulls the taty—part—out o' my pocket. An when it sees the taty, it says, Yes. An whiles it's eating its taty, I moves off; but not so fast—but it can keep up wi' me. But before it's done eating its taty, I takes care to be in my shop. An it follows me into my shop for another taty. An as sure as it comes in once, it comes again.'"

"The dear old man!"

"And Dr. Guthrie was wrong in another point of his—otherwise excellent eulogy:—when he says of John Pounds:—'He knew the love of an Irishman for a potato; and might be seen running alongside an unwilling boy with one held under his nose, with a temper as hot and a coat as ragged as his own.'

"To say nothing of the too violent action;—altogether out of character with John Pounds:—John Pounds knew nothing of such distinctions as to national difference. He saw the poor children starving, and he fed them."

"Whenever you begin telling me any thing that John Pounds said himself; you always drop at once into provincialisms or vulgarisms. Was this always his way of speaking?"

"Always. I never knew it different."

"It seems astonishing, that while he had such sterling excellencies in other respects; some, of high order;—he should have remained through so long a life so coarse and vulgar in his manner of speaking."

"We must bear in mind, that he had next to no education as a boy; and that he lived all his life, or thereabout, in that low neighbourhood, and in constant intercourse with the low and degraded.

"Living so long in the very midst of that low contentious neighbourhood, he lived kindly disposed to all; and he had not an enemy. In the wretched brawls, notoriously frequent and violent in that street and neighbourhood, often bursting out from the dark alleys and back courts like a blast of furies;—terrible by day, but more terrible in the darkness of night;—wrought up to madness and desperation by intemperance and ungovernable passions; dangerous to life:—no one ever heard of their ill-treating poor old John Pounds, or molesting his humble abode."

"A fine local testimony.

"Has the same good work been carried on since the old man's death?"

"Voluntary schools have been enthusiastically instituted for the like purpose;—and also as Memorials of the good old man; and have been gratuitously worked with generous persevering earnestness; and are now doing excellent service in gathering into their cherishing care many of the poorest, most destitute children. But the old man's school was never re-assembled—after that terrible dispersion, when the dead body was lifted in among the children."

XL.

On the evening of the tea-party in February, in reference to the monument;—during the proceedings after tea, a young Marine Artilleryman was seen to enter the room, quietly, and with lively interest. He had been one of the scholars of John Pounds; and had now recently returned from the Baltic, in the Duke of Wellington; where he had served on board during the Crimean War. "I could not get in sooner," he told me some days after; "for I am stationed at Fort Cumberland: and that, you know, is about four miles off. I stayed as long as duty would let me, for I was very much interested; but at a quarter past seven o'clock I had to run off; and I ran all the way back to Fort Cumberland. There was snow on the ground all the way. I got in just before the gate was shut. The gate shuts at eight; and if I had not got in before eight, I should have been punished for being out after time; and should have lost my bombardier's stripe off my arm."

April 25th. The same young Marine Artilleryman called upon me this afternoon;—now a Corporal;—to arrange for his marriage at Chapel the next Sunday morning. When all was arranged for the marriage, something happened to be said that called John Pounds to mind:—"Ah, dear good Mr. Pounds!" the young Corporal exclaimed with affectionate ardour; his open countenance colouring generously. "You know, Sir, I was one of his scholars!"

"Yes. How was it, William, that you first went to his school?"

"Father had noticed the old man as he passed his shop, and was pleased with him altogether; and gave him a pair of shoes to mend for him."

"What did he charge?"

"He soled and heeled them, and charged only two shillings. Other shoemakers would have charged three shillings."

"What sort of work was it?"

"Strong and good. They wore well for a long time after."

"Now, just tell me, William, how Mr. Pounds began with you;—and how did he treat you, when you first entered his shop?"

"Father took me by the hand;—I was a very little boy then;—and we went to Mr. Pounds, in that little shop in St. Mary's Street. It was full of children; as full as it could hold; there did not seem room for another; and good Mr. Pounds was sitting amongst them, on his bench, at the window, working. And father says to him: 'Mr. Pounds, I've brought my boy; if you'll be so kind as to take him as a scholar, I shall be very much obliged to you.' So he looks up from his work, and says; 'Yes, Sir.' So I went in, and father left me there; and I was a scholar from that time."

"And how did he begin with you? What was his first lesson he gave you?"

"He says:—oh, so kindly!—and lovingly!—drawing me gently to him: —'Now, come, my little fellow:—In the beginning God created the heaven and the earth.'"

"But could you read in the Bible when you first went to him?"

"Oh, no, Sir! I couldn't read at all. I scarcely knew all my letters. But he always began so. He began so with every one. Whether they could read or not, he always began with the first chapter of Genesis. I astonished them at home; for I could go through the first chapter of Genesis, before I well knew all my letters.

"Sometimes he would explain it to all the school at once,—without book,—the fifth chapter of Genesis,—how God created the heavens and the earth. He delighted in explaining this. There were some tall girls and boys that could not read;—much taller than I was;—and they stood behind, and listened to these explanations to the whole school, and so learnt in this manner. There was another chapter that was one of his great favourites, the fifth chapter of Matthew, the beginning of our Lord's Sermon on the Mount. He was very fond of giving us these two chapters to read. These two we had the oftenest."

"And how did he go on with you, as you began to advance a little?"

"Oh, he made it very pleasant; we all liked it very much. He would talk to us; and explain things to us; and tell us interesting stories; and make things for us. One day he said; 'Now, every one of you as likes to bring me a carrot, I'll make him a boat of it!' So most of us brought him a carrot;—I was one of them;—and he took his knife, and he made me a boat;—such a nice one!—You'd hardly believe how nicely he cut it out. For he took great pains with it."

"What is your chief impression now,—so many years after,—of his manner of teaching?"

"That he was very kind, and very attentive to us. He would sometimes hear us our lessons while he was going on with his own work; and though he had no book to look at, he knew at once if we made a blunder, and would correct us."

"Were you ever punished by him?"

"Yes, once;" and he coloured and smiled.

"How was that?"

"One morning, when my mother sent me to school, a regiment of soldiers happened to be coming along the road, with their band playing, and I went on the Common with them, instead of going to school. When I went home to dinner, it was not quite twelve o'clock; and I skulked under the window as I passed, that mother might not see me. But when I came in, and it was so early, mother said, looking at me, 'You've not been to school this morning.' 'No, mother;' I said; 'I've not.' 'How's that? Where have you been? What have you been doing?' So I told her the truth; I told her all about my going on the Common with the soldiers. When I went to school in the afternoon, she told me to tell Mr. Pounds why I was not there in the morning."

"And did you?"

"Yes; I told him mother had sent me off to school, but that I had gone on the Common with the regiment of soldiers instead.

"'I hope you've told no lies about it?' he said. 'No,' I said; 'I've told no lies about it; but I confessed I had endeavoured to deceive my mother when I came back before twelve. 'Well,' he said; 'for your trying to deceive your mother, I shall give you one stroke with my stick on your back. But if you'd told any lies too, I'd have thrashed you right well, I would.''

"And did he give you the stroke with his stick?"

"Yes; he gave me one stroke on my back."

"Did it hurt you much?"

"No, it didn't hurt me; but it frightened me very much."

"How did he generally manage the refractory ones? He must have had some very difficult ones to deal with."

"Chiefly by kind words. He would often lift up his stick, and shake it at them, and threaten them; but he very seldom used it. It was chiefly by kindness."

"What do you remember with the most lively interest that he did for you?"

"The last thing he made for me—was an old guy—out of a carrot."

"He did that, I believe, for a good many?"

"Yes. The day before the fifth of November, he would say to the whole school in the morning; 'Now, as many of you as like to bring me a carrot this afternoon, I'll make him an old guy of it by to-morrow morning. And sometimes they would bring him so many, that he would sit up all night, cutting them into the shape of old guys. For he always kept his word with us. Whatever he promised, we knew he'd do it. Every carrot we brought him, he gave us back, in the morning, as an old guy. Not one was disappointed. He had them all ready.

"Mr. Pounds often went out suddenly during school hours; and he'd leave us all alone,—boys and girls together; and say to us, 'Now, you bide here, while I come back; and mind you be good. And then he'd tell one of the oldest boys, perhaps, to take care of us. And he went out to some poor neighbour; perhaps to take them a dinner that he had been cooking for them; or else to take some broth, or some gruel, or something nice, when any body was ill."

"And had you no disturbances during his absence;—no bits of noisy fun?"

"No;—scarcely ever. Sometimes he would tell one of the older girls to take care of us. And she had no trouble with us. We always attended to her with the same respect. We were as quiet and orderly as if he was with us. There was a feeling of honour amongst us,—at such times,—that made us the more careful—not to do anything amiss. Our love and respect for our kind dear old master made us the more careful to conduct ourselves well,—almost better!"—he said, with a colouring smile on his manly cheek, and a sudden warming up of enthusiasm: —"almost better!—during his absence, than when he was with us! We desired to please him, and do—what we knew he wished. And he knew this; and had confidence in us. To have incurred his displeasure by any misconduct would have been a misery to us.

"It was so that morning,—New Year's morning,—when he went out with Ashton to Mr. Carter's, to show them some of Ashton's sums, and get something to put on his sore heel. I remember; it was a fine frosty morning; the sun was shining bright; and there was snow and ice all along the street. He got up from his bench about ten o'clock, and took Ashton out with him. And there we were,—all as quiet and happy as could be;—waiting for him to come back. Very soon after, Ashton came running back in a terror, and said, 'Mr. Pounds's fallen down in a fit at Mr. Carter's.—They think he's dead—and they're bringing him back in a fly.' Directly after—(I shall never forget it,—I was so frightened—)—the fly stopped at the door. Mr. Pounds was sitting up in it—dead;—and Dr. Martell was sitting on one side of him, and another gentleman on the other, propping him up. They opened the top of the fly, and—it seemed to me—they lifted him up out of the top of the fly—I could see no more; I was so frightened. All was confusion and terror. I ran home without my hat;—I forgot it in my fright,—and durst not go back to fetch it. I hardly knew what I did. Oh, it was a terrible day! I shall never forget it. Poor old man!—We loved him so!

"I seem to remember nothing after—till the funeral. I was there, when you buried him. And so were all the scholars; with that crowd of their parents and friends, and many others; for all the neighbourhood felt they had lost a Friend in good Mr. Pounds."

XLI.

It was now about two years since the suggestion was adopted, that if there should be any surplus remaining after the completion of the monument, it should be devoted to the instituting a Memorial Library in connection with it. From the first, we never doubted that this Memorial Library would be eventually founded; and during the interval, the Teachers had given to it their earnest consideration, and from time to time had held meetings, with the view of providing for its solid and permanent effectiveness. We had long had two libraries in immediate connexion with the Sunday Schools; one, designated "The Sunday School Library," for the use of the scholars; the other, "The Teachers' Library," for the purpose of accumulating works suitable for helping Teachers, in their work as Teachers. Both these libraries we resolved should be merged in the Memorial Library, when instituted. It was also decided, that the Sunday School Committee for the time being should have the management of the Memorial Library; that the use of the books should be gratuitous; that all the Teachers, and such of the scholars as the Committee might think proper, should be entitled to take out books; and that this privilege should be thrown open as extensively as practicable for poor children beyond the limits of our schools. The question as to what should be the name of the new Library caused some little diversity of opinion for a considerable time; but it was finally agreed, that it should be called—"The John Pounds Library." There was much variety of opinion on many points during these deliberations; but all our final decisions were unanimous.

When the time seemed to be drawing near for the completion of the monument, the School Committee were the more assiduous in preparatory work for the intended Library in connexion with it. For some months they held frequent meetings for the purpose of improving the Children's Library before merging it into the new one; carefully selecting new books for it; such as they deemed well adapted to give desirable instruction to children in a pleasant way, and for their morally healthy amusement. Books that none of us were sufficiently acquainted with were distributed among the Teachers, to take home and read, and report upon them at a future meeting. These meetings were very pleasant to all of us:—simple in spirit and proceeding, with a high and sacred appreciation of the responsibilities we had thus undertaken. All were thoroughly in earnest; patient and persevering; and conscientiously discriminative in the selection of books; endeavouring to guard against sending forth any evil influence, for want of care on our part; and to do our utmost to provide for the good influences of the new Library; essentially adding, from meeting to meeting, to what we hoped would prove excellent and very varied sources for future and long-extending improvement and happiness, for successive generations of poor children; and in the spirit of the good old Friend of Poor Children, to whose Memory the Library was to be consecrated.

April 25th. The Sunday School Teachers held their Annual Meeting this evening; happily taking tea together in the Upper School-room. The erection of the monument on the grave of John Pounds had been completed. Every body that saw it was delighted with it. And we rejoiced to anticipate, that when the pleasant trees and shrubs about it, which were now unfolding their buds, were come to their full growth, the monument would look still more beautiful, in the midst of their embowering shade.

After tea, when the Secretary had read the Committee's Report of the School proceedings for the past year; the Treasurer rose, and said; that the cost of the monument left a small surplus in hand:—on which, it was unanimously and briefly resolved : "That the John Pounds Library be now founded."

On this,—we all rose in solemn silence:—deeply impressed with reverence for the memory of the good old man;—and in fervent gratefulness to God,—that this Library,—which we hoped would live after us,—and be largely useful—to an indefinite futurity,—was now founded. These few moments—when we were all standing—silent—and still—were very impressive:—not soon to be forgotten.

After an interval of pleasant conversation, full of deep, happy feeling; we resumed business; and merged the Children's Library and the Teachers' Library into the John Pounds Library; and confided the working of the new Library to the School Committee.

At the request of the Teachers, I sent a letter to the Christian Reformer, and other periodicals, mentioning for the satisfaction of contributors at a distance, that the monument was completed, and that the Memorial Library was founded in connexion with it. The letter appeared in the June number of the Christian Reformer, and in other periodicals about the same time.

There are two inscriptions on the monument: one, on the south front; the other, on the east side.

INSCRIPTION ON THE SOUTH FRONT.

Underneath this Monument rest the mortal remains of John Pounds, the philanthropic Shoemaker, of St. Mary's Street, Portsmouth, who, while working at his trade in a very small room, gratuitously instructed in a useful education, and partly clothed and fed, some hundreds of girls and boys. He died suddenly, on New Year's Day, MDCCCXXXIX, while in his active beneficence, aged LXXII years.

"Well done, thou good and faithful servant; enter thou into the joy of thy Lord!"

"Verily I say unto thee, inasmuch as thou hast done it unto one of the least of these, thou hast done it unto me."

INSCRIPTION ON THE EAST SIDE.

This Monument has been erected chiefly by means of penny subscriptions, not only from the Christian Brotherhood with whom John Pounds habitually worshipped in the adjoining Chapel, but from persons of widely differing religious opinion throughout Great Britain, and from the most distant parts of the world.

In connexion with this Monument has also been founded in like manner within these precincts a Library to his memory, designed to extend to an indefinite futurity the solid mental and moral usefulness to which the philanthropic Shoemaker was so earnestly devoted to the last day of his life.

Pray for the blessing of God to prosper it.

XLII.

One beautiful Sunday evening, as I turned round the corner of the Chapel to go to the vestry, I saw Mr. Lemmon standing before the monument of his friend. He stood with his back to me. As I touched him gently on the shoulder,—"Ah, Sir," he said, with deep feeling, his eyes glistening with tears; "I was reading these inscriptions again. Johnny never thought it would come to this. Who'd have thought it?—The Founder of Ragged Schools!—And now they're springing up in all parts of the country!—And lords and ladies are proud to help!—Johnny never thought of all this!—But I think—they should have put on,—he was Founder of Ragged Schools." He said this with a tone and look of dissatisfaction and regret.

"That thought occurred to me, Mr. Lemmon, as I was writing the inscriptions. And I hesitated some time. He is so commonly spoken of as the Founder of Ragged Schools, that it was not till I had given it my best and lengthened consideration, that I could decide to leave it out. But I felt it would not be in character with his quiet way of doing good. He never thought of being Founder of Ragged Schools;—or of any schools. He only thought of his own little school—in his own little shop;—and doing all the good he could among his poor neighbours."

"Yes!—You're right, Sir!—You're right!"—he said, with hearty concurrence. And a generous glow brightened his old cheek.

My approaching duties now required me to bid him good evening for the present.

XLIII.

In the year 1860, Dr. Guthrie published his "Third Plea for Ragged Schools." In a tone of generous triumph, he contrasts the Ragged School Movement now, with what it was when first he entered upon it. "I remember the day," he says, "when they were but a beautiful theory; in the eyes of many, but the rainbow-coloured dream of benevolent enthusiasts. In those days it was necessary to lay bare the bleeding wounds of humanity; to move the public by tales of misery, and raise, if we could, a flood of feeling to float us over the pecuniary difficulties that barred our way." "Ragged Schools have now had a full trial; and their benefits," to use the words of Dr. Chalmers, "are matter not of experiment but of experience. The tree, said our Lord, is known by its fruit; and by that unerring test we are willing, and indeed anxious that they should be tried. For this purpose, I might crowd these pages with statistics drawn from the provincial towns, as well as from the largest cities of the kingdom; and all demonstrating their entire success. These institutions are everywhere."

The year following, Dr. Guthrie went to London, on behalf of Ragged Schools. And from London—"he made a special pilgrimage, for old John Pounds' sake, to Portsmouth:"—as his Sons touchingly expressed it, in their very interesting Memoir of their Father.

Writing to one of his Daughters, April 13th, Dr. Guthrie says of this visit to Portsmouth:—"We went through the Victory and saw the cockpit, three stories below the quarter-deck, where Nelson expired. This was interesting, but to me it was more interesting still, when we left the scenes associated with Nelson and his battles, to go away to an old-fashioned humble street, and in a small shop, in a two-storied house, built of wood, not above seven feet broad and some fifteen long, to stand on the scene of John Pounds' labours. He would have, sometimes, thirty or forty boys there; the place so crowded with children (whom he was saving from ruin without fee or reward, and, indeed, long without the notice or praise of any man), that they occasionally sat outside on the street. It was the humble birth-place of a great scheme."

XLIV.

A highly esteemed lady, who was one of our constant Sunday School Teachers all the time John Pounds took so earnest an interest in bringing his chosen scholars to have them entered, but who had since been residing many years in Tasmania; a blessing to all about her:—writing to me from Tasmania, in May, 1878, says, drawing near the close of her letter:—"I never had a happier occupation than that of teaching in the Sunday School; and I often think of it with pleasure now. Good old Mr. T— is not at all forgotten. As for John Pounds,—that Prince of the Poor!—I could not forget him, if I would; as I meet with his honourable mention in so many publications. It fairly set me crying once, when one of my boys came unexpectedly on it,—in reading aloud. He, the cobbler, had the honour of leading Dr. Guthrie into his Ragged School work."

XLV.

May 3rd, 1879. As I was walking along the Esplanade this morning, enjoying the sea breeze and the fine open view over Spithead and the Isle of Wight, I met a gentleman near the castle, of high aristocratic notions, who seemed to be out for the like purpose.

"You're out earlier than usual, are not you, this morning?" he said with an inquiring smile.

"I go out," I said, "not by the clock, but according to my feelings. I've been at composition all morning; and when I felt I'd had enough, I put up my things, and turned out for a little fresh air and exercise. And what do you think I've been writing about? But you'll not guess; so I'll tell you:—poor old John Pounds!"

"Ha!—the good old man!"—he exclaimed, with an instant warmth of admiration; which surprised me. For I had never seen any thing of the kind in him before; though I had known him many years, and often met him, and conversed with him. His habitual manner was quiet, calm, perfectly self-possessed, cool and even, with no tendency to any thing like enthusiasm; with a sort of indolent languor in his utterance. But now he suddenly brightened up, his eye filled with life and vigour, and he spoke with a generous eagerness, that seemed as if he could not express himself fast enough. "Poor old John Pounds!"—he exclaimed, with a spring and fulness in his voice,—a bound of enthusiasm. I listened astonished.—"Suppose he were to come to life again now!—What a change!—The old man wouldn't know himself!—To hear every body talking of John Pounds!—To hear himself praised every where—for his philanthropy, and the great good he has done! Extolled by all classes of society; eulogised in public meetings by powerful philanthropists,—mentioned by learned writers in their printed books,—and by great statesmen in their speeches on grand occasions; pictured in illustrated newspapers and magazines; talked of with admiration in the drawing-room by refined ladies and gentlemen; his portrait hung up in handsome houses, to stimulate others to works of philanthropy!—all sects of religion, all political parties, joining to extol John Pounds!—Known and valued in other nations, as well as our own! His fame gone to the other side of the globe!—They talk of John Pounds there!—the philanthropic old cobbler!—Such large results,—and even now so largely growing,—spreading so fast in the world!—all sprung from his example!—Memorial schools erected to his honour, and called by his name!—The Founder of Ragged Schools!—And now they are springing up everywhere!

"If the old man were to rise up now, and were told, that all these great things were his doing!—and hear every body talking so of John Pounds!—he would say:—'This can't be me they're talking of so:—this must be another John Pounds. I never did great things. I worked at my trade in my shop in St. Mary's Street; and taught poor children that nobody cared for!"

Delighted at this sudden outburst of generous admiration, I pursued my walk along the seashore towards Fort Cumberland.

XLVI.

POSTSCRIPT.

This Narrative is chiefly a statement of facts, simply as they occurred; and the rest that is said in it to illustrate John Pounds, I know to be thoroughly in character with his spirit and doings.

HENRY HAWKES
Southsea, Portsmouth.

A Brief Timeline of the Ragged Schools Movement

1766 – Birth of John Pounds.
1818 – Pounds begins to teach his nephew and neighbour's children.
1835 – London City Mission founded in London to provide aid and education to the poor.
1837 – Publication of Charles Dickens's *Oliver Twist*, which shows the state of the working class poor.
1839 – Death of John Pounds.
1840 – The term "Ragged School" first applied after a report on the London City Mission's work.
1843 – Charles Dickens visits Field Lane School.
1844 – Lord Shaftesbury helps inaugurate the Ragged Schools Union. By now at least 20 such schools exist.
1846 – Charles Dickens writes of his trip to Field Lane School.
1847 – *A Plea for Ragged Schools* by Rev Thomas Guthrie published.
1848 – An estimated 60 Ragged Schools exist, mainly in London.
1849 – Portsmouth's first Ragged School is founded.
1852 – Parliament forms a Select Committee to "inquire into the condition of criminal and destitute juveniles in this country, and what changes are desirable in their present treatment in order to supply industrial training, and to combine reformation with the due correction of juvenile crime".
1853 – Thomas Guthrie pushes for State support for Ragged Schools to the Select Committee as a solution to child criminality and poverty.
1856 – The Privy Council decides to pay Ragged Schools 50 shillings per year per child.
1857 – Privy Council reverses decision.
1867 – Over 200 Ragged Schools have been established.
1870 – Inspired by the example of Ragged Schools, the School Board Act ensures that local authorities have a statutory duty to provide an education to all children.
1902 – The Local Education Act abolishes school boards. By now many Ragged Schools have been superseded and have closed.
1944 – Ragged Schools Union renamed the Shaftesbury Society. Its focus has shifted to education for the under-privileged at night schools and to informal education.
2007 – The Shaftesbury Society merges with John Grooms to become Livability.

Contemporary Newspaper Extracts

The following are selected newspaper articles and extracts which give a flavour of the growth of Pounds' reputation and influence after his death.

The Hampshire Telegraph, 7th January, 1839

THE LATE JOHN POUNDS.

SHORTLY will be published, by WILLIAM HENRY CHARPENTIER, 50, High-street, Portsmouth, a CORRECT LIKENESS of the late JOHN POUNDS, Shoemender, as seated at his work in the midst of his Scholars, from an original Painting, by Mr Sheaf.

*

The following article is the one referred to by Henry Hawkes as appearing in the *Hampshire Telegraph.*

The Hampshire Chronicle - Monday 07 January 1839

PHILANTHROPY AND REAL CHARITY IN HUMBLE LIFE.—Died suddenly, Tuesday last, at the advanced age of 72 years. Mr. John Pounds, a man whose deeds of beneficence exercised in a humble sphere of life are worthy of lasting remembrance. His father, who was a shipwright employed in the mould-loft, in the Dock-yard, apprenticed him to the same trade; but at the age of 15, by falling into one of the dry docks, his thigh became dislocated, and he was rendered for life a cripple. When he had recovered sufficient strength, he acquired the art of shoe-mending, and placing himself in small shop in St. Mary's-street, Portsmouth, continued to earn an honest subsistence by it until the end of his days. Unable to share in out-door pursuits, he amused himself by rearing singing birds, and being of a cheerful social disposition, loved lo gather round him in his stall the children of his neighbours, to talk with them as he sat at work, and teach them to read as well as he could by means of hand bills and such leaves of old school books as he could obtain; and so in time became schoolmaster general to all in the neighbourhood, whose parents were too poor or careless to provide for them better, and had generally about 40 such under his care. So far was he from seeking any reward, that some of his pupils were occasionally saved from starvation, only by partaking of his own homely meal. Mr Sheath, of Landport, a self-taught artist, has lately executed in oil colours an admirable portrait of the old man, surrounded by his pupils, which has been purchased by Mr Edward Carter, Esq. On Tuesday morning the deceased had gone to the house of Mr. C. to acknowledge some kindnesses conferred, and to shew specimens of the children's writing when, on moving to leave the house, after a gratifying reception, he suddenly fell down and expired. Medical assistance was immediately procured, but without success, and he was taken back to his home, where the unexpected calamity overwhelmed with sorrow about 30 of his little band, who were then waiting for their daily lessons. Christmas Eve, as was his custom, being a single man, he carried to a female relative the materials for making a large plum pudding, to be distributed among his pupils, and on that occasion declared that he was never happier, that he had no want in life unsatisfied, and repeated a wish, often before expressed, that whenever he should be unable to support himself by his own industry, and to continue to do some good in the world, might be removed suddenly, "as a bird drops from his perch." His wish has been accomplished, and he is gone to await the award of Him who said "Inasmuch as ye did unto one of the least of these, ye did it unto me." His remains have been interred, by desire and at the expense of Mr. Carter, in the burial ground of the Unitarian Chapel, where had been an attendant for some years. To the lasting praise of the late Mr. Pounds it ought to be recorded that he also taught many of his boys to cook their own plain food, to mend their own shoes; sent them to Sunday Schools for religious instruction; and in order to encourage them and enable them to make a creditable appearance, with the aid of friends, procured clothing, which they were allowed to put on at his house on Sunday mornings and restore to his custody again in the evening.

[This article also appeared in *The Morning Advertiser* on 9th January 1839.]

*

Hampshire Advertiser - Saturday 12th January 1839

DEATH OF JOHN POUNDS. —We had not space last week to record the death of one of the humblest, though certainly one of the most philanthropic inhabitants of Portsmouth—John Pounds, aged 72, known and universally respected as the cobbler of St. Mary's Street. In early life he was apprenticed to a shipwright in the Dock yard, but became lame through the injury sustained in one of his hips by a fall from the side of the Narcissus frigate, upon which he was at work: in consequence of which he was compelled lo leave the Dock Yard, and owing to the unjust regulation, of that day without a pension. After continuing some years in a confidential service, where he had the control of money and goods to an unlimited extent, and in circumstances of no ordinary temptation, but in which he preserved the most undeviating integrity, he commenced shoemaking at the well-known shop in Saint Mary-street, where for near thirty years, he has beguiled the hours of his labor by rearing birds, and more especially by giving the destitute the rudiments of education. It has been his habit to collect at his cabin all the wretched—we may almost say the houseless—of the district which includes Prospect Row—children whose parents were often vagabonds, and children often without any—his own observation often being "I don't want good boys, give me bad ones, and I'll make 'em good." He taught them to read the Bible, to write a little, and gave them some idea of the first rules of arithmetic—and his benevolent exertions were not in vain. Among the many hundreds to whom, in the long course of years, he was the means of imparting some portion of knowledge, not a few have attained highly respectable stations in society, and several who have become masters of West Indiamen and other ships have returned to express their thanks for the moral principles he inculcated, and the instruction he afforded. In his habits he has always been extremely abstemious, and generally disposed of the broken victuals which some of the benevolent families of the town afforded him in rewarding the best among his pupils, to whom food was often a desideratum. He died suddenly with disease of the heart on Tuesday, last week, at the residence of Edward Carter, esq., in the High-street, whither he had gone with one of his protegees to shew that gentleman, whose benevolence often assisted him, the extent of the boy's proficiency. The funeral took place on Saturday afternoon, at the Unitarian burial ground, and we believe at the expence of Miss Carter, and from the high estimation in which the old man was held, was attended by very many of the inhabitants. It is singular that on Christmas day last, when speaking to a gentleman about his age, he said that whenever it should please Providence to take him hence, he hoped he should not be a burden to his friends. We cannot let the subject pass without remarking on the extent of good which this man, notwithstanding his very humble means, has been the instrument of effecting; and what a reflection does it involve upon those who, in their various stations, neglect the opportunities in their power of improving the moral and social condition of their fellows. At this peculiar juncture, when the demand for education is at such a height, and when it is plain that if children be not well taught they will be evil taught, the event to that district is a serious one. The children oft in rags and destitution cannot be got to a regular school, but we sincerely trust that some measure will be adopted without delay for the supply of the loss of this truly philanthropic man.

*

The article below was extracted from *The Gentleman's Magazine* by the *Manchester Courier and Lancashire General Advertiser. The Gentleman's Magazine* was a fashionable high class periodical which reported on national and international affairs.

Manchester Courier and Lancashire General Advertiser - Saturday 16th March 1839

AN EXAMPLE OF BENEVOLENCE IN HUMBLE LIFE.— It has been justly remarked, "the more we have to do, and the more we do, the happier we are." The case, indeed, is the same with all us,—the busier we are the happier we find ourselves. The truth of the above remark, (extracted from a private letter,) was happily exemplified in the character of John Pounds, shoemaker, who died at Portsmouth, somewhat suddenly, January 1, 1839. The good deeds performed by this humble artisan are worthy of lasting remembrance. On Christmas Eve, 1838, he carried, as was his usual custom, to a female relative of his, the materials of a large plum pudding, to be distributed among his pupils, both boys and girls, all of whom he taught gratuitously, declaring, on this occasion, that he never was happier all his life, and that he had no wants left unsatisfied. He repeated a wish he often expressed before, that whenever he should be unable to support himself by his own labour, and to continue doing good in the world, he might be removed suddenly, "*as a bird drops from its perch.*" His wish was in a great measure realised, and he has gone to await the award of

Him who went about doing good, and who has said, "inasmuch as ye did it to the least of these my brethren, ye did it unto me."—A lithographic print has been taken from his portrait, to which is appended the following inscription: "John Pounds, late of Portsmouth; who, while he earned an honest subsistence by mending shoes, was also a schoolmaster, instructing gratuitously some hundreds of the children of his poor neighbours. 'They cannot recompense thee, for thou shalt be recompensed at the resurrection of the just.' Born, June 17th, 1766,—died, January 1st, 1839. Aged 72."—*Gentleman's Magazine, Feb., 1839.*

*

Interest in John Pounds renewed 8 years later after Rev Thomas Guthrie began to use him as an exemplary figure. In March and April 1847, *Howitt's Journal* advertised in numerous British newspapers that its April edition would contain a portrait of "John Pounds, the Founder of the Ragged Schools, amongst his Scholars." The advertisement appeared in *The Freeman's Journal*, Dublin; *The Nottingham Review and General Advertiser for the Midland Counties; The Pilot*, Dublin; *The Liverpool Mercury*; *Northern Star and Leeds General Advertiser*; *Northern Whig*, Antrim, Ireland; *Sheffield Independent*; *The Ipswich Journal*; *The Western Times*, Devon and many other publications.

*

The following article shows how by this time knowledge of John Pounds had started to spread around the world.

The Leeds Mercury, Saturday, June 19th, 1847

A COMPANION TO JOHN POUNDS.—A gentleman in this neighbourhood has communicated to us the following particulars, referring to a Boston shoemaker, well worthy of a name and fame by the side of John Pounds, the Bristol *[sic]* shoemaker, and founder of the ragged schools. The account is extracted from a letter lately received from a friend residing in Boston, U.S.:—"The picture of John Pounds, the founder of the ragged school, is capital; I conld look upon it for hours. We have in this city a shoemaker named John Augustus. He has been for some years in the habit of attending the municipal court, and offering himself as bail for the re-appearance or good behaviour of wretched, drunken, outcast prostitutes, who have been brought up by the police as violators of the city laws. His unpretending shop is close by the Court-house, and when he sees an array of prisoners marched in, he drops his lapstone, and is soon found their advocate and friend. When he first commenced, he was told that be would soon run his purse out, and that little would he see of the wretches he bailed out of the House of Correction. But it turned out otherwise, he not only has lost little, but has been the means of reforming a great many."—*Staffordshire Mercury*.

*

This article, taken from *Howitt's Journal* also appeared throughout the country:

Elgin Courier - Friday, 9th July, 1847

JOHN POUNDS, THE FOUNDER OF THE RAGGED SCHOOLS.

John Pounds, the cripple and the cobbler, yet at the same time one of nature's true nobility, was born in Portsmouth, in 1766. His father was a sawyer, employed in the royal dock-yard. At fifteen, young Pounds met with an accident, which disabled him for life. During the greater part of his benevolent career, he lived in a small weather-boarded tenement St Mary's Street, Portsmouth, where he might be seen every day, seated on his stool, mending shoes in the midst of his busy little school. One of his amusements was that of rearing singing-birds, jays, and parrots, which he so perfectly domesticated, that they lived harmoniously with his cats and guinea-pigs. Often, it is said, might a canary-bird be seen perched upon one shoulder, and a cat upon the other. During the latter part of his life, however, when his scholars became so numerous, he was able to keep fewer of these domestic creatures. Poor he was, and entirely dependent upon the hard labour of his hands, he nevertheless adopted a little crippled nephew, whom he educated, and cared for with truly paternal love, and, in the end, established comfortably in life. It was out of this connection that his attempts and success in the work of education arose. He thought, in the first instance, that the boy would learn better with a companion; he obtained one, the son of wretchedly poor mother; then another and another was added, and he found so much pleasure in his employment, and was the means thereby of effecting so much good, that in the end, the number of his scholars amounted to about forty, including a dozen little girls.

His humble workshop was about six feet by eighteen, in the midst of which would sit, engaged in that labour by which he won his bread, and attending, at the same time, to the studies of the little crowd around him. So efficient was John Pound's mode of education, to say nothing about its being perfectly gratuitous, that the candidates were always numerous. He, however, invariably gave the preference to the *worst*, as well as the poorest children,—to the "little blackguards," as he called them. He has been known to follow such to the Town Quay, and offer them the bribe of a roasted potato, if they would come to his school. His influence on these degraded children was extraordinary.

As a teacher, his manners were pleasant and facetious. He amused the "little blackguards" while he taught them. Many hundred persons, now living usefully and creditably in life, owe the whole formation of their character to him. He gave them "book-learning," and taught them also to cook their own victuals, and mend their shoes. He was not only frequently their doctor and nurse, but their playfellow; no wonder was it, therefore, that when, on New Year's day, 1839, he suddenly died, at the age seventy-two, the children wept, and even fainted, hearing of their loss, and for a long time were overwhelmed with sorrow and consternation. They, indeed, had lost a friend and benefactor. Such was the noble founder the first ragged school.

*

This paragraph is extracted from a long article on the history and successes of Ragged Schools.

Hereford Times - Saturday 1st January, 1848

THE CHILDREN OF THE POOR – RAGGED AND INDUSTRIAL SCHOOLS

...Among the various machinery for the reclamation of the children of beggary and crime, none has proved so effectual as the Ragged and Industrial School. This institution owes its existence to the benevolence of John Pounds, a poor shoemaker of Bath [*sic*], who, being annoyed by a set of ragged urchins living in his neighbourhood, took a godlike revenge upon them by gathering them around his stall and imparting them the rudiments of knowledge. His example has been imitated in London, Birmingham, Manchester, Edinburgh, Glasgow, Aberdeen, Bristol, and many other large cities and towns. The Ragged School supplies the place the Sunday or the common Day school to the class below that on which they act. The very fact the child is unfit for admission into them constitutes his claim upon the Ragged School. It is simply a school for the impartation of elementary knowledge, intellectual, moral, and religious, to those children who belong to the very dregs of society.

*

Aberdeen Herald and General Advertiser - Saturday 29 January 1848

JOHN POUNDS,
THE SCHOOLMASTER AND SHOE-MENDER
(From the Alloa Monthly Advertiser)

In these days, when so much attention is being devoted to Ragged and Industrial Schools, it may be interesting to peruse a brief notice of the founder of such benevolent institutions. But for the celebrity which seminaries for the neglected and abandoned of our juvenile population have attained in the present day, it is very possible that the humble, though honoured name of John Pounds, would have been buried in obscurity, and his disinterested deeds of kindness to the destitute amongst the young have found no very prominent place among "the short and simple annals of the poor."

John Pounds was a native of Portsmouth, and was born in the year 1766. His great merit—and that which will make his name be long held in honourable remembrance—was this, that though in the very humblest position in life, and with no means, save what his own industry enabled him to acquire, at his command, nevertheless contrived to render himself an invaluable blessing to the community among whom his lot in life was cast. His father was employed as a sawyer in the royal dockyard of Portsmouth, and it was intended that the son pursue the same occupation. He was not long in the dockyard, however, ere he met with an accident, which disabled him for life, and rendered it necessary that some other vocation than that of a labourer in the dockyard be sought for. It so happened that he apprenticed himself to a shoemaker, but, from some cause or other, John never rose higher in his profession than to be merely a shoe-mender— or, in common *parlance, a cobbler.*

It was not until he had reached his thirty-fifth year that the benevolent career of John Pounds became conspicuous. At that period of his life, he took a house and commenced business, in a humble way, on his own account. The dwelling which took at that time he never left, until death called upon him seven-and thirty years thereafter; and, during all that period, he might any day have been seen sitting on his stool at a low window, busy at his shoe-mending operations, and around him him groups of ragged little boys and girls, all driving away at the lessons which their kind-hearted and gratuitous schoolmaster, John Pounds, had assigned them to learn.

The circumstance which first directed the attention of the subject of our present sketch to the tuition of the young, was the affection which he formed for a sickly boy of a brother of his own. John Pounds (who never married) took this boy to his own home, and undertook to furnish him gratuitously with bed, board, and education. The boy, during the day, was in the employment of a fashionable shoemaker, and in the evening he returned to his uncle, with whom, indeed, he lived on the happiest terms till the end of his days. While acting the part of schoolmaster to his nephew, John Pounds very judiciously thought that the boy's progress would not be at all retarded, but rather accelerated, were he to have the company of another. At length, another boy was got, and, the plan succeeding, a second, and a third, and a fourth, and son on, until good John Pounds became schoolmaster-general to all those in his neighbourhood whose parents were either too poor or too careless to send their children to school. His love for the work of training the young never cooled, and it was his custom to go out to the lanes and byways of the place in which he lived, and solicit, if not compel, the neglected children—children without shoes or bonnets—children with hungry looks and dirty faces —to come with him to his house, and become members of his school. In prosecuting his philanthropic work, John Pounds, when there were several candidates for admission, always gave the preference to the "little blackguards," and, by so doing, doubtless rescued many from a downward and ignoble career.

In a remarkably short time, the number of John Pounds' scholars increased from one to forty, and among these there were about a dozen girls. The place in which the schoolmaster and the cobbler pursued his combined though very dissimilar avocations, was humble in the extreme. In size it was only six feet by eighteen, yet it admirably served the purpose, the best argument against those who always advocate for delay in opening a ragged school, on the ground of no proper building being available. Almost *any* kind of tenement is suitable for the purpose. *John Pounds had his heart in his work*, and because of that, a dwelling, whose dimensions were only six feet by eighteen, adequate not only for conducting the education of forty children, but also sufficient for him to earn his own bread as a shoemender.

Some may be apt to think that the education given to these children by a man in such poor circumstances, and while pursuing his own trade, could not be of much utility. This is a mistake. While John Pounds was busy with his last on his knee, he had his whole school sitting around him, and reading, writing, and arithmetic, were very efficiently instilled into his young charge. He listened to boys reading, and checked them when they went wrong; those in the arithmetic came to him with their slates, and showed him their ciphering, and he pointed out their blunders; and those in the writing class had their copy lines before them, and after they had finished, he scrutinised their work, pointing out its good and bad features. In this way, without almost ever rising from his seat, John Pounds went through an immense deal of valuable work. He was often sadly at a loss for school books, however, and this led him to pick up all the handbills, &c., he could lay his hands upon, and these he made the most of. The interrogatory system of tuition was much in favour with our amateur teacher. He asked his scholars the names of particular parts of their bodies, of houses, &c., and then made them spell them.

But for the tuition given to hundreds of neglected children, in Portsmouth by John Pounds, no education would have been given at all, and as the man advanced in years, it gladdened him to find those who in early life were his pupils, pay him a visit in his humble dwelling, give him a cordial shake of the hand, and thank him for his great kindness to them when young. By the labours of John Pounds, many were fitted to enter creditably upon the business of life, to become apprentices to respectable tradesmen, and to fill offices of trust. Nor did John Pounds ether ask or receive fee or reward for his labours. Though a man in humble life, he felt that there was true happiness to be found in the pleasure arising from doing good, and, therefore, he never wearied in well-doing up to the latest day of his life. Nor must we omit to mention that credit is due to John Pounds for more than the communicating to his scholars of a knowledge of reading, writing and arithmetic. Many of the ragged and forlorn children, under his charge, were taught by him to mend their own clothes, to cook their own victuals, and, to gain religious instruction, they were sent by him to a Sunday school. When they were sick, he attended to their ailments, and they partook of his own homely fare. If he succeeded in getting for any of the children a present of a Sunday suit of clothes, the children had to go to the house of John Pounds, on the Sabbath morning, put on their new habiliments, and, after Church came out, they had to restore their good dress to the teacher, to be taken care of by him. In fact, John Pounds was father and mother, schoolmaster and doctor, to great numbers of neglected children.

But the day arrived when this benevolent man was to die, and the circumstances attending his death appear to us to be singularly affecting. On New-Year's Day, 1839, the school assembled as usual, and John Pounds left home for a short time, to wait upon a gentleman (Edward Carter, Esq) to solicit some aid for a boy, who was very destitute and in delicate health. John Pounds was accompanied by the boy, and while in the act of showing to Mr. Carter the boy's handwriting, and also some of his ciphering, he suddenly fell on the floor. A surgeon was promptly in attendance, but life had fled. The little boy ran back to the school, and all the scholars were happy, thinking it was a signal for the speedy appearance of their much-loved teacher. The boy, however, had scarcely narrated the melancholy event that had transpired, ere the entire scholars, overwhelmed with grief and consternation, saw the dead body of their master brought in at the door, and at the sight of it many of the children wept bitterly, and one or two fainted.

Such is a brief sketch of the benevolent founder of ragged schools, and the great good which this poor man accomplished, certainly affords much encouragement to those who have better means, and better opportunities at their command for imitating his example. John Pounds effectually succeeded in winning the affections of the children, and perhaps nothing can more clearly evince this than the grief manifested at his death, and the fact that groups of young children went to the school house several successive days after the death of their teacher, and, not finding him went away disconsolate. His means did not allow him to give *food* regularly to his ragged pupils, and so it could not be for the loaves and the fishes that so many young children, for so many years, were devotedly attached to their master. John Pounds has been known, however, on seeing some little "blackguard" in the street, to go out and tempt him with a roasted potato to become one of his scholars, and the bait oftentimes succeeded. It is somewhat singular that this poor man was as much a favourite with the brute creation as he was with little boys and girls. Many a time might a cat have been seen sitting upon one his shoulders, and a canary perched upon the other. His was indeed a happy, though an humble, family, and one cannot peruse the simple story of the life of John Pounds without being sensibly the better for it.

[Many other similar accounts of John Pounds' life appeared over the following years in many newspapers, sometimes mistaking the place of his birth, often drawing biblical parallels always highlighting his patience and selflessness and the devotion of his pupils to him. All proclaimed him the "founder of Ragged Schools". There are too many to include here, but the above are representative.]

*

The following extract is from a report on a talk, part of *the Geldeston Winter Lectures*, entitled *The Power Of A Single Individual,* John Pounds is described in these glowing terms:

The Norfolk News, Saturday 18th March 1848

...the cripple of Portsmouth Docks, the cobbler of a crazy wooden shed, with his dirty, demoralized, desperate little pupils round him, "glorious old John Pounds," the master and projector of the first Ragged School, who may be said to have almost consecrated cobbling, to whom the rich and beneficent are indebted for the best hint they ever acted on, and whose name is, this day, written in letters of glowing gratefulness and blessing, on many a poor man's early principled heart!

*

The Hampshire Advertiser, Saturday 8th July 1848

RAGGED SCHOOLS LECTURE AT NEWPORT

An interesting lecture was delivered at the National School, on Monday week last, to a numerous assembly (the Mayor in the chair) by Mr. Ware, the Hon. Secretary of the Ragged School in Field-lane, Holborn, on the "History, Plans, and Usefulness of Ragged Schools," from which we gained the following information:— Ragged Schools originated at Portsmouth, an old shoe-maker (John Pounds) having, by various stratagems, induced a great number of poor, dirty, idle children to come to his stall for the purpose of being taught to read and write. By his single exertions, for years in this way, hundreds of lads in Portsmouth were educated. This philanthropic old man died suddenly in January, 1839, and about that time Ragged Schools were first started in London, of which Field-lane was about the first, and there are now sixty, receiving boys and girls, most of whom would not be allowed to attend any other school, on account of their vile habits. The streets and lanes are thronged with such characters, whose parents care nothing but that they bring money home to them somehow—they make a trade of their children. To prove what class of children they were, Lord Ashley, a few evenings ago, in his place in Parliament, gave the result of an examination of fifteen Ragged Schools in London. He found that the number of persons on the books was 2345, ranging between 5 and 17 years of age; but the average attendance might be taken at 1600. Of these, there were 162 who confessed that they had been in prison several times; 116 had run away from their homes; 170 slept in lodging-houses, which were nests of every abomination that the mind of man could imagine; 253 confessed that they had lived altogether by beggary; 216 had neither shoes nor stockings; 280 had no hat or cap, or covering for the head; 101 had no linen; 249 had never slept in a bed, from recollection; 68 were children of convicts; 125 had stepmothers, to whom much of the misery of the poor children might be traced; 306 had either lost one or both parents. The average attendance last year in all the schools was 4000, (but there were altogether 7000 children under this teaching) and on inquiry they found that 400 confessed that they had been in prison, 660 lived in beggary, 178 were the children of convicts, and 800 had lost one or both parents. Most of these were pale, thin, emaciated, and squalid; they were irritable, and in place of talent was a remarkable species of low cunning. There were 30,000 such children, living by theft and fraud, in the metropolis, and 3000 receivers of goods which they pilfer, dealers in marine stores, brokers, slopsellers, &c. and 4000 were annually committed for criminal offences. This being the case, and there being altogether 100,000 children destitute of education, the object of these schools was to alter such a state of things. They were open morning, noon, and night, and the Refuge at Westminster actually fed, clothed, and gave trades to several of the most unfortunate. The yearly report of this institution was most encouraging. They had succeeded in rendering a mass of depraved children cleanly, industrious, and increasing in knowledge (particularly religious) to such an extent that it was strikingly apparent in the whole neighbourhood. The entries in the "Visitors' Book" made by the nobility, gentry, and clergy, who had attended these schools, were also most gratifying. Interesting letters had likewise been received by the teachers (now amounting to upwards of 700) from several scholars who were now doing well in the world through their instrumentality.

The lecturer having concluded his interesting address, the REV. J. MAUDE rose and confirmed his statements. He had a personal knowledge of these facts from having himself assisted as Minister in a large parish, in the metropolis, for years.

DR. WAVELL said he should like to see something of the sort established in our town. There were many means of usefulness, but none so paramount as this.

THE CHAIRMAN (J. ELDRIDGE, esq.) said there was one incident mentioned in the lecture of which they had cause to be proud—namely, that the originator of these schools, John Pound *[sic]*, was a Hampshire man. He could not but be struck with the disinterested exertions of 700 teachers, who voluntarily go among these wretched children.

*

The West Kent Guardian, Saturday 2nd September, 1848

From: EAST AND WEST GREENWICH RAGGED SCHOOLS

[The following extract is part of a report on a lecture on Ragged Schools given at the Institution, Royal-hill, Greenwich. The lecturer said the early history of the ragged school movement was obscure, but he "believed that the founder of the ragged school system was born at Portsmouth." He gave a short history of Pounds' work and went on:]

...History would record in her brightest page the name of the moral hero who had done all this—of whose blameless life, and bloodless victories over many of the most wretched of his fellow creatures—little thieves and vagrants whom he moulded into children of order and led into the paths of peace—they have just now heard: the name—need it be said—was John Pounds! (The announcement elicited much applause.) The lecture remarked that if one poor man effected so much for the cause which they were met to support, what might not be expected from the co-operation of such an assembly he saw around him! It was a goodly cause—that of the ragged schools: see the embryo evil nipped in the bud by the agency of the ragged school union society! Mark those outcast children that throng our crowded cities and towns, left upon the world by the hand of death depriving them of their natural protectors, driven forth by unnatural parents as thieves or beggars! with the cravings of hunger impelling them to crime! with no moral principle to control—no religious principles to guide, console, or sustain them. Education is not for them; apprenticeship to useful trades whereby they may get a living is not for such as these, for them is not the Sabbath school. What parents would sit their child down beside a dirty little thief—none. The ragged school plan meets the case. Support then this plan; engage in the work of teaching, encouraging, and reclaiming the children of crime and of poverty. Open new schools and you will have scholars. They may be difficult to train, and are so, but love conquers all things. Great were the difficulties in the London schools, but they were overcome by the affectionate energy of the teachers whose reward was the pleasure of doing good. Many were the instances in which the scheme has succeeded beyond the most sanguine expectation of its friends. To whom were the name and actions cf Lord Ashley not known? (Applause) See Lord Ashley at the Field-lane school, and follow his example. (Renewed applause)! The lecturer then entered into statistical details to show the evils of crime, the thousands of children of tender years of both sexes on the streets of London, feeding the lower steam of crime which was hurrying them to ruin and sapping the foundations of society...

*

It is perhaps appropriate that this final extract comes from that other son of Portsmouth, Charles Dickens. He had visited the Field Lane ragged school on a number of occasions, and wrote about his visits in *Household Words* in 1852:

Household Words, March 13, 1852

...I found my first Ragged School in an obscure place called West Street, Saffron Hill, pitifully struggling for life under every disadvantage. It had no means; it had no suitable room; it derived no power or protection from being recognized by any authority; it attracted within its walls a fluctuating swarm of faces—young in years, but youthful in nothing else—that scowled Hope out of countenance. It was held in a low-roofed den, in a sickening atmosphere, in the midst of taint, and dirt, and pestilence; with all the deadly sins let loose, howling and shrieking at the doors. Zeal did not supply the place of method and training; the teachers knew little of their office; the pupils, with an evil sharpness, found them out, got the better of them, derided them, made blasphemous answers to Scriptural questions, sang, fought, danced, robbed each other—seemed possessed by legions of devils. The place was stormed and carried, over and over again; the lights were blown out, the books strewn in the gutters, and the female scholars carried off triumphantly to their old wickedness. With no strength in it but its purpose, the school stood it all out, and made its way. Some two years since I found it quiet and orderly, full, lighted with gas, well white-washed, numerously attended, and thoroughly established...

Charles Dickens

THE END

A New Pupil for John Pounds, *The Illustrated London News*. Sept 19th, 1857

Lightning Source UK Ltd.
Milton Keynes UK
UKOW06f0133110616

276046UK00001B/115/P